LOUISBOURG JOURNALS

From the original (in colors) in the Society's Collection.

Louisbourg Journals 1745

Edited by
Louis Effingham DeForest, M.A., J.D.

HERITAGE BOOKS
2008

HERITAGE BOOKS
AN IMPRINT OF HERITAGE BOOKS, INC.

Books, CDs, and more—Worldwide

For our listing of thousands of titles see our website
at
www.HeritageBooks.com

A Facsimile Reprint
Published 2008 by
HERITAGE BOOKS, INC.
Publishing Division
100 Railroad Ave. #104
Westminster, Maryland 21157

Copyright © 1932 The Society of Colonial Wars
in the State of New York

Originally Compiled for and Published by The
Society of Colonial Wars in the State of
New York, through Its Committee
on Historical Documents

New York
1932

— Publisher's Notice —

In reprints such as this, it is often not possible to remove blemishes from the original. We feel the contents of this book warrant its reissue despite these blemishes and hope you will agree and read it with pleasure.

International Standard Book Numbers
Paperbound: 978-0-7884-1015-4
Clothbound: 978-0-7884-7339-5

LOUISBOURG JOURNALS

PUBLISHED BY THE SOCIETY OF COLONIAL WARS IN THE STATE OF NEW YORK AS THE FIRST VOLUME TO BE PRINTED FROM THE INCOME OF THE PUBLICATION FUND UNDER THE CONDITIONS SET FORTH IN A CIRCULAR SENT TO THE MEMBERS, DATED APRIL 5, 1927.

Founders of the Publication Fund

EDWARD LASELL PARTRIDGE, M.D.
CHARLES THOMPSON MATHEWS
MYRON CHARLES TAYLOR

Committee on Historical Documents

HERBERT TREADWELL WADE, *Chairman*
ELECTUS DARWIN LITCHFIELD

FOREWORD

Few events in the history of the British Colonies in North America have aroused more interest among the members of the Society of Colonial Wars than the Capture of Louisbourg in 1745. Naturally as the most important military achievement of the American Colonists before the Revolution it has been felt most appropriate that it should be honored and commemorated by the Society. Accordingly on March 25, 1895, at the first church service to be held by the New York Society the one-hundred and fiftieth anniversary of the Departure of the New England Troops for Louisbourg was duly commemorated and a sermon preached by the Right Reverend Thomas Dudley, D.D., D.C.L., Bishop of Kentucky. Then on June 17th of the same year there was unveiled on the historic ground of the old fortress the Louisbourg Monument erected by the General Society of Colonial Wars to commemorate the surrender of this strong fortification of the New World to the New England troops under Lieutenant General Pepperrell assisted by the British fleet under Commodore Warren. In connection with this celebration it is here not inappropriate to refer to the leading part taken by the indefatigable chairman of the committee, the Honorary Governor General, Major Howland Pell. In the printed "Report of the Committee on Louisbourg Memorial" published in 1896, there are reproduced the interesting historical and other addresses delivered on this occasion prepared by Frederic J. de Peyster, Governor General of the Society of Colonial Wars, by representatives of the various State societies, by representatives of the Royal Society of Canada and of the Historical Society of Nova Scotia, and by others. In addition the Chairman of the Committee wrote for the *American Historical Register* several interesting papers on the Siege of Louisbourg, and collected considerable new and special information which along with standard works and maps in this field has found a permanent place in the Library of the New York Society of Colonial Wars.

Interest in this most important action never has been allowed to flag, and from time to time papers have been presented before

FOREWORD

the Society by members and others interested in historical research, including discussions of "The Siege of Louisbourg" by Robert D. Benedict, Esq. (November 25, 1895), and "The Siege of Louisbourg and its Effect on the American Colonies" by the Honorable Everett Pepperrell Wheeler (December 19, 1895). "The Siege and Second Capture of Louisbourg in 1758" was the subject of a paper by Frederic H. Betts, Esq. (March 20, 1899). In addition to the many books on Louisbourg in our Library there are hung on its wall several original maps together with some reproductions and prints which are memorials from bequests of former members of the Society along with others which are the gifts of interested members. All the illustrations in this volume are reproduced from originals in the possession of the New York Society.

With such a background of interest it is not difficult to explain the decision of the Council to apply the income of the Partridge bequest along with that of the Publication Fund to the preparation and distribution of a historical monograph containing certain unpublished journals of actual participants in this important expedition. This volume does not pretend to be a historical summary of the Siege, nor are the documents now presented all of the available material, but in the opinion of the Committee on Publication of Historical Documents they do represent a distinct contribution to the history of the expedition as well as being narratives of general interest. When read in connection with some, at least, of the authorities marshalled by the Editor in his comprehensive bibliography it is hoped that these journals will arouse renewed interest on the part of many of our members and stimulate reading and research into a most interesting epoch of American history to which this Society is specially devoted. Accordingly the Committee commends to the members of the Society of Colonial Wars in the State of New York and other readers the accompanying material so interestingly arranged and edited by Major de Forest.

        Electus Darwin Litchfield
        Herbert Treadwell Wade, Chairman
Committee on Publication of Historical Documents *

* The lamented death of Augustus Hewlett Skillin, a member of the Committee, on March 1, 1932, explains the missing name as given in the list of the Committee.

EDITORIAL NOTE

In order to make the text of the Louisbourg Journals more easily readable, and in accordance with the best current practice, various textual changes have been made.

Raised letters (Coll¹¹, Capᵗⁿ) have not been used, and as they were generally used in abbreviations, the missing letters have been supplied, although the spelling of the diarist has not been altered (Collonell, Captain).

Such abbreviations as are still in general use (Mr., Capt., sd., Feb., i.e., N.B.,) are retained.

Abbreviations not generally used in printed books now (cd, shd, wd, nt, wnd, &,) have been written in full (could, should, would or wind, night, wind, and).

Certain old forms (yt, ym, ye) have been modernized (that, them, the).

Missing letters in the middle or end of a word, when the context makes no doubt possible as to the meaning have been supplied (gre—est has been written greatest). Missing letters have been inserted if the word seemed intended as a contraction or abbreviation, but generally matters of spelling have been untouched.

Parentheses are the diarists', square brackets have been used by the editor to supply names, or the correct or alternative spellings of names; to supply an hiatus in the manuscript, such as a number left blank by the diarist; or for doubtful readings, in the last case usually followed by a question mark.

A dash ——— indicates a space left blank by the diarist, while illegible matter is thus indicated [———?].

Italics have been used for *li, s,* and *d,* while *li* has taken the place of the symbol for the pound sterling (£), as the New England pound was not identical with the pound sterling.

When the use of J for I seemed likely to prove confusing, the letter has been changed. It has generally been changed to I for the first person singular, otherwise the spelling (including u and v, and

EDITORIAL NOTE

i and j), and the punctuation and capitalization have been used according to the taste of the original writer.

There has been extreme difficulty in deciphering some of the handwriting, and in distinguishing between abbreviations and private fancies in spelling. Great pains have been taken to preserve the individuality of each writer's orthography, and at the same time to make the text easily readable, but for the errors that have unavoidably crept in the editor expresses his regrets.

The editor acknowledges his indebtedness to Julius H. Tuttle, Esq., Librarian of the Massachusetts Historical Society, and to Alexander J. Wall, Esq., Librarian of the New York Historical Society, for their courteous assistance in making available manuscripts from their respective institutions. He is also particularly grateful to his wife, Anne Lawrence de Forest, for her expert services in reading and transcribing manuscripts and in preparing the index.

L. E. de F.

TABLE OF CONTENTS

	PAGE
FOREWORD	vii
EDITORIAL NOTE	ix
HISTORICAL INTRODUCTION	xv

LOUISBOURG JOURNALS

First Journal — Anonymous	1
Second Journal — Captain Joseph Sherburne	55
Third Journal — Anonymous	61
Fourth Journal — Anonymous	67
Fifth Journal — Anonymous	73
Sixth Journal — Anonymous	80
Seventh Journal — Privates George Mygate and Caleb Lamb	97
Eighth Journal — Anonymous	109
Ninth Journal — Chaplain Stephen Williams	121
Tenth Journal — Colonel John Bradstreet	170

APPENDICES

I	The Fleet	181
II	Peter Warren Letters	184
III	The Expedition as Seen in Contemporary New York	201
IV	Labor Account	222
V	List of Equipment	225
VI	The Present Louisbourg	226
VII	The Society of Colonial Wars and Louisbourg	228

BIBLIOGRAPHY	231
INDEX	241

LIST OF ILLUSTRATIONS

A View of the Landing the New England Forces in ye Expedition against Cape Breton, 1745 . . . . *frontispiece*

	FACING PAGE
Plan du Port et Ville de Louisbourg, dans l'Isle Royale	20
A Plan of the City & Harbour of Louisburg	44
A Plan of the City & Fortifications of Louisburg	76
The Louisbourg Monument	100
A View of Louisburg in North America	132
Plan of Louisbourg in Cape Breton	156
The Louisbourg Flag	172
Plan of the Town and Harbour of Louisburg	204
The Society's Grave-Marker (The Louisbourg Cross)	228

actuated, France spent a sum equivalent today to ten million dollars in erecting a fortress which would be impregnable. Under the shelter of Louisbourg's great guns rode a large fleet of ships which was a constant menace to all of New England. When France declared war the garrison at Louisbourg, supported by the French fleet, threatened to exterminate entirely the fisheries which were the foundation of New England's maritime trade.

For these reasons the desire to capture Louisbourg long was close to the hearts of the people of New England. The impulse to take active offensive measures came with the arrival of news at Boston in 1744 that the garrison was small, the Swiss contingent mutinous, and the French discontented, and that there was a scarcity of supplies. There has long been dispute as to the person to whom the credit is due for proposing the expedition. Some have given it to Judge Auchmuty of Boston, Pepperrell said it was John Bradstreet (who states his own case in this volume), but Parkman, Fiske, Hutchinson, Belknap, Douglas, and other historians declare that William Vaughan of New Hampshire was responsible. Governor Shirley organized the expedition and selected William Pepperrell of Kittery, known and respected throughout New England, as the commanding general.

The journals given in this work supply the graphic details of the campaign, but perhaps do not explain why the expedition succeeded, despite the picture they give of heroism under great hardship and crushing difficulties. Parkman wrote that the triumph was "the result of mere audacity and hardihood, backed by the rarest good luck" and this seems a reasonable statement. Fortune surely favored the English. In the first place the weather was perfect. Every sail arrived safely at Canso harbor and for forty-seven days the army enjoyed ideal fighting conditions in a country usually notable for storms. Secondly, the work of repair being done on the Grand Battery just at this time made it necessary for the French to abandon what was normally a strong fort. The rashness of the commander of the French relief ship, the *Vigilant,* led to its unnecessary capture. These events, with the mutinous spirit in the French garrison and the lack of pay and supplies, undoubtedly greatly assisted the vigorous attack.

There should not be overlooked the presence of Commodore

HISTORICAL INTRODUCTION

The capture of Louisbourg in 1745 was the most important military achievement of the American Colonists prior to the War of the Revolution and, in fact, the only British success of any importance during the entire War of the Austrian Succession. It was an amazing victory and had a profound effect on the spirit and temper of the times.

Parkman called the expedition "a mad scheme" and "a project of wild audacity," and used these terms with justification. The expedition was planned by Governor Shirley, a lawyer, entirely ignorant of the art of war, who even gave directions in advance as to just how and when the fort was to be taken by surprise. It was commanded by a rich merchant, William Pepperrell, who had seen only a brief and uneventful service in the milita. The army was composed of farmers, fishermen, shopkeepers and artisans, with no conception of discipline. They went to face the regulars of the standing army of the first military power of Europe, protected by the walls of one of the great fortresses of the day. When Louisbourg fell the civilized world recognized that a new military power had risen in America. As for the Americans, it gave them a confidence in themselves which they never lost. At Bunker Hill where the patriots' fortifications were laid out by Richard Gridley, who was an artillery officer at Louisbourg, the Americans laughed at the earthworks of the British and compared them to the great walls of the citadel on Cape Breton.

Too much has been written of the expedition of 1745 to call for more than a brief account here, but something may well be said of the causes which provoked the campaign.

France considered the possession of Louisbourg absolutely necessary to the control of her Canadian possessions. Holding that excellent harbor on Cape Breton, which was easily defended, she could command the entrance to the gulf and river St. Lawrence and have a clear port for imports as well as exports. Thus

Peter Warren, an able officer, with an effective fleet. Warren and Pepperrell were, fortunately, men of tact and patience and the difficulties of a joint command shared by a British naval officer and a Provincial militia general were never permitted to interfere with the purposes of the operations.

L. E. de F.

LOUISBOURG JOURNALS

FIRST JOURNAL

Anonymous

The author of this long and detailed account is unknown. He was a soldier in the Fourth Massachusetts Regiment, of which Samuel Willard was the colonel. He was probably in the Third Company, commanded by Major Seth Pomeroy and Captain Ebenezer Alexander, as on August 17th he refers to the death of John Taylor of Hadley as "of our Company," and it is known that Taylor was a member of the Third Company. From other notes made by the diarist it is certain that he was a resident of Hampshire County, Massachusetts, and it seems probable that he was a resident of Springfield. He names several cousins, and gives the first names of his brothers, but he still remains unidentified.

The soldier was evidently intelligent, candid and enterprising, and his journal is particularly interesting for its length and the wealth of its observations. There was usually little formality between ranks among the Provincial troops but this man seems to have been especially friendly with his officers and to have had somewhat surprising sources of information.

Beginning the journal was a page entitled "Preface" which was badly torn and had so little legible matter left that it has been omitted from the text. Of the few words of it left there can be read, "What I have wrote, was for my own Private Use that I might'ent So Soon forget the Great things I've [seen?] wich Otherwise I might have done."

The present location of the original manuscript is unknown. It was bought at auction some fifteen years ago by the late George D. Smith of New York City, a well-known dealer in rare books. Mr. Smith at that time very generously gave the Society of Colonial Wars permission to photostat and publish the complete journal.

THE JOURNAL

The News of our Goverment's Raising an army, (Together with the Help of the other Neighbouing Goverments) In order to the Reduction of Cape Breton. (Viz) Louisbourg, which was Like to prove Detremental if not Destroying to our Country. So affected the minds of many. (together with The Expectation of Seeing Great things, etc.) — As to Incline many, yea, Very Many to Venture themselves and Enlist into the Service Among whom, I was one, which was the, 14th of March 1745. I And having had the Consent of my friends, (and asking their Prayers), (Which was A great Comfort to me. Even all the Time of my being Asent.) I set out for Boston, Tuesday March 19th. wee was well Entertained Upon the road, and arrived, the fryday following On Saterday, wee all Appeared before Coll. [Benjamin] Pollard, to be Veiw'd. Both our Persons And arms, Those that found their own, and Those that had none, were ordered to Mr. Wheelright's (Commissary General) to get Equipt. That being Done, wee Receiv'd our Blankets At the Sametime, and Return'd to our Lodging

24. Sabbath Day, wee had Liberty to go to Meeting But in the Afternoon wee was Obliged, to get [our] Chest's and go Aboard. which wee Did the Greatest part of us. The fleet Set Sail this day from Nantasket

25 Monday. Our Capt (Viz) John Le Croix (Which was the Packet, His Excellency Sent for Commodore [Peter] Warren, when Lying att Antequa [Antigua] Was Ordered To forthwith to be Under Sail, Our Company not Being ready they Sail'd all the forenoon About the Harbour. Just att 12 O.Clock wee all went on Board, wee went a Little way beyond the Castle [William], Wind being against us, wee Cast Achor and Rhode.

26 Tuesday. in the Morning Lieutenant Mun [John Man] the M[— ?] and my Self. went to See Castle William and I thought (With my Self) if Capebreton in Louisbourg were Strong as that, wee Should hardly take 'em. wee was well Entertain'd, while wee tarried. by Cousin Chapin wee wrote home to our friends. and then Return'd to the Vessel. And About 3:O Clock. P:M. wee Weighed Anchor and Away wee Sail'd, before a Pleasent Gale of South South West Wind — Wee had'ent Sailed, above 3 or 4 Leagues, before Some were Sea Sick. wee kept Upon Deck Good part of this Night To prevent our being Sick.

27 Wednesday this day our Vessel was A Very Hospital, wee were all Sick, in a Greater or lesser Degree. Wee Sail'd a good pace all Day, Towards Night, the Wind Began to rise, it also Grew foggy and Something rainy. So That wee Could not be Upon Deck, as the Night before — But was Shut down in the hold; and a Long, Dark and Teadious night wee had, Such a one I Never See before: Wee was also Much Crouded, even So as to Lay, one on Another. Sick etc. My Friends, you can Scarsely think What Distress wee were in. —

Thursday 28 Our disstress Encreas'd, inasmuch as our Sickness, not only Continued, but the weather Grew, Thicker and more Stormy. And our Captain Upon whom (Under God) was our dependence Began to Drink too hard. As the Storm Encreas'd, (As is too frequently the Manner of Seamen) So that he was Altogether Uncapeable to mannage the Vessel, Neither was he able to go Down in to the Cabbin, but Lay Great part of the Last Night Upon the Quarter Deck: the Mate also was Something Disguised with Liquor: So that our Dependence was — Upon An Old fisherman: to Stear her, which he Could well do: altho he knew nothing of Navigation; About 1 O'Clock P:M: wee Spied a Privateer, Coming toward's Us, Against which wee had Like to Stove. which we Should have done, had'ent Old Peter (as wee Call'd him) Taken the Helm, Out of the Captains hand; by her Coming So near Us, wee began to think it was an Enemie, (Altho it was only to Speak with Us, to know where he Was. I Remember our Captain told him wee Was on Georges Bank's) But wee was So Sick and Concern'd etc., that being taken Seem'd No great Matter. As wee then Said one to another Going to France is no great matters. But notwithstanding our Difficulties yet wee had Searoom Enough which was one of the Greatest Outward Comforts wee Had: yet wee was not without many fears, wee Should, See Land no more: it made the Most Rude Amongst Us, Sober and thoutfull; I had'ent That to Reflect Upon That it was Against the Advice of my friends, I Came etc Which was no Small Comfort to me. (As I've before Said.) I would'ent had our Friends known how it fared. With Us by no means: for help us they Could not — Beyond what prayers Might Do, and I Doubted not, of our having them. —

29 Fryday. A.M. Wee had a pleasent Gale of Wind — the weather Somewhat Clear, wee had Most of Us Recover'd of our Sickness, So as to Eat which wee had'ent done in near Eight and forty hours Past I was So well as write my Journal, for the two Last days past. I Could then Evidence to the truth of The 100 and Seventh Psalm. Dr. Watts's Version (But more Especially the 1, 2 3 and 5 Verses — 4th Part — Comman Metre) having the Book then with me I Could With a great deal of Pleasure Read and Wonder At the Admirable Author.) P.M: it began to Thicken Up again and Snow Very fast which made me fear The Storm was Returnning Again Upon Us. But Desire to put our trust in Him who has appear'd for Us hitherto. —

30 Saterday — Wee had a good Gale of wind. and Most Or all of Us Recover'd of our Sickness. had a good Stomach to our Victuals. Wee all Seem'd Like New Men. Wee Discover'd three Sail, which were Some of the fleet. Towards Night, wee Sail'd into A Harbour, Call'd Liscombs Harbour' (This Day wee Sail'd 30 Leagues in Sight of Land) where wee found Seven, Belonging to the fleet. one of which to Our Joy, was Captain [Thomas] Sanders, who was A Privateer and wee hop'd now, to Sail to Canso, Safely Under his Convoy. N. B. He Carried the Hon. Bridgadeer [Joseph] Dwight Mr Hauley [Joseph Hawley] and Doctor [Charles] Pynchon.

31 Sabbath A: M: wee pray'd and Sung Psalms in our Vessel. P. M: Mr Hauley Preach'd. The Same was the first Sermon Ever He Delivered

Monday April 1st. There being Little or no Wind, we Continu'd all Day in the Harbour-and an Excellent one it is; Being A Short turn, it opens to the South: East and Runs. North: West where Comes in a River, I've forgot the Name the Passage into it is Narrow but after wee are in it's Very Large. A 1000 Sail Might well Ride at Anchor. I went not AShore but it appear'd a hidious Country, as I found the Eastern Shore Generally was. We are now 20: Leagues from Canso —

Tuesday. 2 About Sunrise (the Wind Being fair) wee Weighed Anchor: Being Warn'd by A Cannon Aboard Our Convoy. wee had the pleasure of Seeing Many Of our fleet Come out of the

Harbours, Between Liscombs And Canso, till wee were in all, Eighteen in Number. Wee cast anchor at Canso, About 4:O:Clock P. M. — Wee found Many Sails there, Altho wee found not the Fleet, which Sail'd two Days before Us. Being Much Crouded in our Vessel Many of our men went Ashore and Lay. —

Wednesday 3 This Morning it was Exceeding Cold — Our Men that Lay Ashore, in their Return to Us in the Morning, made more Adoe with the Cold, than I've Seen any the winter past. and had there been Snow Two u'd have been Smart Winter. it Seem'd Like war and Drums beatting. Trumpets Sounding, Gun Roaring etc. But wee were Soon forbid to fire or any other war Like Noise; for fear wee Should Thereby, Discover our Design to the Indians Thereabouts. and they Should tell it at Louisbourg. wee knew there was Indians there For Captain [David] Donnahoo had taken four which were with us in Canso, the Manner of his taking 'em Was thus. He went Ashore to 'em, and told 'em he was Sent by the Govenour of Cape [Breto]-n- to Bring The Indians provision: they Observing an English Vessel with him, were loath to go aboard for fear of Treatchery, But He told 'em he had taken it from The English. and had Aboard 25 good fat English Doggs all his Prisoners, and So Persuaded them Aboard

N : B : He Could Speak French well. —

4 Thursday this Day Cousin Benjamin Stebbins was Taken Sick which made me fear wee Should have Sickness in our fleet and army. There was a man died this day Aboard. The Massechusetts Capt [Edward] Tyng Commander. Lying just by Us. — They Buried him on A Little Island in the Midst of the Harbour. This day I went A Shore and See the Ruins of Canso. it was much Larger i. e. had Consisted of More, Buildings than I Expected but it was Reduced to Ashes (the Sight of which fill'd me with Some Indignation against the People of Cape Breton.) it was a Very pleasent place, and the Land was good the South End of the Island where it had been Inhabited. it's a Small I-land Lying in the Mouth of the Bay, that runs Up to Cannada River, it's Call'd the Gut of Canso it Cuts of Cape-[Bre]-tn from our Eastern Shore. — New Hampshire Soldiers were all Come they were Ordered Ashore this day. they was Imbodied and Taught How to Use the firelock by Major [Ezekiel] Gilman. Being in Numbers about Three Hundred

— Sun 2 Hours high Came in the General [Pepperell]; and many of our fleet are in Sight. A man Carelessly handling his Gun, Shot it off, and the Bullet went thro a Mans Cap on his head. I heard he was Laid Neck and Heels. (not for his Pains) but for his Carelesness. —

5 Fryday. Wee had Orders to go Ashore to Train, and the fleet being Chiefly Come in wee was a Very Large Band. wee had Thirty Six Drummers, who was Ordered to Beat at once, which wee Did for a Considerable time, altho I knew no Reason for it. There was also many Fidlers. Trumpetters. etc. which were pleasing. But Considering the Occasion of our Being together Prevented, in a great measure, The Delight wee Otherwise could have took.

7 Sabbath wee was again all Ordered Ashore to Be View'd Concerning our Arms and Amunition — Wee had two Sermons preatch'd this Day. A: M: By Mr. [Samuel] Langdon. .P: M: By the Rev Mr [Samuel] Moody — I Judge there was'ent Less than four thousand men that heard him. as 'twas his Usial way to read A Chapter before Sermon. So he did now which was 2 Cronicles: 14. His text was in 110 Psalms: 3 Verse — After Exersise was Over there was a Vast Deal More Drumming and Trumpiting than was needful Which I Trust Displeased a great many, while others Tollarated it.

Tuesday The General has order'd A fourt to be Built att Canso. There was Six Cannon Left There and a Captain with 80 Men. I'm inform'd that — Our Cruisers, have taken a Prize thought to be Worth — *li*8000. which is Going Directly for Boston —

Wednesday. 10 it has Snow'd all Last Night and So Does now. it Either Snows or Rains half the time I think Since we've been here. I understand the-Council of War Laid out a Sceme How to take—The Citty (Viz) to Come Upon it Upon Surprise and Scallade the Walls. Not waiting for Commodore Warren or Connetticut forces. and accordingly had Given The Captains their Particular orders where to Attack—Yet after all if they'r apprised of our Design wee are to Lay a Regular Siege I hear wee'r to Set Sail Early in the morning and whether wee go or Stay I hope God will be with us to prosper Us.—

Fryday. 12 There was Discover'd as was Thought two Sail of at Sea, But was found to be Vast Bodies of Ice. this Day wee Chose out Cranideers Four out of Each Company Mr. John Terry of ———— was Chose Capt over 'em. I'm inform'd that all the fleet is now Come in. As I was Going Ashore This Day I See a man Buried on the Island I've Mentioned already. his Being Buried without a Coffin was what I had'ent Seen before. and therefore was Somewhat Affecting. and thot it might greive our friends to hear the Like of any of Us (Even Upon Such An Account as that). But what matter thou't I is't where or how the Body is Laid when Dead (Altho wee Make So Much of it now) if Christ be it's keeper and it has a Remembrance in the Resurection of the Just. A Little After, there was another Buried, it was Suppos'd he Killed himself with Drink. This Day: P:M: it Thundred and Lightned, with Some Snow. and afterwards rain, it was also Very Cold. I Cant but Think Much Colder than 'tis in New England Water will Freeze over on Deck in a Quarter of An Hour. this Day a Regiment was Pitch'td upon to take St. Peter['s] [1]

Sabbath 14 Wee had no preaching this day — P: M: Came in Captain [David] Donnohoo who had taken Eight Indians. I hear one of 'em gives the following Account — that he was at Louisbourg 14 Days Ago That, then, Provision was Very Scarce Almost A Famine he Says wee Can Easily take them But I fear too good News (for us) to be true. —

Monday. 15 Very Pleasent, wee han't had So fine a Day Since wee Left Boston.

Wednesday 17 Notwithstanding wee'd Orders to Sail yet wee Continue Still in this Harbour, the Wind has been fair which wee Did'ent Improve, which Made Many of Us Uneasy. But I hope all will be for the best. Wee had Certain, news Afterwards that the Ice was'nt gone. There was a Snow of Ten Guns taken By Captain [William] Flecher. B Clear'd out from Martineco [Martinique] Loaden with Rhum and Sugar. Bound for Cape Breton. She had a Little before taken a fisherman Belonging to Cape Ann. They'd taken the hands aboard the Snow and put a Number of Frenchman Aboard the Scooners So that our own men are Brought in here. and there is Some, also in Persuit of the Scooner. — Some

---

[1] A French settlement near Canso (originally Canceau) Strait. The proposed attack was abandoned when the Indians captured on April 14th stated that St. Peter's was practically deserted.

of Our Company were atravelling by the waterSide at Canso found A Coffin floating in the water Wee Concluded it to be one Buried in the Sea.

18th Thursday another Prize was Brought in to day Loaden with Rhum and Mollasses which The General has Order'd for the Use of the fleet they Came in with Great Shoutting having not lost a man in the Engagement. Wee now Hear a fight at Sea Upon Which Capt [John] Rouse and Captain [Thomas] Sanders are Gone out, the General went not with him, But the Rev Mr [Samuel] Moodey is Gone. Doctor Charles Pynchon is also gone with Captain [Thomas] Sanders. they Soon Joyn'd Capt. Tiyng,[2] [Jonathan] Snelling and [William] Fletcher. But She outran all But Capt [John] Rouse and he Says She Struck to him But Upon Improving Some Advantage Afterwards and it being Night She got Clear of, him and he Saw her no more.

20 Saterday A Warm and Pleasent day, wee was all Order'd A Shore to be View'd by the General. wee were Strictly forbidden fireing — I am uneasy that wee are Doing nothing that Seems to forward the Design'd Expedition. —

21 Sabbath Four men of Coll. [Samuel] Willards Company[3] Went AShore to get Some wood, Neither of 'em Carried their Guns, and while at work Were Shot Upon by A Indian and two frenchman, and Being Under Such disadvantages were taken Prisoners. and was Compell'd to go with 'em which was About Six Mile. But Setting down to Eat were Careless of their Guns our men, fell upon 'em and Overcame 'em But Did'ent bind 'em. and as they was in the way back One of the frenchman took Up a Large Club and Struck one of our men on the head, and wounded him whereUpon they all fell A fighting Again But our Men Conquer'd and was Was going to Kill the Indian But he begging for Quarter, they Granted it and he afterwards in the Scuffle got away,

---

[2] Capt. Edward Tyng of the frigate *Massachusetts* was senior Provincial naval officer. This naval engagement was between nine Provincial vessels and the French frigate *Renommée,* which escaped.

[3] Willard not only commanded a regiment but the first company therein. All general officers and field officers had companies. This was the rule in the British Army. The company commander had valuable perquisites and the senior subaltern performed the duties.

But the two Frenchmen they've Brought home with them, the men I knew —

Tuesday 23 After Many Reports, Discouragements. and a Fear'd Disappointment. The Much Desire'd and Long'd for Commadore [Peter] Warren is Come and, With him three other Ships whose help wee very Much need. they Come not into the Harbour but go Directly to Cape [Breto]-n to prevent help's Going in to them.

Wednesday Wee have all the help now that wee Expect. Connetticut Regiment Being Come [4] But what are Numbers, what is Man that wee Should put Confidence in him. I Humbly Desire to Put my trust in Him who Has Sav'd (See Thursday March the 28th) and is Still Able to Save.

25 Thursday I went Aboard A Brigg Belonging to Conneticutt finding A Leabanon man there, Which gave me the Sorrowful News of the Death of Cousin Mary (Bliss) but now Lommis one I, Well respected But must never See more. It Made me think I Might never See all my friends that I Left Behind me in our family, or Place if it Should Please Providence to Return me But my hopes are that God will Preserve both Them and me. I heard also that Father was, Better than when I Left home for which I Desire to be Thankful. —

27 Saterday it has Rained the three Days Past Wee have a great Deal of Such Weather here

28 Sabbath. Mr [Joseph] Hauley Preatch'd A M: from Deuteronomy 32, 29 — P M: from Revelations 3. 17 I hear the Commadore has taken one or two Prizes since he Left Us, wich Would Otherwise have gone into the Harbour

Monday-29 After wee have tarried 27 Days In this Harbour wee Are now Set Sail for Cape Breton, We did Rejoice. But Considering what Our Design was, Might'nt it Justly be with trembling O! our Friends (Tho't I) Did you but know that this day wee were sailling forth to Encounter with Our Enemies how wou'd you pray for Us. I have Indeed Such Confidence in you That I Can Request nothing Greater than to have you're Request's Granted. —

---

[4] The Connecticut transport fleet, arriving April 24th, consisted of four sloops, a brigantine, and a schooner. Major General Roger Wolcott of Windsor was second in command under Pepperrell. Col. Andrew Burr commanded the regiment.

Tuesday 30 Early This Morning Wee had A View of the Citty i.e. the Steeples etc. A Calm and Pleasent Morning wee have But by A 11.O'Clock the Surffs — Ran high which Made it Dificult Landing etc. — and altho the Enemie had'ent heard of our Comming Before wee Came into Chapparough Bay [5] — (Which Indeed is Very Wonderful.) Yet before wee had landed they had time Enough to Come from the City (which was About 4 Miles from where wee Landed and About two and a half from where wee Encamped) So that there Came Out to Oppose Our Landing (As was Judg'd by Some) 150 Men [6] And had wee A Landed where they Expected, and where wee at first made an Attempt wee Should Almost Certainly Susstain'd the Loss of A great Many men. But wee had orders to Land in Quite A Differrent place than what wee had Made a pretence of. Which gave them the Trouble of Travelling Above A Mile, in which time, A few of Us got Ashore, and altho the Number was but about 17 which met 'em att first yet they was Enabled to Defeat their Design and to turn 'em back by the way they Came. And not without the Loss of Several Men Slain, and Some taken, The Vessels also, which Where of force, Shot Upon 'em which Kill'd one while We Susstain'd no Loss Except one wounded in His knee and that Slightily. for which Let God have the Praise and Glory. I travelled Directly Up to the top of A high Hill (Lying a Mile And a Quarter West of the Citty) where wee had a fair View of it. The french Shot att Us Several times. one of the Balls wee took Up while it was a roalling (wee Judge'd it to be A 24 Pounder) wee Lay this Night in the open air — But wee Cut A few boughs to keep Us from the ground. Vastly the most Comfortable Nights Lodging This! Since I left Boston. There was Singing and Great Rejoicing. And there was Indeed great Cause But wee Should be Carefull to Rejoice in the Lord which has Done all for Us. it was a Very pleasent Evening it was the first time I've heard any froggs Peep or Birds Sing for there was none at Canso. The North Pole. Appears higher to Us.

[5] Gabarus (or Chapeaurouge) Bay, selected as the landing point. It was 3 miles from the town and 4 miles from the Grand Battery.

[6] Actually 24 soldiers under Mesillac du Chambon and 50 civilians under Morpain, the port captain.

than it Does in New England. Wee are in Latitude 46. and 27 Minutes or thereabouts. —

Wednesday May 1st. Wee Removed from This place and went about A Mile West. and had almost Made our Selves Tents. But Just at Night wee had Orders from the General to Remove half A Mile East. that wee Might be nearer to gether — and in A better Posture for Defence, against our Enemies Round About Us. one Can Hardly Conceive what Spoil wee Make Upon the wood — for houses, for fires etc. one thing I Particularly Remark — (Viz.) that it was Vastly better Landing and Likewise More Conveniences for our Living on the Island Than was Represented to Us; while att Home Altho the Island (Especially on Some Places) is the Most Stony, of any Place on Earth. This Night, Many of the Army Went Up towards the Grand Battry to Plunder (and Indeed! wee fill'd the Country (for as Yet, wee had no Particular Orders, — But Everyone Did what was Right in his own Eyes) Among which I was one. There was also a Number went Up, A Little North of the Grand Battry and fired Several houses (16). Some of which were Store-houses fill'd with Sails Cables and other Ship, Tackling, Many that were there Suppos'd what Was Burnt was worth li100000. they was Much Blamed for Destroying So Much of what wee had got in Possession and I think very Justly — for I Cant Suppose they had any Prospect of Doing Any good thereby Altho wee Generally Thou't Afterwards it was A Means of the French's Deserting the Grand Battrey and if So, the Loss, was to us gain. About 2: O:Clock in the Morning I Return'd to the Camp. There had been an Alarm in the Night and The Capt and all our men but one or two were gone to Discover the Enemie. But Return'd without Seeing Any. There was also A great tumult and Noise all this Night. —

Thursday-2. This Morning there Being A few Men Near the Grand Battrey and Perceiving no Smoke Come out of the Chimneys Ventur'd in and took Possession.[7] they hung an old Red Coat for Coullars and Which the french Perceiving. Came with A Con-

---

[7] De Thierry, Captain of the Royal or Grand Battery, had reported it untenable. Lieut. Col. William Vaughan of New Hampshire, who claimed to his death the credit for conceiving the expedition, marched into the battery

siderable Number. Across the water in Shalloways [Shallops] — Designing to Retake it But A Small Number of Our Men Made 'em Retreat back to the Citty and now Seeing they Could not Recover it again They was Minded to Destroy it and began to Thow Balls and bombs both from the Town and I-land Battry — Note. they had Stop'd their Cannons with Iron, that So wee Might-ent Use 'em Against the Town

Fryday 3 Wee Began now to Land our Cannon, and Mortars. and are Getting them Up to the Green Hill (commonly So called-) wee are fetching our tents ashore and Likewise Setting of 'em Up. Landing our Powder also, and (having Clear'd one Cannon att the Grand Battry) Were ordered to Carry Powder Up there wee all Seem'd to be of one heart and things are in A Good Posture. This Day the french Shot very Much from the Town our Men Kept an Account of the Cannons and it Amounts to 2400 Weight of Powder This day wee took Prisoners, four Men and a Boy — The Biggest part of this day I was in A house about half way Between the Town and Grand Batty So that I had A fair Prospect of the Battle The House Shook Exceedingly altho it was a half Mile from the Town. —

4 Saterday. This Day I went to Carry Powder we took one Prisoner as we was a going Up to the Grand Battry. While I Was there (Which Was the Biggest part of the day) was Brought in from the woods. five more French men. and a French Negro. We had now Cleared Three Cannons All the Smiths was also Sent for that Was found in the Army. this day we Shot 84 Cannons against the Town. and I Suppose Sixty of 'em went — inside the Walls. Many Struck on the water 40 rods from the Citty which would rise and go over the wall Afterwards this day the Enemie Shot but Little Wee had but two Cannons from the Town and one and Twenty Bombs from the I-land Battry and but one of them fell inside the Walls. and that without Doing the Least Dammage. Our Scout Just

on the 2d. One of his men, William Tufts, nailed his red coat to the staff. (Cf. this diarist's statement under May 18th that Joshua Pierce was the first to place the English colors over the Grand Battery.) The French sent four boat-loads of men to recapture the battery, whom Vaughan beat off. The battery and its thirty cannon when cleaned out gave the New England army practical control of the inner harbor.

FIRST JOURNAL

now Come in which Brought in Eleven Prisoners and have Kill'd two — Two of Sd Prisoners were young women —

Sabbath. 5 Mr [Joseph] Hauley Preach't to Our Company From Psalm 90th-Even According to —

[Remainder of page missing. The manuscript is badly torn and several pages are mutilated in this section.]

There was a man found dead in a french house Near the Citty it was Tho't he Died in a Drunken fit. This Day the Commodore Brought in a Large prize Loaded with Bread Meat and Flour which was Bound for Cape Breton I hear there's Several Prizes taken and Carried into Canso.

7 Tuesday About 3 OClock A. M: I went up to The Green Hill to Guard the Artillarie towards noon We Moved Our Cohorn Morters Within About A10-

Town, But Just as we Got to the Little
on. We was Shot Upon by
Perceived Our D

[Page torn and remainder of page missing].

Which is as follows.—[8] Summons Sent in. To the Commanding Officer in Louisbourg

The Camp before Louisbourg May 7th 1745

Whereas there is now Encamped Upon the Island of Cape Breton Near the City of Louisbourg. A Number of His Brittannic Majesties troops. Under the Command of the Hon-Leut. General Pepprell. A Squadron of His Majesties Ships of War Under the Command of the Hon. Peter Warrin Esqr now Lying before of the Sd City

[Remainder of page missing].

In Consequence of which Wee Sd William Pepprell and Peter Warrin. In the Name of Sd Sovereign Do asure you that all the Subjects of the French King now in Sd City and Territories. Shall

---

[8] A substantially correct copy of the demand for surrender made May 7th here follows. For full text see *Mass. Hist. Soc. Colls., 6th ser., 10:14.* This demand was sent against the advice of several senior officers who held it was unjustified in view of the confusion of the plan of attack and operation and the general lack of success on the part of the Provincial Army.

be treated with the Utmost Humanity. Have their Personal Estates Secured To them, and have Leave to transport them Selves and Sd Effects to any part of the French Kings Dominion in Europe — Your Answer Hereto is Demanded at or before five of the Clock this Afternoon.

Commander in Chief of the { W. Pepprell
P. Warrin

[Remainder of page missing]

---

which time we Ceas'd Firing Whereupon the Women and Children came Up on the Walls to See Us About 2. O:Clock P. M. our Flagg Return'd with The Following Ans. (Viz)

N.S. Louisbourg May 18th 1745

Wee Lovis Du Chambon. — Knight, of the Millitary Orders of — St. Lovis Kings Lieut. Commanding The Royal I-land. St. John's, Canso and the Adjacent I-lands. On the Behalf of His Most Christian Majesty.

Upon the Summons Sent Us this 7th Day of May O. S. By the Hon. Leut. General Pepprill Esqr Commanding The Troops which form the Siege of — Louisbourg. And the Honorable Peter Warren Esquire Commanding the King of Great Britton's Squadron of Ships Anchor'd near the Port of Sd. Town. To Surrender the Sd. Town with its Dependencies. Artillary Arms and warlike Stores. To be in subjection to the King their Master In as Much as the King Our Master Has Betrusted Us with the Defence of Sd Island Wee Cannot hearken to any Such Proposals till after the Most Vigorous Attack. nor have wee any Other answer to make to this Demand but by the Mouth's of Our Cannon

To Messers Pepprill and Warren, Commanding the Troops and Ships, of the King of Great Britton

Translated by Mr N. [Nathaniel] Walter [9] (of Roxbury) Transscribed by St. Croix.

And now Seeing the Terms was not Complied with We Gave a

---

[9] Chaplain, 6th Mass. Regiment, Commissioned official interpreter, March 22, 1745. Harvard, B.A., 1729.

FIRST JOURNAL 15

Great Shout and Began to fire Upon the town Again. A great number Enlisted to make a trial for the Island Battry but Did'nt go the Night Appointed.

Wednesday 8 one Captain's Company went up into the Woods and took a Small Village, they Kill'd 20ty and Brought away 25 Prisoners. Also brought away A Number of Neat Cattle etc Without the Loss of one of our Men.

Thursday 9 there is A great Firing from our Fashien [fascine] Battries and from the Grand Battry the Town also Fires Considerably at Us. About 10 O'Clock A M: We had Orders to Prepare our Selves to Scallade the walls this Night. I Must Confess I was Sorry to hear there was Such A Determination. Before We had Used our Cannons and Mortars Longer But if it is'nt for the best I hope it will be Defeated. and if it is I hope and trust God will be with Us and Prosper Us. And accordingly Sun About a hour high (at Night) The Whole Army Was Gathered together, for the Design before Mentioned. But there was a Great Uneasiness Appear'd Thro out the army (and that for the Reason I Mentioned (Viz) that we had'ent tried Enough With Our Artillarie having taken a great Deal of Pains to get it Ashore and Draw it Up to our Battries and then Might'ent Use it) Which Commodore Warren Perceived as he Walk'd Back and forth in the front of the army. (Note: he had a Capt with A 100 of his Granideers going with Us) and Said (to a Number of Offisers as they Stood talking together) Gentlemen; what is your Communication? to which, Leut. Mun [John Man] Made this Reply. I Suppose your Honor's Aquainted with our Design Against the Town this Night. and I Always tho't Actions of this Nature Should Be Done with the Greatest Vigour and Resolution. (to Be Sure, Replied the Commodore) But Seeing Such a General Uneasiness, — Makes me fear what the Consequences of This Night Will Be. The Commodore then Left 'em and went and walk'd A while with the General-and Soon after, there Came word for all the Captains to go in to the Council and Speak their Minds. and I was told there was'nt So Much as one Vote in favour of it.[10] This Night Captain Joshua

[10] This whole incident is illustrative of the informality and lack of discipline prevailing in the Army. At the morning meeting of the Council, with all general officers and regimental commanders present — 17 in all — and with Warren also there, the vote was unanimous to attack that night. The dis-

Pierce. went with a Number of Men and Built A Fashiene Battry (which went by the name of -Cohorn Battry) Where We Placed three Cannon (Eighteen Pounder's) and to which, we Moved our Large Morter afterwards. We have made, Three Attemps to take the Island Battry but Have been Disappointed (Once Leut. [Samuel] Chandler went a Captain etc.)

Saterday 11 There went twenty Men Up about Eight Miles in the woods and had taken A Small Place and was Carrying away the Spoil. But there being a French Dr. among the Prisoners He Seem'd to Rejoice that he was Taken and Desired Liberty to go and Call his family and they put that Confidence in him as to grant him his Request but Instead of his Family he Brought an Hundred french and Indians Upon 'em which Killed Eighteen of the Twenty that went out. Yea Bucher'd 'em at an Inhumane Rate. One of which was Captain Peter Prescoot [Prescott] of Col. Jeremy Molton's [Jeremiah Moulton] Regiment —

P. M. There was a man had his Legg Shot off by a Cannon Ball and he Died before he Could be Brought down to the Camp. Another Receiv'd a Muskett Ball in his Elbow which Caus'd his Arm Emeadiately to be taken off. Another was Shot in his knee and Doctor [Charles] Pynchon tells me He dont Expect he'll Live. It is now Very Cold and has Snow'd for Several hours together [11]

12 Sabbath Mr. [Joseph] Hauley Preached to our Company in the P. M. from John 3 17 [16] for God So Loved the World etc. having an Oppertunity to Send a Letter to New England I wrote one this Day-

Monday 13 A great Deal of firing This Day From the Town. the Grand Battry and the fashiens [fascines] now while I write Eighty Cannons have been Discharg'd in a Quarter of an hour

Wednesday 15 I went to Guard the Artillarie where I tarried 48 hours. This day in the P. M: — fell a Cold Hail it Seem'd like a

covery that the subalterns and enlisted men objected was enough to cause the Council to reverse itself at its afternoon session.

[11] The Council this date, affected with discouragement, virtually decided to abandon the offensive and to wait for reinforcements. Comparative inaction was general until the capture of the *Vigilant* changed the whole outlook (see May 21).

Storm in March I Rec'd a Letter from Brother Moses Dated April 19th.

Thursday 16 We have Split 3 Cannon at the Grand Battry but Did no great harm to the Gunners. I Suppose they were Overloaded which Caus'd 'em to break (Using lb15½ when lb14 was a Common Charge) We also Broke on Cannon at our Cohorn Battry which Sorely wounded the Chief Gunner So that his Leg was Cut off Soon After but is Likely to Live. A Large Piece of Sd Gun flew forty rods and Buried it Self in the Ground the Piece I've often Seen.

Friday As I was by the water Side A washing My Cloath's I See a Dead man carred along To be buried he was Kill'd by A Piece of A Bomb Shell that Came from the Town it fell on his head and broke his Skull. He belonged to Piscattoway. Note. I have not told of all the Prisonners we have taken, I Suppose by (at Least) one Third. I hear the Commodore Does not think it Prudence to try any more for the I-land Battry. but Sayes that if the help Comes that He Expects Very Shortly He'll go Directly into the Harbour. Upon which the General has Determined to Let the Matters Rest for the Present This Night we Made Another Battry Just Forty Rods from the west Gate, (which Goes by The Name of, Advanc'd Battry) and are Drawing Down Cannon from the Grand Battry with A Design to break the Town to Pieces if they Don't Surrender. And now while I am writing none but those that hear (or that have been in Some such an Engagement) Can Think how much firing there is here, Cannons Constantly A going, and Bombs etc. and Altho I'm Two Miles from 'em they Don't Seem to be above Sixty rods they are So powerful. While I am writing there is great Firing with Small arms and People ran for we had word that the french was Come out to Drive Us from Our Batteries. but it was the men from the wall Shot Upon our Men, while at work (See Last page) and wounded one of our men in his arm but not Like to prove Mortal. There was also a Small fight over to the Light Point (Viz) a 100-French Came against forty of ours They Kill'd one Indian which belonged to Us. But our Men Soon Drave 'em into the woods Again — Our Men found a Number of Cannon Sunk in the water Near the Light House, I understand the French were A Going to build A Fort there to Defend the Harbour (Which I think is almost Impregnable now) But our Men are Endeavouring to get 'em Up to Use them against the I-land Battry. I hear we have Broke another Cannon at the Grand Battry. which Sorely wounded Capt [Daniel] Hale of Newberry — and is Since Dead A Large Piece of Sd Gun About Six Hundred weight flew up in the air and fell on the House and fell thro' all the floors to the Bottom of the Cellar. There was A Bomb Came from the I-land Battry which fell by the Edge of the water at low Tide which blew Up a Large rock and Carried a Piece of Sd Rock (About 300 weight) Up over The Wall and house which is att Least twenty rods the rock I've often Seen and Lifted.

☞ ———— When we was Making our Battry Last Mentioned. there was a Larg Rock in the way Where we wanted Much to fix A Gun but it Was Immoveable by Us. But at Length there Came A bomb from our Enemies which fell on This Very Rock and So broke it to Pieces that we was able to move it at our Pleasure. —

18 Saterday We have Cause of Joy and Sorrow both We Seem to gain ground of our Enemies we've almost broke the west Gate So that we Could Drive in A team. altho we have but one Gun att the Advance'd Battry to Play Upon 'em as yet There has been an Exceeding hot Battle this Day from Break of day till Night not only Cannons (which we had Plentifully from the Town) But also Small arms far Enough beyond what I Could Number. I Doubt not but their has been As many Guns fired This Day as I have Draw'd Breaths. We have Kill'd Some from off the wall How many we Can't tell But we also have Lost two men (Viz) one of our Gunners who had This awful Circumstance atending his Death (Viz) Having made a Shot that Did'ent please him Said God Damn me if I Don't Strike the Gate this time But while he was taking Sight Almost Ready to fire there Came a Ball from The Town and Split his head that one the parts fell on Each Shoulder and he Died. Another was Capt. Joshua Pierce of Lanchester one I Very well knew He was Col. [Samuel] Willard's Capt A Truly Brave and Noble Captain and therefore is Much Lamented It was he first put Up English Collours in the Grand Battry the 2nd of May His birthday Being 27 Year Old Just — Year to a day as he then Said He put up English Collours in Cathragene [Cartagena] in

New Spain. There being Several Attempts made to take I-land Battry (as I've before Mentioned) it was Generally tho't The Officers were Afraid to go — And the Night before Last Capt [Joshua] Pierce had a Commission to go and men in great Numbers Appear'd to go with him (Several of Capt [Joseph] Millers etc.) I Remember he Said while he was at our Tent that He'd never Return till he'd made a Thorough Trial and Accordingly went up to the Grand Battery to set out. But they were forbid by the General. Upon what Commodore Warren had Said (See Friday 17 Day) and So it was he did never return but was Shot at the Advanc'd Battry with a Cannon Ball thro his Bowels he was able to Speak many things for he Lived 16 minnites he is now Brought down to the Camp. There was four men Kill'd this day besides Capt Pierce one or two of which were kill'd By a Barril of our own Powder's Accidentally Catching fire.

Sabbath 19 A. M. I attended Capt [Joshua] Pierce's Funeral after — which I went and heard — Rector [Elisha] Williams Preach He took his Text in Samuell 30-6. but David Incouraged himself in the lord His God — He applied it to the present Case Both A M. and P M. he preach'd Exceeding well. I also heard Mr. [Nathaniel] Walter of Roxbury from Peter 2-11 Dearly beloved I beseech you as Strangers and Pilgrims Abstain from fleshly lusts which war against the Soul — I am Inform'd that we have Lost five men at our batteries This day. one was Kill'd by the breaking of a Cannon Being Carried by a Larg Piece of it (about 400 Weight) About Eight rods and then fell and Ground him to Pieces — P. M: the Commodore is Just Set out in Persuit of a Large Ship, and begins to fire Briskly at her. A very Cold Day I See it Snow Some.

Monday 20 The fight at Sea Still Continues we hear that there's Several french men of war on the Coast.

Tuesday 21 This Day the Commodore Brot in the Ship he has been after and a Very Large one it is, it Carries Sixty Guns, with 600 hands, and also A great Quantity of Stores, with a thousand Barrels of Powder (as I was told) and also Rigging for a thirty Gun Privateer which was then Building att Quebeck; A Number of Men went out yesterday which have bro't in ten Prisoners, they also Kill'd two. one of Sd Prisoners is Suspected to be that french Doctor I Mentioned (See Saterday May 11th) and if it is Prov'd he Will Suffer Death. He is now in Irons About 6. OClock P M. the whole army was Called Together to make a Shout for the Prize the Commodore Had taken (Viz the Vigelent [12]) at which time the Battries was also to fire. (I Suppose without Ball) — Our Scout having Discover'd about 200 french and Indians at a Small place, 4 Miles Up North Sent Down to the General for help whereupon there Went up a great Number of Men. but before they Got there the French had Led off Except two which was Left behind for a Spie. and being So thick woods they Could not take 'em Howbeit they Shot Upon 'em and Suppose'd they broke one's arm for he Let His Gun fall and Escap'd without it — Dr Morrisson and Dr [Charles] Pyncheon went Chyrgeons etc.

Wednesday 22 Went up thirteen Men which belong'd to Capt [William] Fletcher. after wood in Chapparoug Bay — and Not being Carefull to take a guard with them. there Came a Number of Indians Upon 'em which Kill'd Seven out Rite, and took 3 Prisoners, two of which, are Since found and Most awfully Butcher'd. Stabb'd thro the heart Several times their Heads also Cut to Pieces etc. wee Trust the Other is Kill'd also. one of the three that Return'd was wounded and is Since Dead. There fell out a Sad Accident this day,[13] About ten Pounds of Powder took fire (at our Advanc'd Battry) which Burnt two men Very Much one of 'em was, John Hooker Belonging to Major [Seth] Pomroy's Company the Other was Jonathan Clary. Capt [Jabez] Omsteads Drummer. I Desire to take Notice (with thankfulness) that while many Companys are Sickly and Some dead our Company are all well and for the Most part have been So (Except Capt [Joseph] Miller) I talk'd with a Capt Who belonged to Boston (Capt Ephraim Baker) who told me he'd Lost Six out of his Company. Distinguishing is the Goodness of God towards us. This Day Died one which belonged to our Goverment I am now Come from the Funeral of another

---

[12] The *Vigilant,* Capt. de la Maisonfort, 64 Guns, 500 men, and loaded with supplies. If she had reached the fortress the siege would almost certainly have been broken. Her capture greatly heartened the attacking forces and depressed the defenders. The *Vigilant* was taken by H.B.M.S. *Mermaid, Superbe,* and *Eltham* and the Provincial *Shirley.*

[13] This accident occurred on May 19th, not the 22nd, according to Pomeroy's Journal.

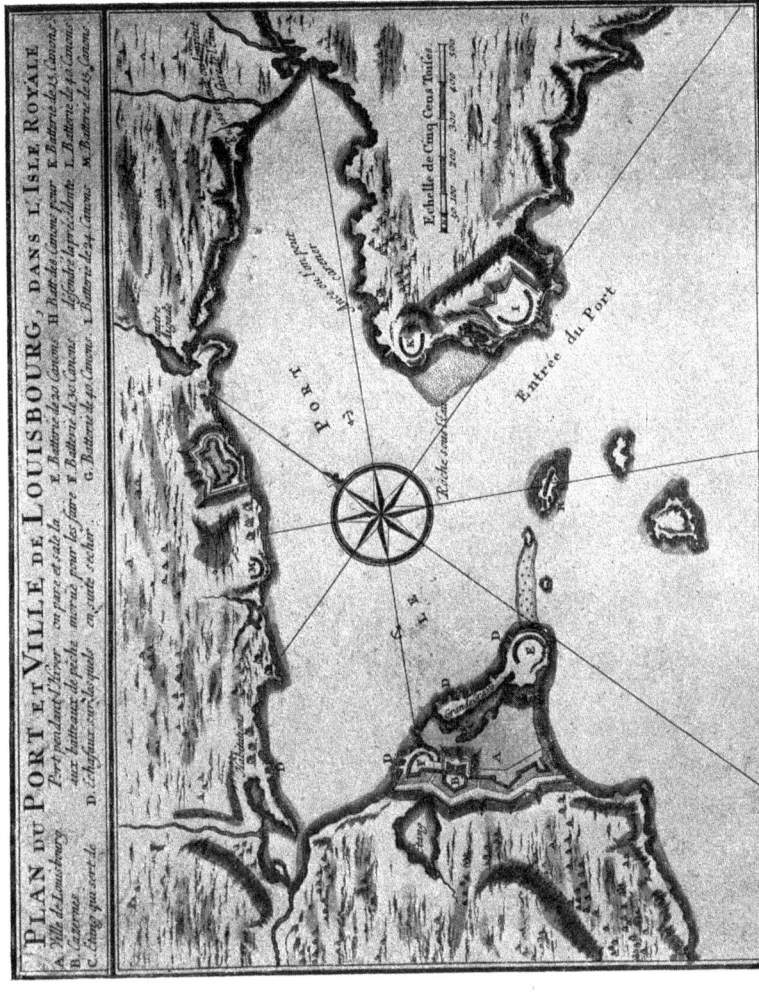

From the Society's Collection.

who Belonged to Bolton of our Province who Died with a Feavour. He was about Eighty year Old.[14] — We was (About a hundred and fifty of us) Order'd to Carry Boats from our Landing place to the Grand Battry which was three Mile. which was the Hardest Service I've Ever Undergone in all my Life. (and So Said they all) but having a Prospect thereby to take the I-land Battry made Us Chearfully Endure our burden [H:M: Col. C — Mr Pa.?]) :

23 Thursday Died Major Newton who has been Sick a Long time. I understand he's Much Lamented Note, He belonged to Conneticut: This Night there was a Remarkable Northern Twilight.

25 Saterday A Number of Men went out upon a Scout which brought in four Prisoners and Kill'd one.

26 Sabbath The Rev. Mr. — Balch (who was Chaplin to our Regiment) who has been Sick a Long while was able to Preach both A M and P M. and a Comfortable Sabbath we had; we was Free'd from Duty etc. This Night we Made an Attempt for the Iland Battry. and wee have great Reason to be humble'd before God. who did not go before us to Prosper us but we were Smitten. Many were Kill'd, Some taken (A) Others Drowned, (b) Many Wounded, (c) There appear'd A Great Concern the next morning thro'out The army Even in their Countenances for we Could not tell how many we had Lost. but Did Expect it to be a great Number.

(A. Wee found in the Citty when it was Surrend'red into Our hands One Hundred and Sixteen Men that was taken At the I-land Battry. There was also three, if I Mistake not, that Died of wounds that they'd Receiv'd altho They Liv'd Some time. So the whole was 1–19).

(b. One (Among the many) that was wounded was Nathaniell Redington Belonging to Goshen Listed Under Capt [Joseph] Miller He Receiv'd a Muskett Ball thro the flesh of his thigh but not Like to be mortal).

(C: This I had from Mr J — Winchel who was an Eye Witness. That Just by them, there was a Boat Cut Asunder and all the men Drownded and although They Cried for help, in Such a Moving Manner As Lord Save Us Lord have Mercy on Us — Dear Friends Come and help Us, etc. and tho they were in oar's Reach of 'em yet Durstent offer 'em the Lest help They also Receiv'd many Balls in

---

[14] Evidence of the extreme age of some of the soldiers.

their own Boat. But it Did not Sink 'em. Nor Did they wound any of their Men He went ashore att the Light house Point and tarried till Morning where they found Eleven (Drove Up) Dead Upon Shore and many was oblig'd to have their Limbs taken off, etc. and Said He; I would'ent be in the Dangers I was then in not one minnit for the whole world [15]).

27 Monday Was taken Eight Frenchmen and one Woman the woman Gives this Account (Viz) That there's an Army of French and Indians coming Down Upon Us which Makes us Strengthen our watch etc.

29 Wednesday This Day It's Election at Boston I hope to Receive Letters from home as Soon as they can be Convey'd from Boston. This Day there fell Seven Men from the top yard arm of Capt [John] Rouse's Snow Three of which were Kill'd in a moment; the other four fell into the water (Missing the Vessel) and Receiv'd no great Hurt —

Thursday 30 Our Scout are Return'd that have Been out Several Days they have had a Smart Engagement with About 200 french and Indians [16] (Double to their Numbers) and being Under Some Disadvantage fought Upon a Retreat. We Lost Six Men Upon the Spot. and one that was wounded Died before They Could bring him home: there were also many wounded. two, of which are Very Dangerous.

Friday May 31 I am Just Come from the Generals Tent where I

---

[15] The Island Battery, closing the harbor entrance, carried 39 guns and had a garrison of 180 to 200 men. The only landing places were two gaps in the rocks. The Provincial army considered the capture of this battery most important and tried repeatedly to organize an expedition against it but the lack of discipline interfered. The first serious attempt was on the night of May 23d. There were northern lights and a moon but the chief difficulties were the lack of junior officers and drunkenness among the men. The next day Lieut. Cols. Arthur Noble and John Gorham were charged with the failure but exonerated. The Council called for volunteers for the next expedition, promising that the men could select their own officers. About 400 volunteered. During the landing a drunken soldier proposed three cheers and aroused the French. The Provincials lost 189 killed or captured and the whole mismanaged affair greatly depressed the spirits of the army. The Island Battery was finally rendered impotent by the fire of the Lighthouse Battery, built by the Provincials.

[16] Actually 100 French and 80 Indians.

FIRST JOURNAL 23

Saw Eight Prisoners taken Last Night. They are Part of that Company I Mentioned. May 30th (Note their fight was on Tuesday May 28th. and these were taken by another Scout that was out) which Say that our Men Kill'd Thirty and wounded forty more. our men Suppos'd they Kill'd Some but Con'd'ent Learn what Number till Now. Note I have not kept an Exact account of all that have Died with Sickness Since we began Our Siege For there was many Died that I Didn't Hear of till Some time after and So Did'nt put it Down in my Journal Note: It was not a Very Dying time Considering the Number there was of us. and also of the Number of Sick. (which was 5-00 as I had it from Dr [Charles] Pyncheon — About this time) [17]

Saterday June 1st it Has been foggy Three days past I Look upon the Weather to be Very Unhealthy. Several of our Company are not well. We Having Split our Biggest Morter. There was a Vessel Sent for one to P. Royal [Annapolis Royal] but was Mollested by Indians and So Return'd Back again Where Upon Capt [John] Rouse is Set Sail for one This Day — But to our Great Joy we had one Sent to Us from Boston which Landed here Just at Night.

2 Sabbath Mr. Balch Preach'd A M. from Revelations 1. 10. I was in the Spirit on the Lords Day P: M: from Matthew 23. 37 O Jerusalem Jerusalem Thou that Killest the prophets etc. —

3 Monday A French Sloop Ran Ashore att the Light House Point and Twenty three men Escap'd But the Sloop we've got Loaden with Provisions for Cape Breton Our Scout have taken Seventen Prisoners [18] which were So faint our Men were Oblig'd to tarry about Eight Miles Back. one Night Longer than they needed otherwise to have Done.

Tuesday 4 I Received a Letter From Boston Dated May 6th — which Informs me that Part of a Day Every Week is Set apart to Seek the Divine Presence and Blessing with our army which Does

---

[17] On June 2d Pepperrell wrote Shirley that about 1500 of his men were sick or wounded.

[18] From a raid made by Capt. James Noble with 160 men, on the fishing settlement of the du Vivier family at Mera (Miré), twenty miles distant from Louisbourg.

Greatly Encourage me and also others that I Read it to. This Day wee was order'd to Move our Tents and Pitch 'em Clost together So that we Might Fortifie our Selves Somwhat against Our Enemy (See Monday May 27) which we Did and forted in about Twenty Acres. Inside which; we all Encamp'd. We had Several Field Pieces which we plac'd in Flanquers, etc.

Wednesday 5 This Day Capt [Joseph] Miller (who has Been Sick a Long while) went on Board to Return to New England. I wrote a Letter to Brother Moses.

Tuesday June 11 (d) Our Scout Came in which had took a Great Number of prisoners they also Kill'd two or three but we Lost not a man nor Receiv'd a wound. This day two of the Swisses [19] ran away From the City and Came to our army and from what they Say we have hopes that the Citty will Break up in a Little time This Day went a Flagg of Truce, or Rather a Letter from the Marquis [de la Maisonfort, of the *Vigilant*] to Inform the Govenour of Cape Breton that he was taken. (which news Seem to Dishearten 'em Very Much) He also told of the Good Usage he had from the English, and Cautioned them against ill behavour towards the English Prisoners. This Day arrived a man, of War and joind to our fleet, and also Says She Left two more but a few days Sail off.[20] This Day The Soldiers had a Treat Givin 'em by the Province it being The Day of Accession of His Majesty King George the 2d to the throne [21] We have made a Battry at the Light House Point to Play Upon the I-land Battry.[22] We had one man Kill'd there this Day. we had a man wounded at the advanc'd Battry (Belonging to our Regiment) But I hope not Mortal

(d. Here Endeth my first Journal which I Sent home, to New England and By Capt Miller and it was Dificult to Get Paper Here and it was Several Days before I Could get any which made the Vacancy from June 5 to June 11 —).

---

[19] Since 1722 there had been at Louisbourg soldiers of the Swiss regiment of Karrer, an auxiliary of the French Army.

[20] The *Chester* from England joined Warren on the 10th. On the 12th arrived the *Sunderland, Canterbury,* and *Lark.*

[21] There was violin, flute, and vocal music and an extra allowance of spirits.

[22] A most important and effective measure, recommended by Capt. Philip Durell, R.N., and Capt. James McDonald who commanded about 300 marines.

FIRST JOURNAL

12 Wednesday while I was at the Battry this day there was a man wounded a Piece of a Bomb Shell took all the flesh off of one of his Thighs (Being about 12 Pound) and it's fear'd He wont Live. Capt [Jabez] Omstead's Drummer (See Wednesday May 22) Died this Day.

Thursday 13 we were ordered Carry one of Our Mortars over to the Light House-Battry (and having a Bombadeer Sent Us from P — [Annapolis] Royal) and it had a Very good Efect, the Bombs being thrown with Extraordinary Exactness So that of 22-19 of 'em fell Inside the Fort. The Other Ships I Mentioned Tuesday June 11 — are arriv'd Here. So that wee Have the Assistance of the Ships Following (Viz) [23]

Names of Ships	of what fire Guns	Name of Captains.	
Superb	60	Peter Warren Esq.	Since made Admiral
Princes Mary	60	Richard Edwards Esq.	Since Made Commodore
Sunderland	60	Capt Britt	There was
Canterbury	60	Capt Hore	also Cap Tiyng
Chester	50	Capt Kemp	Cap Snelling
Hector	40	Capt Cornwell	Cap Fletcher
Mairmaid	40	Capt. Dugless	Capt Prentice Coniticut
Lanceston	40	Lord Montique	Capt Donnahoo
Eltham	40	Capt Dural	Note Capt Smothers
Lark	40	....	was Lost before
Vigelent Fr.	60	French Ship	this time

We are great Numbers of us Emploi'd in Getting Moss to Defend, the Ships,[24] for the Commodore Designs Shortly to go in to the Harbour If the French Don't Yeild and So prevent it

14 Friday There was orders. Thro the army to have four Men

---

[23] See Appendix I, *The Fleet,* for correct names of ships and officers.

[24] Warren to Pepperrell, June 12th, "As it will be of the greatest consequence to barrocade our ships well against the enemy's small shott, I desire you will please to employ as many men as you can spare in getting a schooner load or two of moss for that purpose."

Drawn out of Each Company to go Aboard the Commodores Ships the Men that went from our Company were Serjent Jonathan Benton. Simon Ames. Nathaniell Horton and Joshua Gere. This Day a Man which belong'd to Andover was Shot thro his Grine and Soon Died The Man Mentioned Wednesday June 12 is alive and to Humane Appeerence is Like to Do well This night I watch'd. The French threw 45 Bombs at our advanc'd Battry but yet (Wonderful it was) there wasn't a Man of us Hurt. —

15 Saterday The whole army was Called together to whom the Commodore made an Excellent Speech Well worth writing down but too Large. to Reed He Says hes now Ready to go in with his Shiping into the Harbour and waits for nothing but a Fair wind and Saies that if nothing Short of his Going at the head of the army (into the Town) Will do. He'll Chearfully Do it. for He'd Rather Leave his Body at Louisbourg, than not take the City. We had orders for making a Great Number of Ladders for Scaling etc. (the Trees, Grass and Flowers are about as forward Here now as they are at New England the Middle of May not Earlier to be sure.) So about Sun Set There Came out a Flagg — from the Town they Requested there Might be a Cessation of arms for a while that So they Might Call a Council to agree upon Some Terms whereby they May Surrender the City into our hands. for So Long as we fire So Smartly they can't Do any Such thing.[25] I Stood by and heard, Commodore Warren Tell the Rev. Mr. Walter [26] to return this answer — that They Should be Dealt well by as Prisoners of War and No Otherwise. The flagg Return'd and had time to Consider of it till: 8 O'Clock Next Morning. and I Earnestly Desire that there may be a Heart givin to 'em to Resign themselves Up That So their May not be that Effusion of Blood. that is Other-wise Determined.

Sabbath 16 The Flagg Came out the hour appointed and have been here Some hours. They offer to Resign the Citty into our hand — Allowing to Every Man His Personal Estate, all the Cap-

---

[25] The fortifications were badly battered, practically all the houses in the city damaged, only forty-seven barrels of powder left in the stores, food was short. Governor du Chambon sent an officer, de la Perelle, asking for a suspension of hostilities to arrange terms.

[26] See footnote 9.

tains Leutenents and Ensigns were Consulted in the (Important) Affair the Question was put whether we should agree Upon Such terms or Directly to Storm the Citty (Note! the wind was fair for the afore-Mentioned Design) and it Pas'd that we Should take 'em at their Offer. and accordingly the Cappitulation was Drawn and Sign'd and Hosstiges Givin from Each Party This is a Day Much to be Remembred by Us, For Our Enemies have Submitted themselves to us and Given Their Strong Holds, into our hands Let————(Read the Cappitulation and Return Back to here again. I had it not till after I had rote this, which is the Reason etc.)

17 Monday The General went in and took Possession of the City of Louisbourg! the greatest Conquest, that Ever was Gain'd by New England

18 Tuesday About break of Day Died one of [Lt] Col. [Thomas] Chandler's Men who has been Sick the greatest part of the Siege. we ought to with Thankfulness take Notice of the Distinguishing Goodness of God towards us of the County of Hampshier, that while, others are Dead by the Enemies hand and by Sickness, we're all Here alive that Came from That County.

The Commodore took a Vessel as She Came Sailling into the Harbour not knowing the Citty was taken we hear that there is Several Merchant Vessels to Come in here in a Short time We are a Notable Trap and I trust Shall be a Considerable time for the

———•———

Terms. Agreed Upon. The Surrender of Louisbourg To His Brittannic Majesties Obedience etc.[27]

Camp before Louisbourg June 16, 1745.

Sir — We have before Us yours of this Date together with the Several Articles of Capitulation On which you have Propos'd to Surrender the Town and Fortifications of Louisbourg. with the Terretories Adjasent Under your Government. To His Brittannic Majesties Obedience to be Deliver'd Up to His Majesties Forces

[27] Here follow copies of correspondence relating to the capitulation. For full records see McLennan's *Louisbourg, 163, 179–180.*

now Beseiging Sd place Under — our Command — which Articles we Can by no means Concede to. But as we are desirous to treat you in a Generous Manner we again make offer of the Terms of Surrender Propos'd by us: in our Summons Sent you the 7 of May Last. And further Consent to allow and promise you the following Articles (Viz)

That if your own Vessels Shall be found Insufficient for the Transportation of your Persons and propos'd Effects to France we will Provide Such a further Number of Vessels as may be Sufficient for that Purpose. also any Provisions for the Voiage that you Cannot Furnish your Selves with.

2 That all the Commission Officers belonging to the Garison. and Inhabitants of the Town may Remain in their Houses. with their Families and Enjoy the Exercise of their Religion and no Person Shall be Suffered to Misuse or Mollest any of them till Such time as they Can be Conveniently transported to France.

3 That the Non Commission Officers and Soldiers Shall Immediately upon the Surrender of the Town and Fortrese's be Sent on board Some of His Brittannic Majesties Ships. till they Can be also Transported to France.

4 That your Sick and Wounded Shall be taken tender Care of in the Same Manner with our own

5 That the Commander in Chief now in the Garrison Shall have Liberty to Send off two Covered Waggons. To be Inspected only by one Officer of Ours. that no war-like Stores may be Contain'd Therein —

6 That if there be any Persons in the town or Garrison. which you Shall Desire May not be Seen by Us. They Shall be permitted to go off Mask'd. The Above we do Consent to Promise. Upon your Compliance with the Following Conditions (Viz)

First the Sd Surrender and Due Performance Every Part of the afore Sd Premises be Made and Compleated as Soon as Possable —

2 That as a Security for the Punctual Performance of the Same the I-land Battry or one of the Batries of the Town Shall be Delivered with all the Artillary and war-like Stores thereunto to belonging into the Possession of His Brittannic Majesties troops this afternoon.

3 That His Brittannic Majesties Ships of War now Lying be-

fore the Port Shall be Permitted to Enter the Harbour of Louisbourg without Mollestation. As Soon after Six of the Clock this afternoon, as the Commander in Chief of Sd Ships Shall think fit

4 That none of the officers nor Soldiers or Inhabitants in Louisbourg. who are Subjects of the French King. Shall take up arms against His Brittannic Majesty. nor any of His Allies untill After the Expiration of twelve Months from this Time

5 — That all Subjects of His Brittannic majesty who are now Prisoners with you Shall be Immediately — Deliver'd up to us.

And in Case of your Non Compliance with These Conditions. We Decline any further treaty with you on the affair: and Shall Deside the Matter by our Arms.

            W. Pepprell
            P. Warren
Monss Du Chambon   — Sr.

      Camp before Louisbourg June 16–1745 —

Sir — I have yours by an Hostage. Signifying your Consent to the Surrender of the Town and fortresse's of Louisbourg and Territories Adjasent etc. On the terms this Day propos'd to you by Commodore and my Self. Excepting only that you Desire your [troops] May march out of the Garrison with their Arms and Colours to be then Deliver'd into our Costody till Sd troops arrival in France at which time to have Returned to them. Which I Consent to and Send you an Hostage for the Security of the Performance of what we — have Promised. and have Sent to Commodore Warrin that if He Consents to it also he Shall Send a Detachment on Shore to take Possession of the Island Battry. —

            William Pepprell
Mons — Du Chambon —

News won't Suddently Reach old France. This Day I went into the City I found it Suprisingly Strong — But the Particular account of it I shall Omit here and Leave for a further Observation. Last Night a Vessel Came in — from Boston — I Received a Letter from Brothers Jonathan and Moses. Bearing Date May 25. none can tell how Glad we are to Receive Letters from New England — it is Exceeding Foggy Now and begins to Rain. —

23 Sabbath The Rev. Mr [Samuel] Moody Preach'd at our Campt From Proverbs 8. 6. Hear for I will Speak of Excellent things. Doctrine That Grace is an Excellent thing —

— *24 Monday* I sent a Letter to Brother Moses — That Inform'd him that Louisbourg was taken.

26 Wednesday The Weather is Clear'd up and is fair

Note! it has been Exceeding foggy and Rainy Ever Since the 18 Instant. (Excepting about two Hours in which we See the Sun.) And altho' I Can't Say, that the Stars in their Courses Have Fought against Our Enemies Yet This I Can Say. Remarkable! has been the weather It was 49 Days after we began our Siege before the General went into the City. and in all that time we had not So Much as 24 Hours Rain. There has not been the Like Since the Citty Has Stood (As they Relate.) which was a Vast advantage to us (not only Upon the Account of our health But also) in Using our artillarie This! in Conjunction with Many Other things, not Less Remarkable Ought not to be forgotten by us (Note He had not as yet, been into the City.

27 Thursday We had an Exceeding hard North-Est storm, and very hard rain.

28 Friday We moved our Sick and Stores into the Town and the whole army was allowed to Move Our Company Mov'd, and Liv'd in a house a Mile North from the City. This Day I went into the City, and The more I View it, the more I Admire it. — Nor Can I Ever tell the Strength, and Cost of this place. and yet I Can tell So Much that perhaps I Sha'nt be Credited. Could I give a Description of it in full I Shou'd'ent Expect to be Beliv'd. There was three Scooners and a Small Sloop taken this day they Came Sailling Into the Harbour Having heard nothing that the Citty was taken, while 1 was in the Citty I went to See the Place where they Buried their Dead. and the french Having Occasion for Earth to fortife them-Selves and it being Easiest Digging there, They had taken Earth from that place which uncover'd Many Coffins. and Bones etc. Since we Besieg'd — There was Such Numbers Kill'd and that Died [28] — with Sickness, that they'd Digg'd

---

[28] Before the siege there were 590 soldiers and 900 civilians in Louisbourg. Fifty were killed and 80 wounded during the siege.

FIRST JOURNAL 31

A Hole about twelve feet Square (and about as Deep) Where they threw in all together, and without Coffins. I was told. —

Saterday: 29 I went into the Citty again, I went To See the Hospital (Du Roy) and a Very Large House it is but the Description of this I Leave till afterward

Sabbath, 30 Mr. Balch Preach'd Both A. M. and P. M: from St. Luke 1.72. to preform the Mercies Promised to our Fathers. and to Remember his Holy Covenant. This Day Came in Eleven Shallowaes [Shallops] and about Seventy, persons. and Subjected them-Selves to us. they Belonged to the Adjacent Villages. There was a Man Died the Next Door to Us. He belonged to the Commodores Ships

Monday July 1. I went to See the I-land Battry. I found it very Strong it's forty rods Long it — Mounts thirty Guns (24 Poundrs [29]) and is Excellently Situated to Defend the Harbour. (but a further Description See afterwards.)

Tuesday 2 Our men taken at the I-land, Battery (who was Kep't in the City.) Inform'd Us that Leut. ——— Perceiving a Switser [Swiss] Uneasie ask'd him the Reason He told Him and withal told him He Design'd to Desert the Citty, and flee to the English Army. Leut ——— Desir'd Him to Carry a Letter to his Friends ashore, He Said he wou'd. But He was Unhappily Discover'd and having the Letter found with Him they Sought no further witness but Hang'd Him next Day —

4 Thursday Came in a Transport from N-England With a Captains Company from Wosster County [30] they Set out from Boston Saterday June 22, they Say there's a Great Number on the way Hither. I am Inform'd that the French have kept an Exact Account of the Cannons. and Bombs that we have Thrown at, and into the City. The Number of Cannon 9–5–56. The Bombs 6-oo, etc.[31] A few of our Company went out into the Harbour to fishing

---

[29] Correct figures. For a full record of artillery, ordnance supplies, etc., in the fortress, see McLennan's *Louisbourg, 408*.

[30] Capt. Ebenezer Edmunds with a company from the 8th Mass. Regt. (Choate's).

[31] Pepperrell stated that the besiegers had fired "upwards of nine thousand cannon balls and about six hundred bombs."

— Where they See two men (which Doubtless were Kill'd at the I-land Battry) floating in the water one had his head took off He had a Wescoat Butten'd about Him. The Other was Naked. His flesh Was Much Bruised of against the Rocks or Else Eat by the fish. who they are is not known. This Day one the Commodores Ships (Viz) the Lanceston (Having Brought Her Guns into the Citty and plac'd 'em there) Set Sail for france and with Him Capt Woster [David Wooster] of New Haven. and three other transports which Carried a Great Number of French Gentlemen and Ladies — I See 'em take their Leave of the City and their friends Still Left behind. in a Very Affecting Manner.

5 Friday. There Came in another Transport of Men from New England.[32]

Saterday 6 This Morning it's as Cold as 'tis Commonly with us at New England in September Several Shallops from the Adjacent Villages Came in and Resign'd them-Selves up This Day Mr. Hauley [Rev. Joseph Hawley] went to Live at the I-land Battery in the P. M. Leut. [Ebenezer] Alexander Leut. Mun [John Man] and my Self — Went to See the I-land Battery and also the Light House a Description of which I Design to give afterwards, Just at Night Came in Capt [Edward] Tyng from Boston — Leut [Samuel] Chandler — Leut. Mun and I went aboard. where to our Great Joy we found the Rev. Mr Williams [33] — and also many of our Acquaintence and friends. by whom I Receiv'd four Letters from Springfield. I also hear Capt. [Isaac] Colton is on the Voiage here.

Sabbath 7 The Rev Mr Williams Came Ashore and was at Meeting at the Citadel A. M. The Rev Mr [Samuel] Moody Preachd from Hebrews 1. 13 But to which of the angels Said He at any time. Sit on my Right Hand, Untill I make thine Enemies thy footstool. Mr Moody Spake of His Faith (which He'd often Discover'd at New England and also at Canso) Not (Said He) That I'de any Secret Impulses But, God, Seldom gives A Remarkable Spirit of Prayer, but Sooner or Later He gives an ans — He also

---

[32] Col. John Choate with two companies of his 8th Mass. Regt.

[33] Both Rev. Stephen and Rev. Elisha Williams were chaplains. This was Stephen Williams. See *Ninth Journal* in this volume. Elisha Williams was called "Rector" as he had been Rector (*i.e.,* President) of Yale College.

was Led to Speak of Swearing. and Cautioned against it (for he Speaks of almost Every thing in Every Sermon) and that He Might Make the Deeper Impression Upon many there who Gave Themselves Up to Such a vile Practice. He Related, what you may See in Saterday May 18. He Said he had it from an Eye Witness. P. M. — Rector — [Elisha] Williams Preach'd from 1 Cronicles 16. 12. Remember His Marvellous works which He hath done His wonders, and the Judgments of his Mouth. Hardly any Can tell what Joy it was — to See God worshiped according to His own appointment where Anti Christ had, Had His Seat to See So many good Ministers (as I had Reason to think.) and Especially our Dear Pastor — I Must Confess it Seem'd to me Like what wee read in the 126 Psalm 1 Verse.

8 Monday I went round the Citty, with those that Came Down with Mr [Stephen] Williams who often would Say if we had'nt Come Down here we never Should — Belived half if it cou'd have been told Us. This Day came in Capt. [David] Donnahoos [34] Sloop which Informs Us that the Capt and Leut. the Chief Gunners and nine more of the best of his Hands were Kill'd Up in Canso Harbour (or Gut) who having Spied a few Indians (which was their Pollacy) Went ashore and when they Came there their was Some Hundreds who Kill'd 'em and Cut 'em all to Pieces. He had Like to have been Kill'd there a Little before (Even a narrow Escape) but was Resqued by another Vessel. So after Many Worthy Actions he Died in Battle. It's Appointed for all Men once to Die. and if So, what Wonder if those that are often Expos'd to Death in war Should Die So. two men Died next Door to us. (belonging to the Princes Mary) one Died with the Consumption He was born in New England — I See the Dr open Him who found his Inwards Very Much Consum'd. Not So Much Affected were his Ship Mates when Digging his Grave as many are only at the Sight of a Dead Horse. But would Curse and Damn Each other while a Doing of it. which to me appear'd Very Maloncholly and Strange.

---

[34] The Indians are reported to have cut open Donahew's chest, to have sucked his blood, and then to have eaten him and five of his slain companions. Only three years before Donahew had miraculously escaped death from other savages when wrecked on the coast of Africa in a slave ship. (*New Eng. Hist. and Gen. Register, 77:103.*)

Wednesday 10 Leut. [Samuel] Chandler Obtain'd Leave to go Home to New England — and with him thirteen of our Company. But I Cou'd'nt get a permit altho' I Endeavour'd for it. and Therefore Must Ev'n be Contented to tarry till the fall of the Year. I'm Inform'd that a Myreen [Marine] got Drunck and Shot of his Gun and wounded two men very Much. . .

11 Thursday. This Day I went into the Hospital to See the French People Say Mass. I Could'ent help wondring to See Gentlemen who were men of Learning (I Suppos'd, and Doubtless of good Natural parts also) So Led Aside as to worship Images, to Bow Down to A Cross of wood. and to See So many of all Ranks Seemingly Devout. when we've Reason to think They never had any Communion with God Through the Course of their Lives. Being Ever So Strict in the Practice of their Religion it is now, and has been for Some Days, Quite Hot Weather.

13 Saterday Our Men which were Dismis'd Set Sail for New England this Day. to whom I wish etc.

14 Sabbath Rev Mr [Stephen] Williams Preach'd in the Cittedal in the A. M : from 1. Cronicles 18 — 22 for there fell Down many Slain because the War, was of God and they Dwelt in their Steads. Untill the Captivity. in the P. M. — Mr Fairweather. (Chaplin to Capt. [Edward] Tiyng) Preach'd From 1 Cronicles 29. 11. 13. — Thine O! Lord is the Greatness, and the Power, and the Glory, and the Victory. — Now therefore our God we thank thee and praise thy Glorious Name — A Prize Came in this Day taken by Cap. [William] Fletcher — Loaden with Flour. from Cannada

17 Wednesday Came in Capt [Isaac] Colton and with Him Many of our Friends from Springfield, Enfield etc. By whom I Receiv'd A Letter from Brother Samuell Brother Jonathan Brother Aaron, and Cousin M — Bliss. I heard also of the Death of Aunt Steel.

18 Thursday. This Day was kept by us as a Day of Rejoicing for the Late Victory the Goverment Allowed two Sheep to a Company and Six Gallons of Wine. P M. The Rector [Elisha Williams] Preach'd whose Sermon was admir'd Very Much altho' I had'ent opportunity to hear Him — I Sent two Letters to New England (By Leut [Samuel] Chandler whom wee all well Respect,

FIRST JOURNAL 35

and wish A Prosperous Voiage) one to my Honord Father and the other to Cousin M — Bliss.

Saterday 20 I Came to the Knowledge of Many things. that I Could not know before the Citty was taken which Set forth their Disstress Beyond what I had tho't of Before among the many I Shall Mention but two or Three which are (Viz) there was a woman Newly Bro't A Bed that was So affrighted by A Bombs falling into The House where She Lay, that She Soon Died. There was a man Playing with his Little Child between his feet. and there Came a Cannon Ball which Cut the Child asunder. (But Hurt not the Man) it went into another Room and Kill'd two more of his Children. (This I Saw not, but I had it Crediably) A woman (Near her Time) was walking in the Street who was Cut asunder by a Cannon Ball, and Died Immeadiately.

(This Added, Since I Came Home (Viz) that the Child is Still Alive in the City and that many Of our Men See it which I wou'd have Done my Self (were it true) Had I heard of it before I Came from thence.) it's now the Heighth of Straw Berrie time. theire Sold in the City for $3d$ Quart.

21 Sabbath. The Friers and Priests being gone the french Left of Worshiping in the Hospital. — Mr [Stephen] Williams Preach'd there. (which was the first time we had met here) from Luke-13. 25. When once the Master of the House hath risen Up and hath Shut to the Door. —

23 Tuesday A Vessel being Discover'd the Commodore Sent out two Ships which Soon took her and without The Loss of one Man. I had a fair Prospect of the Battle being up in Highest Steeple in City. (The Barracks or Cittadel).

24 Wednesday Came in the Prize which Came from the East Indias Exceeding Rich. I Spoke with an Officer which Belonged to the Princes Mary (which went out) who told me the Prize was worth 1-20-000 Pound Sterling. Being aboard a Vast Quantity of Pepper. Embroider'd Cambricks. Sattins East India Handkerchiefs etc. They Discharg'd A great Number of Cannon. As they Came in. The Commodore Return'd an answer, and also fifteen Guns from the City.

25 Thursday Died a man next Door to us belonging to the

Princes Mary. I've been Several Days Emploid In Raising Vessels which the French had Sunk — The Soldiers were allowed 6*s* per Day.

28 Sabbath Mr [Stephen] Williams Preach'd up at the Grand Battry. From Luke-15-24 For this my Son was Dead And is Alive again —

Monday 29 The whole army was Call'd together. and The General Read to Us A Letter His Excellencie Had Sent to him which Inform'd Us that He Design'd to See Us by the Last of this Month.[35] which Should it be, Would Greatly Rejoice Us. — A Vast Deal of Buisiness is Carried on in the Citty in Repairing what wee'd Batter'd Down. Note! In the time of the Siege we Broke A Very Larg Bell which Hung in the Cittidal into four Pieces, By a Cannon Ball, we have found a Very Good one in the Store House and have Hung it in the Room of that which was broke. —

Tuesday 30 Another Large East India Ship was taken But I han't heard what She is Tho't to be worth — This Day we had a Pint of Wine Given to Each of Us To Drink His Majesties His Excellencies the Generals and Commodores Good Health which I Should be glad to Do oftner if they Should Think fitt. —

Friday August 2nd There was A Prize Brought in Vastly Rich Which Came from the South Sea — Worth Both the former Prizes. I hear She's thought to be worth — 4-0-0-000 Pound Sterling. —

4 Sabbath Rector — [Elisha] Williams Preach'd from Deuteronomy 32–29 — O! that my People were wise that they Understood this that they would Consider their Latter End Doctrine that God Does with great Earnestness Wish or Desire the Happiness of Man. . . . . .

8 Thursday it has been Exceeding Foggy. and Some Very hard rain for five Days Last Past. This Day two of Capt. Ebenezer-ALexadrs [Alexander] Men Were Dismis'd and Set Sail About 6. O Clock. P M: Dr C [Charles] Pyncheon was a Coming out to our House to see Joshua Geree (whose Life wee Dont Much Ex-

---

[35] On June 26th the Council asked Pepperrell to urge Governor Shirley "to come as soon as possible." Pepperrell wrote Shirley to that effect June 29th. Shirley answered July 7th.

pect) and as He was a riding over the Trench at the West Gate a plank Broke Under him. So that He fell Thro' and Broke His (Left) Legg Both Bones But it was Soon Reduced again, which Gives Reason to hope He'll Soon get well

9 Friday it's Colder than 'tis Comonly at New England the Latter part of Sept.

12 Monday Leut. Mun [John Man] and I finish'd Measuring the Citty Height of the walls Thickness Bigness also with many other Circumstances, as also the Grand Battry, I-land Battery and Light House and also the Road from the Grand Battry Down to the Citty. and also from Each fashine to the Citty. and I trust in A Little time we Shall have a perfect plan.

Tuesday 13 This Day I went into the Citty to Live. and to Tend Dr. [Charles] Pyncheon.

Wednesday 14 Last Night fell a man (which Belong'd to Some of the Ships) off of the wall which Doubtless Broke Some of his Inwards He was Brought into the Hospital He liv'd in Extream pain about four Days and Died — His Being in Drink I Suppose was the Occasion of His fall

Friday 16 Just at Dusk Came in the Hector. which Brought His Excellency — and His Lady, the Commodores Lady and many other Gentlemen. and Women etc.

Saturday 17 8. O Clock A M. His Excellency Came ashore Who was Receiv'd with Great Respect and Great tokens of Joy being Salluted by the men of war 17 Cannon from the Superb. and 17 from the Hector. the whole army was Call'd together to attend upon His Excellency while He was walking thro' the Street Up to His House. and as Soon as He had Set His feet Upon Louisbourg the Cannons in the Citty were Discharg'd. With a great Deal of Drumming Trumpiting and other Instrument of Musick Was this Day fill'd up. This Day Died one of our Company Viz John Taylor of Hadley — the first that has Died which Belong'd to the County of Hampshire Since the Expedition was form'd. Many of that County are Sick at present and what God Designs for Us in a Way of Righteous Judgment (for our Iniquties) I know not.

18 Sabbath A M. Mr [Stephen] Williams Preached in the Hospital from Matthew 19. 22 But when the Young Man heard that Saying He went away Sorrowfull for he had Great Possessions.

P M. Rector [Elisha] Williams Preached at the Cittadel (Before His Excellency) from. 1 Corinthians 2.2 for I Determined not to know any thing among you Save Jesus Christ and Him Crusified. —towards Night Came in Capt [Jonathan] Snelling from Boston and with Him many Gentlemen — Some of the Council and Some of the House — one of which was Dr. Joseph Pyncheon, which Did — Rejoice Dr Charles [Pyncheon] Very Much and my Self also. By whom also I Receiv'd two Letters from Home Dated July 17. and 18.

19 Monday A M: Wind South and rainy P M. Clear'd off and Very Pleasent. Died in the Royal Hospital three (Viz) Leut — Gross (Belonging to Conneticut County Sloop) one — Garisun — and one — Dakins

20 Tuesday Wind West — and a Very pleasent Day Nothing Remarkable this Day — Unless the Funeral of Leut. Gross which was attended by Firing around of Guns (from the Sloop to which He Heretofore belong'd) and that in a Mournful manner being a minnit — Between 'em. —

21 Wednesday A Very pleasent Day. This Day His Excellency went to See the Grand Battry. which fired Seventeen Cannon at His Arrival (that Number being A Royal Sallute) and the Same at His Departure Died in the Royal Hospital this Day. 3 —

22 Thursday His Excellency went to See the I-land which Salluted Him as the Grand Battry Did while the Ensigns were all Displac'd etc. —

23 Friday A Very pleasent Day Especially in the A M

24 Saterday the Whole army was Call'd together and His Excellency Made an Excellent Speech Both to Officers and Soldiers But all Insufficient to make 'em Really willing and Contented to tarry all Winter. He Gave the Soldiers two Hodgsheads of Rhum to Drink His Majesties Health. After which He with the Generall and Sundry other Gentlemen walk'd all round Upon the Wall of the Citty, while the Ensigns with their Collours [36] were plac'd at Each Angle of the Wall and all the Soldiers in proportion. who fired in Volleys as They pas'd along. to hear Such Numbers of Guns Even for an Hour or two together it Seem'd almost Like

---

[36] The Ensign, a line officer, relative rank of present 2nd Lieutenant, was the color bearer.

FIRST JOURNAL 39

the Late Siege. This Day I Reciev'd a Letter from Sir Warham Williams which Inform'd me of the Death of Job Cotton — I Trust our Loss is his Gain. I Think I Can truly Say I simpathize and mourn with the Mourning and Bereiv'd parents and friends.

25 Sabbath A. M: Wind South: and Rainy. — Mr [Stephen] Williams Preach'd in the Royal Hospital from Luke 18-9 — and He Spake this parible unto Certain which trusted in them-Selves that they were Righteous and Despised Others — P. M. the Wind North West and Clear — The — Rector [Elisha Williams] Preach'd in the Cittadel before His Excellency and his family (e) from Psalms 8: 4 What is man that thou art Mindful of him and the Son of Man that thou Visitest Him. Towards Night were Buried 3 which Died in the Hospital Belonging to the Commodores Ships. . . .

(e. He always attended Divine Service there, and also the Commodore. Hearing our Chaplins one part of the Day. and the Commodores the other, as Did also the General etc.).

26 Monday Died one belonging to the Ships (Note. I have not Set Down all that have Died in the City But by what Observation I Had of the Funerals — I Judge there Dies 3 or 4 in a Day one Day with another This Day Dr [Charles] Pyncheon was Able to Set in A Chair for Some Hours. which was the first of his Getting Up. Since he Receiv'd His fall, which is Eighteen Days.

Tuesday 27 A Vessel Going out of the Harbour — after wood was Driven by the wind against the Rocks at the I-land Battry. which Stove it So that it Sunk No Lives were Lost. But there was a Considerable many things Lost, which were in the Vessel. one of our Sloops as She was a Going after Coal was taken by A French Scooner — who took away all the Mens Cloaths and their Guns. But Gave a Deed of the Vessel to Some Certain Gentlemen which they were — Acquainted with and So Let 'em go. and She Came into this City to Day Note. the French Enquir'd whether Louisbourg — was taken. our men told 'em they knew not that it was — Whereupon the Sd French Vessel Came in Sight of the Harbour But not Liking the Looks of things etc. are tack'd about — Cap. [William] Fletcher is now gone in persuit of her. etc. This Day Set Sail for England, Capt. [Frederick] Cornwell. Belonging to the Hector. who has Assisted Us in our Siege against Louisbourg this Day I wrote A Letter to F—d [Friend?] E— at New England. —

Wednesday 28 Wind South and an Exceeding pleasent Day. —

Thursday 29 Dr [Charles] Pyncheon and I, Reciev'd a Premit to Return to New England by the first Convenient Oppertunity — none Died in the Royal Hospital this Day. —

Friday 30 A M: Clear weather. P. M: about 3 O'Clock — Cloudey and rainy Dr Joseph Pynchon went on board and also Capt. [Isaac] Colton to go to New England by whom I Sent Three Letters. to my Friends there, none Died in the Royal Hospital this Day.

31 Saterday. about 6: O Clock A M: Capt [Edward] Tiyng Set Sail (with a fair Wind) for Boston This Day Died Nathaniell Dike. Belonging to Capt [John] Heustons Company —

1 Sabbath, Sept 1. — Mr [Stephen] Williams Preach'd in the Royal Hospital from — See Last Lords Day. P. M: I — Heard — Rev Mr Wood (Chaplin to Commodore Warren) from Proverbs 10.9. He that walketh Uprightly walketh Surely. Sickness prevails and Deaths Multiply This Day Died Jonathan Fox of Suffield Listed under Capt. [John] Huston. Died in the Royal Hospital one of Capt. [John] Warners men of Lanchester and one belonging to the Ships.

2 Monday A Very pleasent Day the Wind North West — This Day Died one which Belonged to Capt [William] Warner of Boston. None Died in the Royal Hospital this Day.

3 Tuesday A pleasent Day and Warm. Died in the Royal Hospital a man Belonging to Capt [Daniel] Fones of Rhode I-land — and one Thomas Wheelright who Listed Under Col. John Storer. this Day Died — Onisimus Nash who belong'd to Sheffield Listed — Under Capt [John] Huston — one of Col. [Samuel] Willard's men went on board in order to return to New England But Being So ill was bro't ashore again and Died this Day His name was Zac Gould — Another Died who belong'd to Roxbury Under Capt [Estes] Hatch. another Died who Listed Under Capt [James] Church of Hartford his name was — Burbanks — We hear there's Several french men of War Lying Near to this place — we have our Intelligence by a Carrolina Ship which Says She Left 'em in Latitude 44 — (Some time ago) Bound for this Port. Whereupon orders were given thro' the Citty by the Beating of a Drum that all Sailors Should Immediately Repair to the Several Ships to which they Belong'd — and if any had absented themselves too Long — or Committed any Crime etc. by Repairing to the Commodore Should be forgiven A Great Number Also of our Land men went Aboard to Assist the Comdrs men.[37] I hear the French Ships Mentioned are two Seventy Gun and two Sixty — and two forty —

Wednesday 4 A Very pleasent Day Died this Day (next Door to the Hospital) Joshua Maxwell He was taken Sick the Last Day of August — He was Delireous near all the time of His Sickness.

Thursday. 5 Overcast weather and foggy. Died one in the Royal Hospital this Day — I wrote a Letter to Sent to — Mr J-C — at New England.

Friday 6 A M : foggy and Very hard rain. Died this morning Capt John Warner of Lanchester Belonging to our Regiment (Viz) Col. [Samuel] Willards He's one that's been very Serviceable in our Late Siege. and therefore it must be a Considerable Loss P M : I am now Come from the Funeral of Capt [John] Warner who was Buried in arm's the General and Several Cols attended the Same Died in the Royal Hospital four which Belong'd to the Commodores Ships. P M : Died Sergt — Walker Listed under Capt John Huston Being the Sixth He's Lost. with a negro that Died Upon Chapparoug Bay who never Came Ashore and another which Died in the Hospital before I Came Here to Live. I Heard this Day. that the Indians have burnt Sheep Coat and George's [Sheepscott and Georges in Maine] Upon Our Eastern Shore — a Man Died this Day which belonged to New-Hampshier Under the Care of Dr. Wood ([A. P. ?] P. M. at 8 Clock)

7 Saterday West and Cool P M. Cloudy and Rainy the air Somewhat warmer. Died this Day at the Grand Battry. Capt James Stevens — Died aboard the Vigelent Mr Samuell Winslow (Who Came from Boston with the Rev. Mr [Stephen] Williams) He was Stationed there as. ——— Died in the Royal Hospital. one. which belong'd to the Ships

8 Sabbath A. M : Mr [Stephen] Williams Preach'd in the Royal

[37] The Council had authorized the voluntary enlistment of not over 600 soldiers as marines on the British men-of-war.

Hospital from Ezekiel 21. 10 — it is Sharpned to make a Sore Slaughter etc. P M. I heard Mr. ——— [Wood] Commodores Chaplin. Wind: North and Quite Cool Weather Capt. [Ebenezer] Alexander Set Sail for Boston. This Day Died Sergt ——— Taylor of Col. [Samuel] Willards Company.

Monday 9 a Cool Day this Day Died Cor: Little-John Belonging to —

Tuesday 10 A pleasent Morning. this Day Died Capt [Robert] Glover and also Adjatent Generall. He Belong'd to Boston. another Died Belonging to Cap. Lane His Name was ——— Wardwel

Wednesday 11 This Day Died Dr Alexander Bulman. I Believe a Truly Godly and Pious man (Chief Chirurgeon to the General's Regiment. He has been Very Serviceable to this army and therefore is a great Loss. and not to Us only But to the Town of York to which He belong'd. But our Loss (I trust) is His Unspeakable Gain. Several others Died. But I knew not where they belong'd. I am Crediably Inform'd that there was Ten Buried this Day. three Coffins went By the Hospital together this Day. P M I went on Board Designing for New England but the Vessel was So throng'd I Came Ashore, and wait for another oppertunity. This Day Dr [Charles] Pyncheon was able to Walk (Upon Cruches) Up to the General's which was about Sixty Rods. it is now thirty four Days Since his Legg was Broke —

Thursday 12 This Day Died Seven which belong'd to the Land Army. it's an Awful and Disstressing time with Us in this Citty. and when I Call to Mind what God has Done for Us Heretofore. I've been Ready to Say in words Much like to Sampsons in Judah 15. 18 Lord thou hast givin this Great Deliverence into the Hands of these Thy Servants and now Shall they Die by the pestilence

13 Friday A. M: got a Bierth for Dr Pyncheon and my-Self. (aboard Capt — [Ephraim] Done) to Return to New England P. M: His Excellency and Commodore Warren, with many-other Gentlemen (and all the Ladies which Came Down with the Governour etc.) went to See the Grand Battry which Fir'd 17 Cannon at their Arrival and the Same Number at their Departure. from there they went to the I-land Battry which Fir'd as the Grand Battry Did. it being A Very Clear air it made the (Very) Citty to tremble. which gave me an Idea How the french felt in the time of Our Siege —

14 Saterday I am Disappointed a Second time for — The Vessel wee were to go in is not permitted to Sail yet. Last Night Died Sergt Jonathan Warriner of Leut Mun's [John Man] Company. He has been Sick Six Days He was taken with a Cramp in his Leggs and afterwards with a Chollick in Bowels He was in Extream pain Great part of his Sickness. But had — (to Humane appearence) a Very Easy Death — He is to be Inter'd this Day but I Can't Attend it My Self — Which I Should be glad to Do.

Lords Day. 15 A M : Mr [Stephen] Williams Preach'd from See Last Lords Sept 8. P : M : the Rector [Elisha Williams] Preach'd from Numbers 14. 17. and now I Beseech thee Let the Power of my Lord be great. etc. there was one — Buried this day. — a Very pleasent Day and warm for the time of the Year. —

Wednesday. 18 His Excellency Made a Speech to the army which (I Conclude) was Occationed by a Great Uneasiness in the army Especially those that Came first in the Expedition. because they were not Dismis'd (as they Suppose) according to Contract. and also Upon Account of His Excellency's not Suffering the Small arms which were found in the City to be Divided among The Solders. I Often heard there was Seven Hundred had Listed to Lay Down their arms — But I Hope His Excellency has Made the Soldiers Much more Easy. He has Promis'd to Return (or Dismiss) all but two Thousand. by the Middle of October and those whose Circumstances most Require them to be at home. further Promis'd that those that tarry Shall have *li2* New Tenor per Month. and Promis'd them Bedding also as far as it could possably be Obtain'd and that they Shall be Return'd to New England in the Spring as Soon as may be with Convenience also Order'd the Small arms to be Immeadiately Deliver'd to the Soldiers. after which He was pleas'd to Give the Soldiers two Hogshead of Rhum to Drink His Majesties Good Health. Commodore Warren Being present — Made a Short (but Excellent) Speech Gave two Hodgsheads of Rhum, for the Same Use.[38]

[38] The situation was much more serious than the journal would indicate. A general mutiny was threatened and some men had already left their

19 Thursday. I went out to See Leut. Mun [John Man] who is not well. it fell to my Lot to have a Gun. —

20 Friday. Cloudy But warm. Sept is more Like it Self. i. e. as 'tis in New England than any Month I've Seen Since I left Home. I Hope Sickness abates Somthing altho' there's been a great many Deaths Since Sept 15th which was the Last I Mentioned. I not Being well my Self have not taken an account of 'em as I Used to Do.

22 Sabbath. Rector [Elisha] Williams Preach'd in the Royal Hospital from. 2 Peter 1 : 17 for he Receiv'd from God the Father Honour and Glory when there Came Such a Voice to Him from the Excellent Glory This is my beloved Son in whom I am well pleased — Doctrine. God puts great Honour upon Christ in being Reconciled to Sinners thro him —

  Proposition : (1) God is Reconciled to many Sinners on Christs account

  (1) God has taken them into a Near Relation to himself. He calls them his Sons —
  (2) God accepts their Services (3) God has Comunion with them God Meets them in ordinances Sometimes in one Duty Sometimes in another —
  (4) God will Finally Take them to Heaven

  (2) Proposition : Herein God puts great Honour upon Christ in that He is Reconciled to Sinners thro' him —

  (1) Herein He gives Testimony to the Saving Vertue of Christs Death and Suffering —
  (2) Here by Christ becomes the Instrument of aboundance of Good improvment

  (1) Use of Reprofe to Such as are not Desirous that Christ

posts. The chief grievances were that the men had been kept beyond their period of enlistment and were likely to be kept much longer, that clothing, rum and other necessaries were lacking, that the men were unpaid, and that the Massachusetts and New Hampshire men were to be paid much less than the Connecticut and Rhode Island troops. Massachusetts had enlisted its men at 25 shillings a month, while Connecticut paid forty and Rhode Island, fifty. Moreover, the Army was in part very angry over the orders to refrain from plundering and the resulting lack of booty, while the Navy was to be greatly enriched with prize money. See the minutes of the Council of War for Sept. 17, 1745. (*6 Mass. Hist. Soc. Colls. 10:45.*)

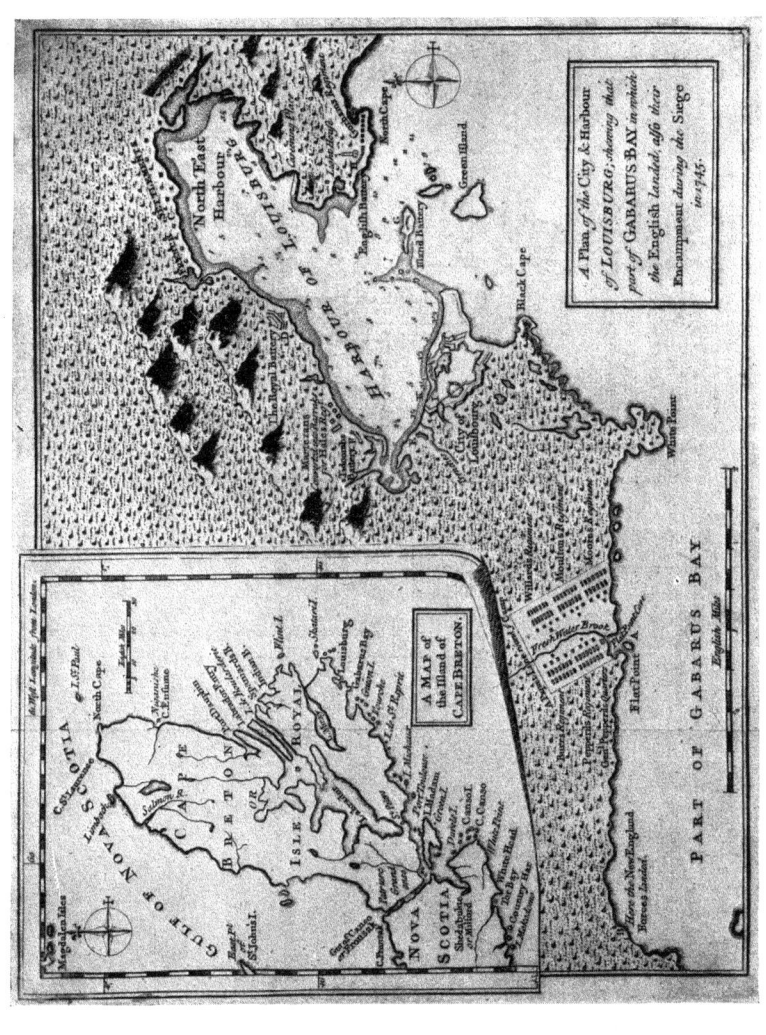

From the Society's Collection.

FIRST JOURNAL

Should have the Honour of their Salvation (1) Such are not Sensible that Christ Deserves this honour (2) Such are Desirous of Having the Honour of Reconciling themselves —

(2) Use of Conviction. God will Never be Reconciled to Siners any other way. (1) God has promised that very Glory to Christ Isaiah 49–6 (2) it would Deprive Christ of his Glory if men Should Receive their Salvation any other way —

(3) Use of Encouragment, to Sensible Siners to Depend on Christ for Reconciliation. (1) Consider Tho you See no Reason for God to Love you, you may See great Reason why God should pardon you It is for the Honour of Christ for God to be Reconciled to Siners (2) Consider the more unworthy you are the Greater Honour your Reconciliation will be to Christ, the Greater your Sin the more honour you put on Christ in believing: and the more Honour God puts on Christ in Pardoning you — (3) Consider Jesus Christ is worthy that God Should put Honour upon Him — (4) God Delights to put Honour Upon Christ —

23 Monday. Capt [John] Rouse Arriv'd in 19 Days from England. He Informs that Capt Bush the Commodores Packet (Viz) — Lord Montigue, arrived there Some Days before him He says England Rang with Joy at the News of Louisbourg's being taken. and that it was as Much as one's Reputation was worth to Speak a word Against the Governments of New England etc. We hear that Commodore Warren is Made Govenour of Louisbourg and the Adjacent I-lands. and also Rear Admiral of the Blue. and that General Peppril, is Made Baronet of Great Britton as also Col. of a Regiment Here. and I-BroadStreet [John Bradstreet] Leut Col., and that [William] Shirley is to have the Care of the Other Regiment.[39] —

---

[39] The victory assured Warren of fame and fortune. He was commissioned Rear Admiral of the Blue, August 8, 1745. Promoted Rear Admiral of the White, 1747, and of the Red, 1748. He might have been a Baronet in 1745 but did not want it as he had no son. He was made a Knight (K.C.B.) in 1747. Also elected M.P. in 1747. He became a very rich man because of the prize money won in 1745. Warren's commission as Governor of Louisbourg was late in arriving and he and Pepperrell jointly administered the town until the spring of 1746. Pepperrell was made a Baronet, and was the first native-born American given an hereditary title. His colonelcy of a new royal regiment was highly profitable as the perquisites were great. He had contributed

24 Tuesday. — Admiral Warren Highsted His Flagg. and all the Ships Salluted Him and also all the Privateers after which he Returnd 'em an aswer: as Did also the Grand-Battry. A Very great firing there was

26 Thursday. Died Dr — [John] Manning Chirurgeon to Col. [John] Choat's Regiment. I have the account from the Rev. Mr. W [Stephen Williams] that there has Died of the Land army Since the 20th of June 110.

27 Friday Went on Board the (Defence) Conncticutt Country Sloop in order to Return to New England took Dr [Charles] Pyncheon's things aboard etc.

28 Saterday. this Morning I went Ashore took my Leave of Friends there. Note many have Died Since 26 Instant. But the Number. I know not — Mr [Stephen] Williams Came into Our Chamber and prayed with Us. took our Leave of Him. Went on Board About 4 O'Clock P M: Just at Night Came on board. Rector [Elisha] Williams Capt Smith Capt [David] Sebury Commissary — [Jeremiah] Miller all Bound for New England The Guns were all Loaded in order for firing. But the wind fell and So we Did'ent go out of the Harbour.

29 Sabbath. at Six a Clock this Morning we weighd Anchor and Set Sail Before a Good gale of North West Wind we run about 6 and 7 and 8 knots we Came by Canso 4 O'Clock P M: we Sail'd 32 Leagues by Day-Light Mr Bidwell [40] the Chaplin Preach'd both A M. and P M:

30 Monday. this morning we was out of Sight of Land not So good a Wind as Yesterday. towards Night the Wind Blew fresh at

---

li10,000 to the expedition but probably recovered it on his perquisites as its commander and otherwise. He later became a major general and then a lieutenant general in the Royal Army. Shirley was anxiously asking the Home Government in a letter as late as September 27, 1745, for the colonelcy of the other proposed regiment. This commission was dated September 11th but did not reach him until October 10th. He is believed to have made himself wealthy out of this and other related opportunities. All three men were of high character and abilities and their enrichment was the customary reward for good service.

[40] Rev. Adonijah Bidwell who kept a journal of which the New York Society of Colonial Wars has a photostatic copy.

FIRST JOURNAL 47

East North East a Smooth Sea we went as Steady as if we'd been upon Land As pleasent an Evening as Ever I See —

Tuesday October 1. Wind the Same as Last Night Weather Clear and an Exceeding pleasent Morning Spied one Sail Bearing the Same Point as we — 1 o'Clock P M: we overtook Her She belong'd to Martins [Martha's] Vinyard. Came from Louisbourg Saturday Night Last this night we Lay Very Much Becalm'd. we are in Lattitude 43-33 Minutes.

2 Wednesday. Sun About an Hour high the Wind Blew fresh at North: North: West we Run. 7 or 8 knots. About noon we Spied A Sail A Head of Us about 3 Leagues Still a fresh gale — We Met with the Sail. it was Capt [Edward] Tiyng — who Came from Boston Monday Last Bound for Louisbourg. to Bring His Excellency etc. About 3 OClock we made the Land altho' at a Great Distance about Sun Set we Came by Cape Sables

3 Thursday. About 12 at Night we Came into the Bay of Phunda [Fundy] we went. 6. knots till 12 Clock at 2. OClock went 4. and So Less and Less till we had Almost a Calm. I think I never See pleasenter Weather in this Month in all my life. not a Cloud to be Seen etc. the air North North West. almost a Calm till 3 O'Clock P M: and then A fine Breeze of South: South East Wind. we went near 5 knots (Said Cap. [John] Prentice while I was waiting)

4 Friday. this Morning we Spoke with a fishing Vessel Belonging to MarbleHead who Said it was But 30 Leagues to Cape Ann — The Wind Shifted to West South West So that we was Oblig'd to tack to make our Coast. Exceeding — pleasent weather tho' almost too Hot.

Saterday 5. This Morning — Made Cape Ann. we Endeavourd to go into the Harbour but the wind fail'd Us. we took out our oars and Roed about an Hour But all in Vain. About Midnight the wind freshned Up we were within 10 leagues of Boston —

Sabbath 6. at 2 OClock we run Direct for Boston as Soon as Day Light we was in Sight of the Light House. we Salluted the Castle with 7 Cannon. they Answer'd Us. we Cast Anchor Just by the Long Wharfe about 10 OClock. About noon I went ashore went to Mr Dwights where I See Ensign John Ely of Sp[ringfiel]d who told me of the Death of Sergt-Atchinson who I had for Sometime Long'd to See. I Desire to be Thankful that while others are Dead I'm not only Alive but Enjoy a good Measure of Health. I went and Heard Revd Mr. Prince He Preach'd from ——— an Excellent Sermon it was.

Thursday. Octo. 10 At 5 O'Clock P M I Set out of Boston. For Home. I kept Sabbath at Leister I Heard Mr Eaton Both A M. and P M.

Thursday Octor. 17 I Reach'd Home. and — Being the Subject of a great many favours and Mercies (which I have not Mentioned) for Seven Months Absence ought to be Remembred. with (Humility, and) Thankfulness. (Psalms — 47 5.6.7)

This Omitted in its proper place. and I put it Down here — one time as I was at the Battries and Stood Just by the Great Mortar as it was Shot off, the Shell. Broke just as 'twas Deliver'd (not being able to Distinguish the Sound of the Morter and Shell) and flew about our heads. But thro' the good Hand of Providence none of us was Hurt. Note the Shell weigh'd 180 Weight. about 3 Hours after this Morter was Carried over to the Light House — Point which Did Such Execution There etc.

The Number of men that we Kill'd in the Citty I could not Learn. But Doubtless 'twas a Great Number. While I was Measuring the wall. and I Observed a great Deal of Blood Sprinkled Upon it. I am inform'd that there was Six men Kill'd By a Cannon and Carriage that By one of our Balls, was thrown off of the Wall. (by the Cittadel where the men was Exceeding thick. Being the Best place for Defence in all the City) Note the wall was, Right Down inside as well as out. altho 'twas'nt So in any other place in the Citty.) the Gun and Carriag I've Seen

I Shall Endeavour in this page to give Some Description, of the Citty of Louisbourg.

and 1. The Citty not being Square it's Longest way is East and West. it is 5.10 Rods in Circumference. it — Contains. 57 Acres. and a Half Quarter.

2 — The walls thereof is of Stone and Lime. in the wall are. 47 Angles. the Heighth of the wall on the Land Side is. from 21 — to 35 — feet. The wall is 36 Feet thick. Square on the top. from which (inside) it Goes Slanting Down to the Street of the Citty —

So that at the foundation it's 60 feet thro' — Note when I Say Square I Don't Intend upon a Leavel There Being Sixteen feet of it Rais'd about five feet aboue the Rest. thro' which the Cannons Port. and the other 20 feet is for the platform. —

3. — There is a trench all around the Citty (i. e. the Land Side) which is 9 or 10 feet Deep. it Generally Bearing a Strait Course (not Angling as the wall) is in the widest places 1–60. feet. and in the other places. 60. the out Side of the trench is wall'd Like a Cellar. about 30 feet from this trench (outward) there's a wall from the Surface of the Earth, in Height about 5 Feet about 1 Foot — Inside (which) there is Pickets which are Higher than the wall. being Exceeding Clost (this is against the Cittadel) together and Very Sharp. From the top of this wall the Earth is Made Slanting till it Descends Down to the Natural Earth (which is about 1–00 Feet —) Under which there was a Powder plot. (I have often been a great way into the Same.)

(this Omitted) on the top of the City wall were 3 Watch Boxes of Hewn Stone. (two of which we Beat Down with our Cannon Balls)

4 — The wall By the water Side (which I Judge is about one third of the whole) is from 12 to 16 feet High — it is 6 feet thick. Made of Stone and Lime. and plank'd on Both Sides and also the top. (on which are 36 Swivel Guns)

5 — There is also 2 Circular Batteries. which Overlook the wall (Last Describ'd) one at the west End of the City, (which Mounts 15 Cannon) the other is at the South East part of the City it Mounts 9 or 10 Cannon.

6 — in the Citty were 1–00 Cannon. 6 of 'em were — Brass. 3 plac'd at the West End of the Citty. and 3 at the South East Corner. there was twenty Emptie Ambezures. (See Thursday July 4 Line 17th) there was 6 Mortars 5 of Which were Brass the Large ones were two feet over. 13 Inches Hollow. —

7 — of the gates on the west was but one Gate (Which Gate we Broke Down) it had no Date that I Cou'd find. there was an Exceeding good Bridge Over the trench. which was about Sixty feet wide: on the South was one Gate. (No Date that I Could find.) A Good Bridge Over the Trench. which was 1–60 feet wide. Note at Each End of S'd trench in order to Shut the water out was a

wall acrost it 6 Feet thick and 12 Feet High made all of Hewn Stone. There was also — two Sally Ports. (as they were Call'd) on the South Side which went Level from the Street of the Citty thro' the wall as Low as it's foundation and opened into the trench: On the East one Gate (Viz) — Porte de Morripass. Built in the year 1740. and an Excellent Fine one it is Built all of Hewn Stone as white as Marble Being Between 40 and 50 Feet High. I think it not–Best to tell what I (and many Others) think this Cost. The King of France's Coat of arms were Cut out in Stone and plased over our heads as We went through at the top of S'd Gate were four Stone Pillars Carv'd out Exceeding Beautifully. (Many other things too many to Mention). On the North or the Water Side are 5 Gates. But the Main Seaport Gate was Port Fredrick Built in the Year. 1742. Being about 30 Feet High Arch'd OverHead. a Piller Each Side one of which a Cannon Ball had Broke Down (Note) this Gate was Built of Wood. the West Circular Battry. Was Dated 1728–1728. — there was a Large pond of water in the Citty over which was a Bridge 26 Rods Long.

8. — I Shall Mention a few Remarkables in the Citty.

and (1) the Cittadel which was a Very Large House. Being 23 Rods Long and about 45 Feet Wide all Built of Stone and Brick. it was Defended By it Self Against the Citty Having a trench between it and the Citty and the Bridge on which we went over (part of it) was Easily Highsted up. (as was all the Bridges I've Mentioned. altho' I neglected to Speak of it) over the Door was Cut out — (See porte De Morripass) in the Middle was A Steeple where Hung an Excellent Bell, the Biggest (By far) that Ever I See. (altho' we Broke it.) at the East End it is three Stories and Several Larg Rooms Well finished. there is also a Chappel in it Larg Enough to hold Large Congregation. I Trust 1-000 Men may Live Comfortably in Said House it was Built in the Year 1720 — Several other things I Could Mention as a Large Stone Dial. the Gate that Leads into it. the Guard House there etc. and Indeed I've Givin but a faint Description

(2) the Hopital Due Roy or Royal Hospital — which is twenty Rods Long the wall about 2 feet thick, Built of Stone and Lime, two Storie High. a Great many Large Sash Windows with Iron Grates to Each of 'em there is 2 Large Lower rooms for

the Sick Well furnished with Beds and Curtains there is the Chambers over these which are for the Same Use. there's also a Great Deal of Linning. As Also a Great many Vessels of Puter etc. In the Middle of S'd House is a Steeple and a good Bell Hanging in the Same. At Each End of the House, are Built a Larg Dwelling House. From which: is a wall Running towards the North — 13. Rods — and then another wall to Meet Each of these, Running East and West So that there is Included within the wall about an Acre of Land which is used for a Garden. at Each Corner of S'd wall (which is 12 feet High and 4 feet thick) is a Large Kitchen and Several Large Coppers for Coocking Brewing etc. and also two wells. the Gate that Opens into it is arch'd over, and a Cross Standing Upon the top. there's 2-Good Sun Dials etc. and many other things But I Shall Mention no more.

3 — La Fortification Or Magizin General Built in the Year 1731 — Being 20 Rods Square. On the South East Corner is a Larg Dwelling House. On the South West a Large Bake House with Good Conveniences as also a Good well within the House. All the West Side is a Store House for Artillary. Bombs. Balls, etc. On the East and North Side is a Very Large Store House for Meat. Flouer. Rhum. Mollasses other Stores that are Eatables etc. all these are Built of Stone. and Cover'd with Slate. — (As are all the other's that I have Describ'd) Note. where the Houses Did'ent Meet. there it was wall'd. there was. 2 Gates Led into the Same which Had Locks and Bolts etc. There were many others Store Houses. and also other Stately Dwelling Houses. Such as the Intendents. (where Commodore Warren Lives) etc. But none Equal to those I've Mentioned. and altho' there were many Very Good and Stately Buildings Yet for the Number there was in the Citty it may Be Call'd a Mean Built place.

4. there were also many Very fine Gardens. (1st) The Kings Garden Just by the Citadel 2 — the Garden in the Magazin General 3. the Hospital — etc. and many others But not Eaquel to these.

5 — There is Six Lanes in the City that run East and West and Six North and South. But not Exclusive of those OutSide.

6. and Lastly. there is a Large Parrade Bigg Eenough to hold twelve Hundred Men Standing in open Order. as Level as we can Suppose Ground to be — which is Laid out by Ranges of Stones.

and Strait as a Line etc. Thus Much Concerning the City —

In the Next place I Shall in Brief Describe The Grand Battry. It Lieth almost North of the City. and is in Distance about a Mile and A quarter to go by water: to go in the Road it's two Mile (Except a few rods). The Battry faces the Coming in of the Harbour — and is in Length 42 Rods and about 8 Rods wide there is 40 ambezures. tho. But. 36-Cannon — (Most or all 42 Pounders) the Barraks or House (in the House is a Chappel. etc.) is 26 Rods Long and 40 feet wide it's Built of Stone the wall of the House is 2 feet and a half thick. there is a trench Round it over which is a Good Bridge — att Each End of S'd House is a Large Tower or Watch House Built Round (Like a Light House etc.) They'r 90 feet Round. Each and Near 60 feet High. Near to the top they'r arch'd over a great Thickness of Hewn Stone So that It's Bomb proofe. (Note) there was a Great Many Bombs and Balls Left in the Battry when 'twas Deserted. the wall of S'd Fort. is 16 feet High and About 10 feet thick. Thus of the Grand Battry —

Nextly of the I-land Battry. it's North East and by North. of the City about 3 Quarters of a Mile Distance Between it and the City there is a Range of Rocks. So that no Vessel Can Come Between it and the City The I-land I Suppose to Be an Entire Rock Containing About 2 acres and a half the fort is 42 Rods Long the wall made of Stone etc. only the top of it about 2 feet thick is of English Turff. (as are all The walls I've Mentioned. Except where I Said plank'd) this was also plank'd Inside and out, tho' not the top. The wall is in Height 10 feet. about 8 feet thick It Mounts 31 Cannon 24 Pounders. there is two Brass Morters. and one. has a Sollid-Brass-Bed-or Platform-Cast with it; So that it's one with the Morter. the Barraks are twenty Rods Long, and about thirty feet wide. there's a well also inside the fort. (As there is also at the Grand Battry) it was Built AD: 1728 —

Last — I Shall give Some Description of the Light House. and it is about three Quarters of a Mile Northward and somewhat Eastward of the I-land Battry. it's near a 100. feet High. it's round — Being 90 Feet in Circuference the wall. 9. . . . . . Feet thick. What is Called the Lantern — (Being at the top) the Glass windows are 12-Feet Long. and Six — wide the Sasshes are all of Iron. it's Bigg enou to (Comfortably) Hold 50-Men. Besides a

FIRST JOURNAL 53

Large Copper in which are Thirty Lamps. (Thus I have in Some Measure Given a Description of the City of Louisbourg with the Fortifications thereunto Belonging —) Note. when I Speak of the Point, the Grand — Battry Lies from the City. and of the I-land — Battry etc. I Speak only my Iudgment for I Neglected to take Minits of Leut Mun [John Man] which had Design'd

An account of the Number of men att the taking of Cape Breton Under the Command of the Hon W-Peppriell Esqr with the Names of the Cols Leut Cols Majors and Captains [41]

Coll—	Captains	Men
John Broadstreet	Peter Staples	52
John Storer	Ephraim Baker	42
Major — Cuts [Richard Cutt]	John Fairfield	45
Note —	[Bray] Deering	52
The Hon Brigdier Joseph Dwight had no Regiment, till after the City was Taken — [42]	John Kinslow [Kinslagh]	43
	John Harmon	42
	Moses Butler	51
	Thomas Pierkins	43
	William Warner	41
	Moses- Pearson	36
	Total	447
Coll—	Captains	Men
Samuell Waldo. Brigdier	Samuel Moodey-	50
Col [Arthur] Noble	John Westen [Watts?]	51
Major [William] Hunt	Philip D[umaresque]	40
	Benjamin Goldthrait	40
	Daniel Hale	43
	Jacob Stephens	36
	James Noble	41
	Richard Jaquesh [Jaques]	49
	Daniel Fogg	39

[41] Cf. *6 Mass. Hist. Coll., 10:497 et seq.*, which corrects the journal in important particulars. The journal, however, is very valuable for its record of the numbers in each company.

[42] Commissioned Colonel of the Artillery Train, Feb. 20, 1744; Brigadier General, Feb. 20, 1745; Colonel of 9th Mass. Regt., June 18, 1745.

Col—	Captains	Men
	Joseph [Jeremiah?] [48] Richardson	44
	John Card	43
	Total	436
Col—	Captains	
Jeremy Moulton	Christopher [Marshall]	42
Nathanial Donnel	James Grant	51
Major Edward Elis	Charles King	49
and also Chief Chirurgeon of the army	Peter Prescot	40
	Ammi Ru[ammah] Cutter	41
	Samuel Roods [Rhodes]	40
	Bartholomew Trow	45
	[Estes] Hatch	39
	Total	347
Col—	Captains	
Samuell Willard	Joshua Pierce	47
Thomas Chandler	John Terry	41
Major Seth Pomroy	Ebenezer Alexader	51
	John Warner	48
Samuel Willard	David Melvin	42
Thomas Chandler	Jabiz Omstead	46
Major Seth Pomroy	John Huston	42
	Joseph Miller	48
	Palmer Goulden [Goulding]	39
	James Stephens	44
	Total	458

[48] Cf. footnote 1, *Sixth Journal*.

SECOND JOURNAL

Captain Joseph Sherburne

Joseph Sherburne was a member of a prominent New Hampshire family and was probably the son of Henry Sherburne of Portsmouth. He is believed to have been about fifty-one years old when he went to Louisbourg in the New Hampshire regiment commanded by Colonel Samuel Moore. At that time Sherburne was apparently a sergeant but on May 17, 1745, he was ordered by General Pepperrell to assume command of one of the two fascine batteries just erected by the Provincial Army. Both batteries faced the west gate of the city and Sherburne's was only two hundred and fifty yards from it. It seems certain that Sherburne had had some previous experience with artillery but it is not known what this might have been. On June 6, 1745, the sergeant was commissioned captain of a company in Moore's regiment, and on the following December first he was commissioned Storekeeper of His Majesty's Ordnance, an office he apparently held until his discharge from the service on June 30, 1746. His pay as captain and storekeeper was four pounds and ten shillings a month.

Sherburne started his journal, or at least that part which is preserved, on the very day he took command of the advance battery and he continued it only to the day he received the flag of truce. The journal gives plain evidence of being part of a longer account which Sherburne had copied for the information of another person.

The journal relates almost entirely to the specific task assigned to the writer but it is important as showing the situation in the battery erected nearest to the walls. The frequent shortage of powder is to be remarked and also the overloading of guns.

The original manuscript of the Sherburne journal is owned by the Massachusetts Historical Society which has courteously placed it in the hands of the Society of Colonial Wars for publication. The journal was noted by Parkman in his *Half Century of Conflict* (*2:126*) and a few sentences were quoted in that work but it has otherwise remained unpublished to this time.

THE JOURNAL

Island Caspey may 17th A D Being fryday

This Evening the Honorable Genneral Pepperrell Gaue me Orders To In List as many Gunners as I could get to go early the next morning to the Advance Battery then Begining —

Satterday morning, I went to the Advance Battery and had with me for Gunners Ebenezer Lawrence William Coomes, Robert Savery John Belustor, John Whitelock and Giffin More a young man, belonging to the Superbe. we had One 18 pounder Mounted but very poor Intrenchments for the most Shelter we had from the french fire (which was very hott) was Some hhds [hogsheads] filled with earth. I had no Cartaridges but was forsed to Load with Loose Powder which was much to our Disadvantage the Fish flakes [1] Lay we tween us and the west Gate was forst to Beat them away with our Shott to haue a fair Sight at the Gate as wee ware Loading the 5th time William Coomes was Killed with a Muskett Ball, we Discharged our Guns 56 times that Day which was as Often as the woud bare ——— (Soldiers Killed) Capt [Joshua] Pearce By a Cannon Shott Joseph Merell Do: one Bickford and Jackson by musket Balles. Thomas Ash by a Bomb Some other Carried of wounded — this Night mounted One 18 Hundred pounder and 2–42 pounders and had pritty Good Intrenchment

the 19: Sunday morning hauing added to my Company John Wadham Valantine Almore and Christopher Blake and four Good Guns Mounted we Began our fire with as much furey as possible and our enemy Returned it with Cannon and Mortars as warmly from the Citidale west: Gate and North:East: Battery with Continual showers of musket. Balls. Their Large Cannons from the Citydale [citadel] flanks us much and often filled our Ambazures

---

[1] "Fish-flakes" were frames for drying cod.

[embrasures] But by a.11 OClock we had beat them all from their Guns — But them at the Citydale we Could not bring any Guns to bare on them John Blaster was Killed half an hour after we Began our fire In the Morning. At 12 oClock was forsed to Seasce our foire for want of Powder they Guns then being very warm. I went with the Gunners to get Some provisions, in the meantime Some person brought Some powder. Soposed to be William Vaughan and Loded the 42 pound by some unskilfull hand which split one and Dismounted another blowed up about 1½ bbs powder Killed Two men and wounded two more The Day for the most part Fogey, — this Night Diged our Trench Down to the South End —

Monday 20th Began to Raise Titcombs Battery [2] — Last night and this morning haled and mounted one 1. 18 pounder and 2:9 pounders from the fashine Battery on our South line against the Citydale, and Began to play them at the Citydall Guns with Such truth that we Soon beat the Enemy from theirs

21 Tuesday thick foggy weather, Little Fire for want of powder.[3]

22d Fairweather and a Supply of Powder and we Expended it as fast as needfull to Do Execution the Fire was very hott on boath Sides till 12 at Noon and Then we Could perceiue we had beat our Enemys from all their Guns. They Seaced their Fire for that Day — John Whitlock was burnt by Siting Fire to a Cartridge of Powder

23d: Fine Fairweather this morning I perceaved the French had mounted Two other Guns on the Citydale, but in four hours ware forsed to leave them, for this day it was observed by our officers and Soldiers that every Shott we fired at them took place in their Ambazures: our men fited again for the Island Battery [4] all the Ships appeared of the City under french Colours.

---

[2] Major Moses Titcomb of 5th Mass. Regt. whose fascine battery, 440 yards from the West Gate, started firing May 15th.

[3] Ammunition was frequently short. On June 2d, Pepperrell wrote to Shirley at Boston that he had no more powder (except a little borrowed from Warren) and was "in want of shott of all sorts."

[4] Cf. *First Journal,* footnote 15, for the attacks on the Island Battery.

24th Thick fogy our Small armes playd in Return of the Enemys, But Little fire with the Cannon only Grape and Longerage [langrage]; Short of Powder.

25 Short of Powder at our Battery — Split the Large Mortar at the fashien Battery

26 A New Recruit of Powder and Shott we played warmly on the walls by the west Gate and the Citydall and the Enemy Did not Spare us for they keept a Continuall Fire with Cannon, Mortars and Small Armes — This Evening our men got Ready to go to the Island Battery being again Dark wether I got in Readiness, to give them a Salute on this Side Also at 12 at Night they Began the Atack and I gaue them what Diuertion I could with Round and Grape Shott —

27 Foggy weather Could here the french work but Could not know what they ware Doing — Little Powder

28 Thick Foggy weather nothing Remarkable —

29 Fair weather Some powder Came Down to our advance Battery and a Gun Battery, Capt [Edward] Brooks being Sick in the Morning By the Request of Colonel Richman [Sylvester Richmond] I went to that Battery to giue their Gunnors some Directions, where I fired some Guns So Returned to my own Station where I Spent the Remaining part of the Day with Pleasure Seeing of our Shott Tumble Down their walls and Flagg Staff —

the 30 Not much fire for want of powder —

31 Thick Foggy weather —

June 1st Thick Foggy weather with Rain —

2.d Ditto ——— a Vessel arrived from Boston with Stores of Shell Shott and Powder —

3.d This morning a Sloop from Cannada was taken near the Harbour Laden with provisions they men got a Shore in their Boat —

4th This moring had some powder and Shott Sent Down and we Sent the most part of the Later at our near Enemys before night and had the Pleasure of Sending many we Received from them Back again

5th Fair weather Little Amunition in the morning early went to the Camps where I got more Supply which I soon made Use of —

6th This Day thick weather In the morning Could see the french had 2 Guns Run out of New Ambruziers Cutt throw the parrapet which soon began to Play with Great Fury and we were Obliged to Turn 3 of our Guns to Silence them which was soon Affected for in three hours we Dismounted one and Silenced the other for that day. mean while they Played very hard from the Citydale and North East Battery their Bumbs Continualy flying to a great Exactness for many fell in our Trench But Did Little Damage —

7th This Day Fair weather we had the Usual Sport of Exchanging Shott Nothing Remarkable they only Broak one of the wheels of a Gun with a Shott and Beat up a platform with a Shell —

8th Thick foggy weather In the morning the Soldiers Came from the Grand Battery fearing a Sally the Small Armes fired so Fast — But nothing in it —

9th Sunday and fair weather Rested on boath Sides till 12 O'Clock I Being much Fiteagued and not well Laid Down on a long Chest wherein we keept our Provisions. I had not Laid Long their Before a Shott Came in throw the End of the House and in at one end of the Chest and out at the other but no other Damage than the Loss of those Necessarys of Life therein Stowed —

10th Fair weather we had a very hott fire on boath Sides Till our Guns ware So hott Could not fire any more — Christopher Blake mortally wounded in the Head Vallentine Almor had Two of his Ribs Broak by a Ball. One of the Gun wheels shott away —

11th This morning had no fire on either Side — Received orders from the Generall In Honour to his Majesty at 12 O'Clock to fire a Salute from our Battery and Capt. [Edward] Brooks to take up the Salute and then the Grand Battery; our Guns being well Shotted and pointed we payed the Complyment all Round which I followed all the Day and am Certain to the Discomfort of our Enemys —

12th This Day we had a very hott fire more than any before which continued all Day and Broak Down much of their Walls.

13th This Day fair weather the Guns and Bumbs played well on boath Sides some men wouned and Carried to the Hospital

14th Had not much fire. but ware making all the preparations for Guiving them hotter work than the Had before — But in the

Evening as we ware haleing an 18 pounder from the fasheen Battery and almost to our trench they Began to heaue their Shells from all their Mortars and hove them so fast that the Elements war almost on flame the Shells fell very thick about us; but we got the Gun mounted on the platform Intending the next after noon To Return their Favours The Houe 47. Shells that night then ware Peasable on our Side and Continued So —

15th This forenoon pleasant weather. By 12 O'Clock got all our platforms Laid ambrazuers mended Guns in Order Stock of full Cartridges Shot in Place Gunners Quartered Dined — matches Lit Ready to return their Last favours but hear their Drums beat a Parley and soon Appeared a flag of Truce which I Received a half way Between our Battery and their Walls which I Conducted to the Green Hill and their Delivered him to Colonel Richman [Richmond] So Returned to my Station at the Advance Battery —

16. Sunday morning at 8 O'Clock Received: and Delivered the Second Flag of Truce In the Like mannour —

The above being some minuets take from the Journal of Sir Your most Obedient Humble

Servant Joseph Sherburn

THIRD JOURNAL

ANONYMOUS

This journal is another of those lent to the Society of Colonial Wars by the Massachusetts Historical Society, which owns the hitherto unpublished original.

The writer cannot be identified. He was probably a sailor. Certainly he was a member of the company of the ship *Hector* which carried Governor Shirley, Mrs. Shirley, Mrs. Peter Warren, and other ladies and gentlemen to Louisbourg, arriving on August 16, 1745, on which date the journal begins. The journal, while brief, adds several details not appearing elsewhere.

THE JOURNAL

3 at 11 hours P. M. sailed from Nantaskett.

Aug: 16 a little after Sun set Anchored in Louisbourgh Harbour

17: 10 A. M. went ashore with the Governor who was rcieved ashore by the Soldiers under Arms and Attended by the General and Commodore [1] to the Citadel where the General delivered him after a short speech in presence of the Commodore the Keys of the Fort. The Commodore made a Speech in Praise of the Officers and Soldiers

:29 a little Sloop looks into the Harbour and then made off [Capt. William] Fletcher in his Vessell and [Capt. Edward] Tyng and Lieutenant in [Robert?] Becket's Sloop went in Quest of them

30 A: M. a Sloop came in taken by This Vessell and informs she stood to the Eastward about Noon [William] Fletcher arrives but is sent out again immediately without coming ashore

---

[1] Governor William Shirley, General William Pepperrell, and Commodore Peter Warren.

31: about twelve oClock a Ship haled in sight from the Eastward acted as if at a loss whether to come in or not at last after continuing in sight four hours went of to the Westward Six men of War none sent N.E. after her. The Chester ordered out, then the Sunderland, afterwards contradicted two Sloops got ready but afterwards countermanded by the Commodore

[*Sept.*] *1:* Wind: North East Capt Spry in a little Sloop of the Commodore's and Capt. [Joseph] Richardson in the Sloop formely [Capt. David] Donahews came to sail about 2 hours P:M. in the Night it rained very hard and blew and was very dark

Sept: 3: 11 hours A. M. a Ship and Sloop appeared to the Westward Wind North:North:West at 3 hours P. M: came to an Anchor in the Harbour proves to be Richardson with the ship that past by Saturday last. She was a Ship bound from Carolina to London, but in her passage about 150 Leagues to the Eastward of Newfoundland Banks fell in three weeks before with a Squadron of French Men of War consisting of seven Sail vizt:

	Guns	
L'Mars	60	Mons: Pernier Commandant
St. Michael	64	
L'Parfaite	46	Mons L'Vivier
L'Argonaut	46	
L'Galaher	32	
L'Renommee	32	
L'Tourveille	32	

bound to this place by whom she was taken and sent to this Port.

4: Capt Spry arrived from his Cruize having seen nothing. this Afternoon a Small Schooner and Sloop sailed to cruze of Scateree [Scatarie] Point to give notice of any large vessell appearing Wind South:West: very Fresh.

5: Wind South:East: very Foggy but sometimes a Glym [Gleam?] Some people say that they saw a large Ship off from the Rampparts, a small Fishing Boat says they saw two large Ships lying too last night were within two or three Miles of them. Several other Vessels that have come in think they saw large Vessels, but cannot be sure on Account of the Fog [Capt.] Clark sailed for Boston with Sick People — An alarm beat in order to bring every man to his Post The Men of War all ready to sail but had the

THIRD JOURNAL

French appeared they could not get out Great joy in Hopes they would come in —

Sept. 5. [Joseph] Richardson was sent to Annapolis to give them information with orders to Cruize of the Bay of Fundy for intelligence and return the latter end of the Month

6: Upon examining the French Prisoners taken in the Carolina Vessell Say that a Fleet of Men of War consisting of twelve Ships from Toulon were arrived at Bouchefort and were to have sailed with them but they were too sickly, that they were Manning them with all expedition to join this Fleet. Capt. [John?] Shaw with a party of thirty men sent to Mera[2] after some French prisoners that had escaped

7: Shaw returned from Mera and brought with him the Captain of the Canada Schooner [John] L'Croix L'Roch and 6 more. L'Croix tho a prisoner upon Parole had made his Escape some time ago L'Roch went away in a Schooner (The Government had Employed him and his Schooner ever since the Place was taken in [Wooding ?]) the fifth instant in the Evening he was to meet L'Croix at Mera, they were then to go to St. Johns and inform them that the Government were about to transport them to encourage them to get as many Indians together as they could, and to endeavour to cut of the Party that should be put by the Government Mons: Castine had had sentrys upon his house from [John] L'Croix's escape but denied he knew anything of the Matter but it now appears that he and his Brother in law were in the Plot and probably a French Priest too — L'Croix had the impudence to pretend that he had not given his Word he is put into Irons on board the Superb the other are confined

9. Arrived Capt. [Daniel] Fones in the Rhoad Island Colony Sloop from Newfoundland where they had heard nothing of the French Fleet a Week before but brings advice that by an English Priest in July they had an Account that the first express from this Place was taken and carried into St. Malo's this night arrived a Schooner from Rhode Island and

10. This Morning give an Account that the 4th instant Cape Sables bearing North:North:East distance 18 or 20 leagues they saw five Sail of Topsail Vessells and one other to Windward of

---

[2] Or Miré, a place 20 miles distant.

them all of which they took to be Ships two of them large tall Ships which they took to be large men of war they were standing about West:North:West at noon The Commodore held a Council of War when it was Unanimously resolved to go in Quest of the French Fleet which it was supposed were gone to Annapolis and desired some land Forces to serve as Marines.

11: This morning The Men of War loosed Their Topsails a Gun was fired for unmooring 600 Land forces all Voluntiers [3] were put on board and every thing in readiness for sailing when advice was given by people from on board two different Vessels that upon the fourth instant they saw a number of Vessels about twenty Leagues to the Southward of Cape Sables consisting of one Ship and five Sloops and Schooners. this was judged to be the same Fleet that we had intelligence of yesterday The Design of the Men of War to go out laid aside for the present and the men sent ashore [William] Fletcher was sent out Yesterday to look into the Harbours on the Cape Sable Shore A Schooner bound to Boston ordered into Annapolis and to send a Whaleboat by the French Ships of there with a Letter to the Govr. to let him know the Men of war were coming counterordered The Ships sailed from Brestt [France] the 6th July O.S. [Old Style]

13. Arrived a Schooner from Boulesang up the Gut of Canso brings Intelligence that all the Indians were gone off to Canada had been out but eight days heard nothing of the French Fleet, but says the Accadians were quiet.

14. Col. Gorham [4] sailed for Boulesang to get intelligence from the Garrison of Annapolis, and to learn the disposition of the Inhabitants.

16. A Great tendency to a General Mutiny amongst the Soldiers it being talked amongst them to Club their arms the next morning and one and all to refuse to mount Guard. A council of War After which the men are promised to have their Wages raised —

17. Things Seemingly quiet. A council of War.

18. Beat to arms the Governor made a Speech to each Regiment Tells them that he has sent to New York and Philadelphia for

---

[3] Cf. *First Journal* under Sept. 3.
[4] Either Col. Shubael Gorham or Lieut. Col. John Gorham, both 7th Mass. Regt.

Cloathing that their Wages should be eight Pounds a Month that as many should be dismist the middle of October as should reduce the Garrison to 2000 that the Army should be paid its Arrars upon his arrival in Boston that they should have liberty to send up any Number not exceeding Fifty to procure them what they should want, represents to them very pathetically the ignominy and Disgrace they would bring upon themselves. the Damage to their Country, the Advantage they would give the Enemy should they leave the place exposed, praises their past good behavior from thence Assures himself of their good behaviour for the future. This Morning Sept: 18. before the Governor made his Speech the Main Guard had clubbed their Firelocks and determined to leave the Guard but were persuaded from it (The Governor did not know it). and there was a general dispotion to a Mutiny. But when the Governor had finished his speech there was a strange alteration and a general air of discontent which appeared in their faces was changed to a general air of content and Satisfaction. This Night Information given that one of the Ringleaders still continued to foment this Mutinous dispotion bragging what they had gained and that if they had been more resolute they should all have been permitted to return home and proposes new Articles to them N.B. The Commodore made a short Speech to them the Governor and Commodore each gave 2 Hogsheads of Rum. —

Sept: 19. The people in general easy and well satisfied. A council of War four of the Ringleaders ordered to be taken up.[5]

23. This afternoon Capt. [John] Rous arrived from England with letters for the General and Mr. Warren. The General is made a Baronet Mr. Warren a Baronet and a blew Flag.[6] Two Regiments are ordered for this place, as likewise Guns for the New England Forces and spare Arms for 2000 more Cannon and all other stores and provisions for 3000 men for eight Months and Cloathing Mr. Warren is recommended by the Lords Justices to the King for Governor of Louisbourgh Commodore Barnet [Baronet] has taken three French China Ships a Manila Ship and a French Privateer. The Fame and [Winchelea?] have taken a French China man and it is reported a Manila ship.

[5] Cf. *First Journal* under September 18.
[6] Cf. *First Journal,* footnote 39.

Sept: 24: This Afternoon Mr. Warren hoisted his blew Flag on board the Superb when he was saluted by all the Ships in the Harbour as likewise by the Grand Battery which last Complement he answered Gun for Gun. Colonel Goreham returned from the Bay of Vert every thing quiet at Nova Scotia.

25: [William] Fletcher returned from his Cruize saw nothing but spoke with two Fishermen who had seen a Ship. The Ordinance Packet arrived from Annapolis but no News

30: This morning News from New Foundland an express who informs that he was taken in the Carolina Ship that was afterwards retaken and brought in here that there was Six Ships in Company till the latter end of August when they separated in a Fog — The Man of war this Deponent was in arrived at Canso Shoals Harbour in Newfoundland to the Northward of St. Johns very short of Water that two more of the Squadron arrived there in a day or two the other three they had not heard of That he with two more made his Escape the ——— of September and arrived at St. Johns in Newfoundland that he was told that the Fleet had taken the Mast Ship that had the Governor of New York and his Family aboard — Mr. Corbet [7] advised Mr. Warren by [John] Rous that they had Intelligence that there were seven Men of War with 100 Merchant men Transports at Rochelle bound to Canada

[John] Rous sailed upon a Cruize to St. Lourence River to get what Intelligence he could

[7] Thomas Corbett, Secretary of the Admiralty.

FOURTH JOURNAL

Anonymous

Nothing is known of the identity of the writer. He was certainly a member of the army and almost certainly an enlisted man. He presumably was in the Massachusetts forces as he sailed from Boston with the first contingent.

The original of the journal is owned by the Massachusetts Historical Society, to which it was presented in 1834 by the heirs of the historian, Rev. Dr. Jeremy Belknap. The Massachusetts Historical Society has very kindly permitted its first publication here.

THE JOURNAL

The Forces etc. sail'd from Boston March 24th — Arrived at Canso Aprill 4th. Were detain'd at Canso 'till Aprill 29th — By reason of contrary Winds, which filled Chapperouge Bay with Ice, and drove it on to the Cape-Breton Shoar, all along the Coast, — so that the Army could not have landed, and the Vessels would have been in the utmost Danger of being dispersed and many of them lost, had they proceeded from Canso any day before that on which they did sail from thence During the Stay of the Troops at Canso they were employ'd in building a Fort there etc. — were often drawn out and exercised, and their arms, ammunition, and Accoutrements examined, and put in Order — and the Army was disposed into Several different Detachments, and the Fleet divided into several Squadrons, with One of the Detachments on board each Squadron, with orders to each how to proceed and land —

April 29th The Fleet sail'd from Canso, with a fair Wind, and were off Chappearouge Point, about Eight of the Clock next Morning — Upon their Appearance, the Garrison made an Alarm to call in the Inhabitants from the Subburbs, and neighbouring

Settlements — The Fleet anchored in Chappearouge Bay about 10 of the Clock, and the Signal was immediately given for landing the Troops — whilst the boats were getting ready — A party of the Enemy (about 200) shew'd themselves on the Shoar, marching towards the place where it was proposed to land our Troops. upon which some Boats filled with men were order'd to make towards the Shoar, as tho they would land, about a mile below the place designd for landing, which diverted the Enemy from proceeding further till they saw the Boats put back and row up the Bay, and by this Means some of the Troops landed and drew up on the Beach before the Enemy got to the place of their Landing — When about 100 of our men were on Shoar, part of them marchd towards the Enemy, and Scouts were orderd to to [sic] search the neighbouring Thicketts — lest a large Body of the Enemy might have Sallied, and concealed themselves, in order to draw on our men too hastily — in the mean time the men continued landing with all the Dispatch possible, — The Enemy advancing along the Shoar were soon met by our Men and after several Vollies exchanged, the Enemy fled, and we took ——— prisoners and killed ——— more,[1] without any Loss on our Side This Day, landed about 2000 Men during which time the Enemy burnt all the Houses without the Walls on the West part of the Town — and Sank the Vessells in the Harbour.[2] The Enemy began also immediately to secure the low Wall at the South East part of the Town by adding on the Top of the Wall a plank with picketts about ——— feet high and placing a range of pickets about ——— feet within that Wall. and planted a great Number of Swivel Guns upon the Wall next to the Harbour —

May 1st Landed the remainder of the Troops and began to encamp — and to get on shoar some provisions and Stores. — NB — The landing of the provisions and Store (as well as the heavy Artillery) was attended with extreme Difficulty and Fatigue for want of a Harbour for the Vessalls, the Surff running very high

---

[1] Seven French were killed, five wounded and one captured. The prisoner was de la Boularderie, a retired officer.

[2] The difficulties and dangers of the landing were very great. To clear the harbor the French sank their vessels at their moorings and demolished houses between the Dauphin Gate and the salt pond called The Barachois.

on the Beach almost contenually, and oftentimes so that there was no landing — so that the Men were obliged to wade into the Water, to their Middles and often higher, for almost every thing they got on Shoar which would other wise have been spoild with the Salt water. — and were obliged when their Labour was over to lay on the Cold Ground in their Wet Cloaths under no better Covering than some Boughs laid to gether — the nights exceeding cold and foggy — but no Signs of Discouragement or Complaint appeared in any of the Men who seemd resolved to surmount all Difficulties. — [3]

May 2nd — Parties were sent out to make Discovery, and intercept the Enemy from getting into the City — who found that they had deserted the Grand Battery — upon which a Detachment was sent to take possession of it, and men employd to clear the Cannon and mend the Carriages — which the Enemy had endeavourd to spoil but in their haste had not done it to any great Degree — Just before the Detachment sent to the Grand Battary arrived there — several Boats full of them armd went cross the Harbour from the Town and attempted to land near that Battery, with Design as is supposed, to have entirely spoilt the Cannons, burnt the Barracks — a small party of our men drew up on the Shoar to receive them, upon which they returnd to the Town and the Enemy began to fire with Cannon and Mortars on that Battery —

May 2nd and 3rd The Troops were employd in landing Stores, and provisions — getting ready to land the Artillery, erecting some Shelters against the Weather and for the Stores intercepting the Inhabitants of the neighbouring Settlements from getting into the Town and a variety of other necessary Employments —

4th Got 3 Cannon at the Grand Battery cleard [4] and began a Fire on the Town from thence — the same Day got 2 Mortars to a Battery about ——— Distant from the Town and some Coehorns and began to Bombard —

May 5th and 6th — Cannonaded from the Grand Battery and bombarded from the new Battery. — Got some of the Great Ar-

[3] The writer does not magnify the conditions.
[4] Major Seth Pomeroy, gunsmith by trade, with twenty-odd smiths cleared the guns. See his journal, edited by L. E. de Forest and published by the Society of Colonial Wars in the State of New York.

tillery on Shoar — and began to transport them — which was attended with incredible Difficulty [5] there being no possibility of drawing them with Horses or oxen if we had had never so many — and the Distance near ——— over rocky Hills — or thro low marshy Grounds where the Cannon were oftentimes almost buried and the Men that hawl'd them, up to their knees in Mire and all to be done in the Nights, which were exceding cold foggy and rainy. — The Enemy did not seem to apprehend the possibility of our transporting Battering Cannon over those Grounds but our men seemd resolvd to surmount all Difficulties — and tho no dry Cloaths nor warm Shelter to sleep in after their Fatigue there were no signs of Disecouragement or Discontent — and in five days time, besides a great Variety of other necessary Services they got 8–22lb Cannon and some smaller ones to the Battery where the Mortars were placed and mounted them in a fascene Battery there —

During this Time viz May 7th a Summons was sent into the Town and an answer returnd —

8th The Enemy made a sally to discover what we were about but were soon repulsed and retreated to the Garrison

11th The new Fascene Battery of 8 22 lb Cannons and 2–9 lb began to fire together with the Mortars Coehorns and the Grand Battery — As soon as the Enemy found we had mounted our battering Cannon they planted ——— cannon thro new Embrazures cut out in the Night on the Rampart of the Citadell and kept a smart fire on our Battery, but without much Effect. —

12th 13 and 14th — In the Nights, we raised another Fascene Battery ——— yards nearer to the Town and removed Six of the 22 lb Cannon (the other 2 being split) and the largest Mortar, to it — and cannonaded and bombarded from thence the 15th 16th and 17th — by which we dismounted several of the Cannon which the Enemy had planted to annoy our Batteries. About this Time the Enemy threw up a Breast Work on the parapet of the Wall at the South East Corner and planted ——— small Cannon there — They also made ——— new Embrasures and planted ——— lb

---

[5] A really astonishing feat and truly believed impossible by the French.

Cannon at the North East Battery to annoy the Ships and Grand Batterie —

17th — In the Night — raised another Fascene Battery within ——— yards of the West Gate and haul'd 2–42 lb Cannon from the Royal Battery, and 2 18 lb Ditto and mounted them that and the next night — and began to fire on the Enemy's Works at and near that Gate with good Success — The Enemy workd constantly at Night to Barricade the Gate Way where we had made a Breach From this Battery we kept a Fire with small arms on the Enemy so that we often beat them from loading their Cannon — and they did the same on us — and several were killed thereby on both sides. the Enemy cut out ——— new Embrazures in the Circular Battery and planted 1 ——— pounder in them to play on this Battery and also made a Breast work cross the middle of the Circular Battery

19th — Continued Cannonading and Bombarding

20th — In the Night another Battery was raised opposite to the North West part of the Town to which the Circular Battery, and several of the Lines of the Town were very open — mounted 2 42 lb Cannon here which the Men hawl'd from the Grand Battery from this Battery and that next the West Gate — the Circular Battery was very much shattered and the Enemy broke from their Lines at the Town. — About this Time the Enemy laid a Boom across the Front of the Town to prevent Boats landing under the Walls — From 20th May to 10th June The Cannon and Mortars continued to play briskly on both sides and the Enemy planted several Cannon to play on our Fascene Batteries — and made two or three faint Sallies towards our Trenches — Scouts were kept out to intercept and rout parties of the Enemy which began to assemble behind us with whom they had several Skirmishes in all which they repulsed the Enemies — A Battery was prepared at the Light house point — and 6 18 lb Cannon landed about a Mile below and hawld there and mounted. — After several Attempts to make an attach on the Island Battery with Boats by night a Detachment of about 400 men made an Attach on that Battery May 26th in the Night but were repulsed, with the Loss of about 60 and 116 Taken prisoners — The variety of Fatigues and the unwholsomeness of the Climate with the poor accomodations — etc. — were too hard for the men at last who were taken down in great Numbers with Fever and Fluxes — so that at some times near 1500 were uncapable of Duty.[6]

[*June*] *11th* — The Battery at the Light house point began to play on the Island Battery with good Success — after frequent Consultations on Shoar and in Concert with Commodore Warren — it was thot adviseable to attempt storming the Town as soon as the necessary preparations could be made in the Mean Time on the 13th 14th and 15th the Batteries continued to fire briskly and with good Success on the Circular Battary which very much commanded the Harbour — Men were employd to get together a Quantity of Moss and what Oacum [oakum] there was for the Ships to barracade their Nettings with and others were employed to make a Quantity of Langrell [langrage] Shot for the Ships and the Transports were employd to clear the Ships Decks — and it was agreed to assist the Ships with 600 men to go on board when they proposed to attempt going into the Harbour — and 3 more 42 Cannon ware hawld from the Grand Battery to the Fascene Battery where the last 2 ware placd — in order to drive the Enemy from their Cannon with Langrell Shot whilst the Ships were entring — and the large Mortar was removed to the Light house point to play on the Island Battery whilst the Ships passed. —

15th — Determined upon Storming by Land and Sea [7] — all preparations made — 600 of the Troops sent on board the Ships — In the afternoon the Enemy sent out a Flag of Truce which produced a Capitulation and Surrender — and on the 17th the Troops enterd the Town and the Ships the Harbour —

[6] About this time only 2100 out of 4000 men were fit for duty. The chief sicknesses were, as stated *supra*, fever and "the bloody fluxes" (dysentery). The accommodations for the men were wretched. The food was chiefly pork and bread with occasional beans and peas. Even the rum was insufficient which occasioned very vigorous complaints.

[7] This bold but unwise proposal to storm the city was never carried out. It was proposed by Warren. See Minutes of the Council of War for May 25th and Warren's General Orders for the attack. (*6 Mass. Hist. Soc. Colls. 10: 21, 220.*)

FIFTH JOURNAL

Anonymous

This is another of the journals lent for publication by the Massachusetts Historical Society to whom the original was given by the heirs of the Rev. Dr. Jeremy Belknap in 1834.

There is nothing in the text to identify the original writer, beyond the fact that he was a member of the first Massachusetts contingent.

THE JOURNAL

March 24 1744/5 The Fleet under Convoy of Capt. [John] Rous set sail

April 4: Arrived at Canso having been separated from some part of his Convoy found the New Hampshire Troops at Canso some Indians taken by [Capt. David] Donahew at Owls Head examined.

12: Men begin to Sicken

13. A Block House ordered to be erected at Canso for Men with a Captain

14: Donahew arrived from the Gut of Canso brought in with him 3 Indian men and women and 3 children whom he took yesterday at the Gut. The 3 men being seperately examined declared that the Inhabitants of St. Peters were almost all drawn of Agreed unanimously in a Council of War, that the intended Attack on St. Peters should be deferred and that those Forces should attend the main Body to Chappeaurouge Bay and that Donahew should proceed a few Leagues before the fleet to prevent our discovery from St. Esprit or Fochee [Forchette?] Orders to sail at break of day if wind and weather permit.

15: Capt Colb [Sylvanus Cobb?] and B in a Whaleboat sent to St. Peters but by reason of Ice there was prevented Landing.

18: A Great Number of Guns heard [John] Rouse [Thomas] Saunders and the Piscataqua Troops sent out —

19: Many Guns heard of heard our Ships had engaged a French Man of War this proved to be a thirty Gun Ship from France to Louisbourgh she was chased by almost all the Vessels of France but outsailed them all but however they prevented her getting into the harbour.

21: Two Sloops with 70 Men sent to St. Peters [Capt. David] Donahew and [Capt. Robert?] Becket sailed for the Bay Vert.

22: Capt [Philip] Durell arrived in the Eltham from N: England.

23: Commodore Warren with one boat and 2 40 Gun ships arrived The Superb Mermaid and Launceston.

23: The Sloops returned from St. Peters, they did nothing but only burnt a few houses and brought away a small Sloop, there being more French and Indians than was expected.

24: The Connecticut forces arrived 8 Transports 500 men. The Rhode Island Sloop was their Convoy who met the same French Ship who attacked her and by that means the Convoy got safe away.

25: Fones [1] arrived

26: [John] Rous and [Daniel] Fones sailed in quest of the French Ship

29: This Morning the Fleet sailed from Canso to Louisbourgh, Colonel [Jeremiah] Moulton with a detachment of about 400 men were ordered to St. Peters to demolish it under Convoy of Capt. [John] Furnell in the New Hampshire Sloop

30: About 9 this morning the Fleet came to an anchor in Chappeaurouge Bay about 2 Miles above flat point. Whilst we were preparing to land a Party of the Enemy of a hundred Morepang [Morpain] commander appeared in arms at Flat point where we made a feint to land and then rowed back towards the Vessels till a Signal was given and then rowed higher up when the Enemy discovered this they immediately marched up the Bay and appeared to oppose our Landing but ——— [100] of our men being landed and immediately attacking them after the first fire they fled precipi-

---

[1] Capt. Daniel Fones of the Rhode Island armed sloop *Tartar.*

FIFTH JOURNAL

tantly away. We killed six men and took an officer and five men prisoners we had only three men wounded — We were covered in our Landing by [William] Fletcher Busch and [Thomas] Saunders. Landed ——— men. In the mean time the French Rang their bells and fired their Canon in the City some of the party recovered the City that night when the French burnt all their out houses near the West Gate.

May 1: The rest of the army landed and pitched their Camp about 1½ or 2 Miles from the Town several prisoners brought in of the Party that made their Sally Yesterday. A Detachment of 400 under cover of the Hills went to North: East: Harbour and burned all their Houses

2: The Enemy having deserted the Royal [or Grand] Battery the Detachment took Possession of it, the Cannon viz 28 42 pounders 9 eighteen Pounders being spoked up and broken 2 Carriages at the Flanks facing the town P: M: The French sent a party in Shalloways [shallops] to regain the Royal Battery but were soon drove back by a small body of our men that were on the Beach, tho' at the same time that the French fired their small arms from the Vessels the Cannon fired upon them from the Town. A few prisoners brought in this day.

3: 5 Prisoners brought in this day two of the Guns at the Grand Battery cleared and began to play upon the Town damaged their Houses and made the Women cry The mortars were haled to Green hill.

4: This day began to bombard the Town from Green Hill and cannonaded them from the Royal Battery more Prisoners brought in

5: Col. [Jeremiah] Moulton and party returned from St. Peters they burnt the Town and demolished the Fort took a few women and children Prisoners one of our Party straggling carelessly into the Woods was killed by an Indian 10 Prisoners brought in. One of the Canon of the Grand Battery split wounded 5 Men

6: Began to hale the Cannon across the Morass Cohorns [Coehorns] placed within 700 yards of the Wall

7: The Summons sent in returned for Answer — That the French King their Master had great dependance on them, and that they would return no answer but from the mouth of their Cannon

This Night a danger to attempt the Island Battery Surf too high and day light came on —

8: Preparing to Attack the Island Battery but did not proceed. Moving large Cannon to Batter the Town A Sally made this Evening by the Enemy but fruitless —

9 Attempt upon the Island Battery but did not proceed —

10: About 20 Prisoners brought in The Bed of the Great Mortar split 20 of our men stragling toward North East Harbour were set upon by a party of French and Indians two only escaped and several killed and the rest after having surrendered themselves inhumanly butchered. Whale Boats carried across the Land the Land [sic] to the Grand Battery in order to Attack the Island Battery but did not proceed a party of Commodore Warren's men with them [2]

11: Began the Eight Gun Battery Sickness Increased Fluxes

May 13: A French Snow from Bourdeaux got in — Two Cannon at the Bomb Battery split and Wounded 4 or 5 Men — Great Mortar Bed mended last night and began to play on the Town — Attempted by a Fire Ship to burn the Snow but in vain The great Mortar moved this night nearer the City

15: This Morning our New Bomb Battery began to fire a Fascone [fascine] Battery ordered to be erected and mounted with 2 42 lb from Grand Battery

17: Last night a party of 100 came from the Town and landed at the North: East harbour and this Afternoon made an Attack upon the Men that were camping on a Battery at the Light House Point but were soon repulsed but few of them gained the Town dismounted some of the Enemy's Cannon from the 8 Gun Battery. This day had the News that our Cruizers had destroyed Bradone Bayonne and St. Anne's

18: Last night the Fascine Battery commonly called the Advanced Battery within less than 200 Yards of the West Gate was finished from whence was fired one Eighteen Pound Cannon that being the only one then mounted there was 3 more not mounted by which the West Gate was soon demolished. Our People fired

---

[2] By carrying the whale boats to the Grand Battery they were within a half-hour's row of the Island Battery.

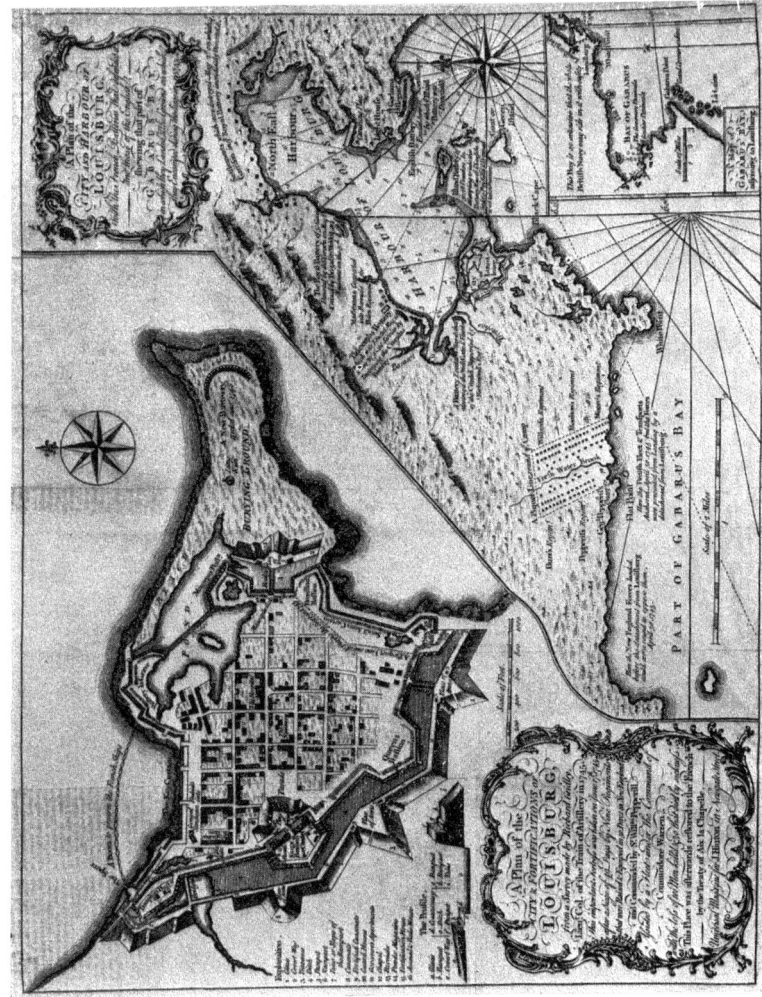

From the Society's Collection.

briskly with their Musketts at the Enemy on the Ramparts, and the Enemy returned a very brisk fire from their Cannon and Musgetts One of our Gunners killed by a Musket Ball, a Captain by a Cannon and several Wounded.

19: A Gunner killed at the Advanced Battery by a Canon shot two Barrels of Powder took fire one man killed 4 miserably burnt a 42 pounder split an engagement of the Harbour in sight of the Camp between a large French Man of War and our Ships

20 News brought to the Camp that [Capt. William] Fletcher in Wattering at Chappau Bay had 8 men killed and 3 taken by the Indians [Major Moses] Titcombs Battery finished

21: A letter from Mr. Warren that he had taken the Vigilant a 64 Gun French man of War. The Mermaid Eltham and Shirly Galley had been aboard her. The Guns from Titcombs Battery do great execution. The Princess Mary and the Bon Ame join the ——— Another Attempt to attack the Island Battery but fell thro

23: We continue our firing briskly the French slacken theirs — Another attempt on the Island Battery under Colonel [Arthur] Noble and Colonel [John] Gorham fell thru — The Commodore sent 200 men ashore to Assist.

24: The Hector joined Commodore Warren

25: Scouts return with a few Prisoners

26: This night an Attack was made upon the Island Battery by ——— [about 400] men were repulsed with about 60 men killed and 112 taken [3] The Great Mortar Split

27: 25 Prisoners brought in from Mera [Miré]

28 a Skirmish between a party of French and Indians and a Scout of ours the French and Indians repulsed we recovered but one of them

29: A Scout sent to Mera

31: The Scout returned brought ten prisoners some of these were of the party that made an attack on our Forces at the Light House — They say that many of their people were killed and Wounded in the late skirmish with our Scout That the Captain of the party that sallied upon the Light House had with five men in

---

[3] See *First Journal,* footnote 15.

a Shallop got into Louisbourgh in the night — two Guns planted last night by the Enemy on new Works near West Gate, silenced by our people's Canon this day.

June 1: Last night the Enemy planted 9 Guns on the Walls near the West Gate A Scout sent to Mera

2: [David] Donahew arrived with a large Mortar — A battery ordered to be erected near the Light House

3: General with some officers Go on board the Commodore to consult a Scout returned with prisoners

4: New Mortar began to play Fired red hot Shot

5: Removed Camp nearer the Water side News that the Siege of Annapolis was raised that the French and Indians were coming to Louisbourg a Deserter came out of the Town [4]

6: Mr. Bastide [5] arrived from Annapolis

9: Two Swiss deserters

10: Arrived the Chester and brought advice of 2 60 Gun ships that she came out with to join the Commodore

June 10. A Scout sent out — the Light House Battery began to play with Very Brisk firing from all Quarters the French threw 65 Bombs only 13 broke the General went on bord the Commodore

12: The Canterbury and Sunderland joined the Commodore, as also the Lark with a store ship bound to Annapolis the Transports ordered on board the Men of War to take of their Lumber in order to go into the Harbour — two 42 lb Guns removed from the Grand Battery to Titcomb's Battery Removed the Great Mortar to the Light House Battery

13: Removed another 42 lb Gun to Titcomb's Battery Very smart Fire

14: A Warrant from Commodore Warren for 150 Barrels of Powder from the Store ship all our Batterys fire briskly more so than ever 3 large Piles of Brush set on three Hills near the Town

---

[4] The French and Indians were besieging Annapolis Royal and lifted the siege May 24th to go to the relief of Louisbourg. This force of 600 or 700 men, under the command of the partisan Marin (Capt. Marin Michel du Bourzt, Marquis de St. Colombe) reached the vicinity of Louisbourg too late and did not try to attack the Provincials.

[5] John Henry Bastide, a British officer, became Principal Engineer of this expedition.

FIFTH JOURNAL 79

for a Becon for Commodore Warren preparations makin for an attack

15: A flag of Truce to desire time to draw up articles granted till tomorrow morning 9 o the clock every thing had been got ready for an attack

16: A Flag of Truce Articles agreed on Hostages exchanged

17: The Town surrendered — .

first [6] night only one 18 lb The People at this Battery killed by Musquts as well as Canon Ball 18 lb Mounted 1 18 lb and 2 42 lb Returned from the West Flank of the Citadel West Gate and some new Embrazures at the North East Battery The West Flank of the Citadel a great Annoyance Beat them from all their Guns by 11 o'Clock — Being much annoyed from the West Flank of the Cittadel a Trench was dug at the South end of this Battery and 1 18 lb 2 9 lb Pounders haled from the 8 Gun Battery and mounted on the South line against the said Flank and fired them with such Truth that the Enemy were soon beat from their Guns

22d. The Fire very hot on both sides till 12 at noon when the French were beat from their Guns fired no more that day

23 The French two other Guns at the Citadel but in four hours were forced to leave them

June 6th The Enemy had 2 Guns run out of new Embrazares cut thru the Parapet which soon began to play with great Fury and we were obliged to turn three Guns against them, and in three Hours we dismounted one and silenced the other for that Day

[6] Evidently additional notes for May 21, 22, 23, and June 6, 1745.

SIXTH JOURNAL

Anonymous

The majority of the soldiers on the Louisbourg expedition, judging from the existing journals, seem to have been interested and impressed by their novel experiences and to have accepted the hardships and dangers courageously and good-naturedly. This soldier on the contrary complained bitterly of the conduct of the officers, and roundly abused the French for not giving battle. He was apparently quite soured about the whole expedition, and although the doggerel rhymes which appear from time to time in the journal show a sense of humor, his closing verses show only distaste and derision for the whole experience.

The identity of the writer is not known. He served in the Second Massachusetts Regiment, commanded by Colonel Samuel Waldo and apparently was in the company under Captain Joseph Richardson.

This is another of the journals given by the heirs of the Rev. Dr. Jeremy Belknap to the Massachusetts Historical Society and by that Society courteously lent for publication here.

THE JOURNAL

1745 Charlstown March 16 1745 this Day Capt. Joseph Richardsons [1] Company Imbercked for the Expedition Intended Against Cape Britton.

Satterday 23 Day we fell Down to Nantasket —

Sabath Day the 24 wind Southwest — this Day a fine gaile of

---

[1] No Joseph Richardson appears in the list of commissions for this expedition until July 1, 1745, when a man of that name was made commander of the sloop *Resolution*. However, a Jeremiah Richardson appears as Captain of the 10th Company in the 2d Mass. Regt.

SIXTH JOURNAL 81

wind and att half an hour Past: 3 we Brok ground and and Sat Saill and the fleet in Number was 53

Monday the 25 — East wind — this morning the Comandore [John Rouse][2] Stood a bout for Cape Pan [Cape Ann] and about 3 of the Clock we Came up a brest of the Cape — and we Stod a Long Shore —

Tusday the 26 East wind — this Day about 12 of the Clock we Came up a Brest with Cape Elsebeth other ways called Caskeobay and at a Quarter past 5 we Came to ancor in Sheepscut River.

Weddensday the 27 — this morning Very fogge and Som Rain Such weather Ended this Day —

Thursday the 28 East wind — this Day Storme and Tempestuos weather So Ended this Day —

Fryday the — 29 Nort wind — this Day att 10 of the Clock we wayed Ancor and Came to Saile and fine gaile we had but Vnhappely one Sloop Ran upon a Roock but got of with out Much Dammage —

SatterDay the 30 Sout wind — this Day a Very high South wind with — Rain and Snow with a Very high See. So that we Lay tow a bout fore of the Clock Vnder a Two Reefe fore saile. Capt. [John] Rouse Lay a bout one Mile off But his Top mast was Not to Be Seene Some Times By Reason of the Seese —

Sabath Day the 31 Est Wind — Last Night we Lost our Comandore [John Rouse] By Reason of the Bad weather this Morningg it Cleard of Very Calm and we were By our Soundings a Bout 10 Leegs to the to the [sic] Sothard of the Sill Islands yn the Bay of funday —

Monday Apriel the 1 North East — this Day a Nor East Storme of Raine So that we Put Into Pubneco a Bout 2 of the Clock In the afternoone with Eight Saile with us —

Tuse-Day the 2 West wind — at 6 of the Clock this Morning we wayed ancor and at 10 we was a Brest of Cape Sables and att 12 we was a Brest of Cape Negrow —

Weddens Day the 3 South wind — this Night we met with a

---

[2] Capt. John Rouse was Commodore of the main Provincial fleet. Capt. Edward Tyng, senior Provincial naval officer, was second in command. Capt. Peter Warren was Commodore of the British fleet which joined the Provincials. See Appendix I, *The Fleet.*

Very feirse Storme of Snow Som Rain and Very Dangeras weather for to Be So Nigh the Shore as we was But we Esscaped the Rock and that was all —

Thurs-Day the 4 Sout wind — Att 6 of the Clock In the after Noone we Came to an ancor In Canso and 12 Saile with us —

Fry-Day the 5 Sou East wind — this Day Capt. [Jonathan] Snelling Came into the harbor and Capt. [William] fletcher with on french Sloop L.D. [laden] with. wine and Rome Shoger

Satter Day the 6 Est wind — Este wind and Storme of Raine Nothing Strange to Day

Sabath Day the 7 East wind — this Day Several Sorts of Bisneses Going on to Day Som a Exersiseing Som a Heareing Preaching So the Day Ends —

Mon Day the 8 Sout west wind — this Brisk wind has Brought in 12 Saile of the fleete I Should Be glad of Such News Every Day.

Weddens Day the 10 East wind — Cloudy and Cold But Nothing Strang this Day

Thurs Day the 11 Nor west wind — this Day 12 more is Com Into the Harbor of our fleet and the Prise is Sat Saile for Bostown —

Fry Day the 12 Sout East — Storm of Snow and Som Raine But No Dammage Don But we had a Larram [alarm] att Night By Reason of a Loose Boate —

Satter Day the 13 Nor Est wind — this Day thund and Litening Very hard Som Rain Last Night 6 or 7 Broad Sids washed of at See But Knew Not the matter.

Sabath Day the 14 Nor west wind — this Day Capt. Donowho [David Donahew] Came In with Eight Indians on of them a King one of them a Queen 4 Saile of Strange Vessels Discouerd of

Mond Day the 15 Est wind — this Day Pleasant and warme which Seemes Very Delite Som to us all. No great News Sturin to Day

Tuse Day the 16 Est wind — A Raine Storme this Day and 2 Shipps Seen of upon the Costs Which are Soposed to be Inglish Vessells —

Weddens Day the 17 — Nor west — This Day Capt. [William] Fletcher Sent In a Brigg of 6 gons [guns] L.D. [laden] with Rum

SIXTH JOURNAL

molasses and a Considerable Quanete of amanision [ammunition] the Prise is Very well Exseptted and we hope that he will Gitt the other that he is in Pursute of —

Thurs Day the 18 Est wind — this Day Capt. Swan and Capt. [David] Donowho Brought In a Brigg of eigh Gons — L : D with Rom, molasses other good stors

Fry: Day the 19 Nor West — this Day [Capts] [Edward] Ting, [Jonathan] Snelling and [John] Rouse are In Pursute after a french Shipp 2 of our Schooners Retaken from the french and Brought In to Day

Satter Day the 20 Sout west — this Day one man Kild him Self — Sr. [Sur, Srr?] Richard Kild him [3]

Sabath Day the 21 — this Morning 4 of Coll. [Samuel] Willards men was Taken by 2 french one Indian But they Ree Toock them Selues and the 2 french men with them the Indian Cleard him Self Capt. [John] Rouse Returned But No Success —

Mon Day the 22 — west wind — this Day Capt. Durall [Philip Durell] Came to the Mouth of the harbor one of 2 Vessel went to take Sant. Peters But No Sucsess and they Returnd

Tuse Day the 23 nor west — this the Joy full Sight of Admaral [Peter] Warren with 3 Shipps Came By the harbor Bound to the Cape he Lay Two one Night for to Speak with us A Small Sloop Brought from Saint Peters Taken by the Inglish —

Wednes Day the 24 west wind — this Day the A : D : [Admiral?] Came to Saile and Went Down a Long Shore — Also the Connetticut flett Came to an ancor In the harbor to Enjoyn our flett this Is well Exseptted By all In ganaral — 9 of them Sloops and Shooners 2 Briggs —

Thurs Day the 25 Souh west — this Day came in Rhod Island Brigg [4] to Injoyn to the fleet — Som Rain this Day But Loocks Likely for more —

Fry Day the 26 Est wind — this Day Capt [John] Rouse went out afte the the [sic] french Priviteare and Rhodisland Priveteares In Company with him Rain and fogg to Day

Satter Day the 27 Est wind — this Day a Nor Este Stoorme But

---

[3] No surgeon Richard appears on existing rolls and this entry is unexplained. It is not even certain that surgeon is meant.

[4] The *Tartar,* Capt. Daniel Fones.

No News But the Men are Vnese for to go to the Cape So we wejght onele for a Sutabl Wind

Sabath Day the 28 West wind — this Day the Reverend Mr. Mood [5] Preachd upon the Island of Canso But So many Sorts of Exersise Going one Little Good there there was to Behad — 1 Corrinthians the 2d Chapt the 2d Vers. Afternoone 1 King the 20 Chapt Vers the 11

Mon Day the 29 West wind — this Morning att 7 of the Clock the Whole fleet Brok Ground and Came to Saile — and att 8 of the Clock we met Commander with all his Shipps of forse the Number 80.

Tuse Day the 30 West wind These Scoundellus french Dogs they Dare not Stay to fite — But Set there houses on fire and So Ran into the Sitty by the Light — This Morning Fine and Pleasant from About 7 of the Clock the 3 Battere was a Larmd: and a Bout 10 we Came to the Place of our Landing and about 100 of the french Com to hender our Design we had But a Small Schurmidg To what we Expectted 3 of our men Wound 3 of thers found Ded 12 of them was Tak 4 Cows 23 houses they Set on fire without the Walls and Sunk there Vessels

Weddens Day the 1sd May West Wind — This We Kild Several Cows and Took Several More — Som horses Sheep and other Sutable things for our Casses Rum wine Molasses Sider But these Thing Was son Scejrse Again —

Thurs Day the 2d West wind — This Morning we had the Success of Taken the Grand Batterre By Land and a 14 Gon Shipp By See L : D : [Laden] With 6 Hodgshead of Powder a Quante of there Sort of Butter — The Grand Batterre had 32 Gons 30 of them was 42 Pound 2 others 32 pound and Several Horses Cows and fouls Takin to Day. It Seems as If the french was In a hurre for they this famos fort Withou any Scorre

Fry Day the 3d West wind — This Day we Took Seueral Men wimin and Children — att Night 20 of Capt [Joseph] Richardson

[5] Rev. Samuel Moody of York, Me., B.A., Harvard, 1697, Chaplain of Pepperrell's regiment. He was aged seventy at this time. He embarked at Boston carrying an axe with which he promised to cut down the "idols" in the Louisbourg churches. He actually did demolish the objects in the churches which offended him.

Company had a Fine walk — we Traveld all Night and a Very-Cold it was This Day 43 Boms Houe and 146 Cannon they Shot att us at Night we got one gon Cleare.

Satter Day the 4 — This Day fine faverable weather for Our Design they houe 30 Boms att us — But Never hurt one Men we Shot 70 Shot att them 6 Boms — we Houe att them this Seemes to Do

Sabath Day the 5 Sou wind — This Day we Met In the Chapel of the Royal Battree. Mr. Newman Chaplin [6] In Psalms the 100 Verse the 4 and 5 one of our Gons Split But hurt None this Day North East harbor [Pak?] taken — 2 of the french Kild one wounded

Monday the 6 Sout west — This Day 100 of the Grand Batterre Men went to the Town Cald Nor. Est Harber the Nomber of there Habitaton was 35 we found Several of theire Camps fild with all Sorts of goods and we Livd upon theire fowls and Sheep Goots Calves we Took 40 Shallawops [shallops] one Sloop one Schooner there

Tuse Day the 7 fair weather — This Day we Plonderd there Camps of all Their goods — a french Doctore Resind him Self up and we went to a Norther Town Contain a Bout 30 Houses we Took 20 men wives and Children also Their Camps of — Prouission one Schooner a Larg Number of Shallawop

Weddens Day the 8 good weather — This Day we found one More Camp with 2 Pritty Gurls In it 3 boys with other good Lomber this Day the Gons went Merryly att the french and the french Struk theire Collers 4 Times this Day att the Iland Battery And the town Shot Several Shot att them

Thurs Day the 9 Good weather — the Night before Last our Men Maid an atemt to Tak the Iseland Batterry but it Was to Late for theire Design So Returnd Back This Day Smart firein one Both Sids — and I Came to the Battery

Fry Day the 10 fogge to Day — this Day a Bout 10 of the Clock 20 of our Side Kild and Carried of By the Indians and french 6 of the others that was In the Same Company got away 2 of the 6 wounded of the Nomber of them was Soposed to Be about 100 the french Shot att our Artillery So Smart that they

---

[6] Rev. John Newman, Harvard, B.A., 1740, of Gloucester, Mass., Chaplain of the 2d (Waldo's) Mass. Regt.

Kild 2 and wounded 2 more — this is the Most Unfortanate Day that has hapned to our Sid yet

Satter Day the — 11 — This Day the Gons went one Both Sides and the men that was att the Town beyond Noth Est harbor Com in which have Told the whole Story

Sabath Day the 12 Nor west wind — the 8th of this month one of our gentleman Catchd Coming out of the Sitty. this Day 2 Sermons Preaehd In our Chapel Hebrews the 9th Vers the 27 the words of the Text for itt is a Pinted for Man once to Die : these Sermons is after the Deth of the 20 men But Little firein to Day.

Mon Day the 13 good weather — this Day Vnfortanately a french Snow Got Into the Harbor all we Could Do we Shot 15 Gons att her In 10 minits But they Shot 53 att us In the Same Time and Capt. [Daniel] Haill was Kild att this Time — Coole Miste fogge Weather a briske wind which favered them 3 more wounded to Day — But are not Mortal and at Night we Sent them a fire Shipp But Did not answer our End —

Tuse Day the 14 Est wind — this Day Is the first fowl Day that we have Had Sense we Landed this Day a man Riding Vpon a horse Vnfortanately A Shot Came from the french and which Not onely Kild the horse But it Took of his Shooe heals and Dismounted the Fallow which was a Great an afrunt as he Saith to hime

Weddens Day the 15 Nor west wind — this Day Pleasant weather But Little fire 59 This Day — No News this Day —

Thurs Day the 16 Nor west wind — this Day one Man Wounded att the Artillery Very Much fair weather and a holsom Air this Day our Cowhorns [Coehorns] Plays well answere the End —

Fry Day the 17 Pleasant weather — this Day one of our 42 Pounders Split that wound 3 one Very much this Day 1 Stone Sloop Came In which gives us the account that yester Day 1 of them was Taken and The french Man Lying In PurSute after Capt. [John] Rouse Did not Bord him and he Put a Bout and Stood Into Canso and So Cleard hur Self of her Enemy att the Lite house Our men found 20 Great Gons In the wattr and a bout 100 french and Indians fell an our Gard and they one of our Men was Wounded Mortall one of them we took.

Satter Day the 18 — this Day Capt. [Joshua] Peirce was Kild by a Larg Shot from the french he Lived 15 minits and then Died which was Very much Lemented this Day one Barrel of Powder Axedentall Took fire and Kild 2 of our men and wounded 3 More Likewise one Gon Split which Kild young Barns and wounded 2 more a new Battery 2 Gons Drawn to it

Sabath Day the 19 fogge — this Day we had the Sucsess of Taken a 64 Gon Shipp which is Called the Vigilence 2 Sermon Preached Exedus the 17 Verse the 11 Last Night I was Set to Geard the Batter [———— ?] of our Men with Me this Day at the Shin [fascine?] Battery one Barrel of Powder Took fire and wounded 2 of them Very Bad Likewise a 30 Gon Shipp Taken and Brought Into Caberose [Gabarus] one of the 42 Pound Split and Kild 2 wound Eight.

Mond: Day the 20 fogge — this Day a Brigg Taken and Brought Into Caberose L:D: [laden] With Stors and and She is Very well Exseptted by us —

Tuse Day the 21 — this Day our Scout Came In from Noth East harbor and Brought In a 11 of the french None of us hurt

Weddens Day the 22 — this Day one of our Men Did: 2 men wound By a Cathridg Taking fire and Burnt them Very Much Likwise theire Watch Box we Shot Down a man of war Came from Bostown Into Caberose — the fashend [fascine] Battery Does good Execution —

Thurs-Day the 23 Pleasant Day — this Night about Eight hundred of us went to Tak the Iseland [Island Battery] But our head offiser Being a Couard we Rowd a Bout all Night and Never Landed — So Every man to his Tent we heard after ward that there was but 130 men of the french one the Iland that Night.

Fry: Day the 24 — this Day D the head offiser was Sent For to go to the General But they Cleard him as If he had Not Ben gilte [7] Smart firein So Ended this Day

Satter Day the 25 — this Day we had the good forten to Tak 4 french men one off them had Mr [Capt. Peter] Prescut Jacet [jacket] and they Gaue fellow to our Indians and they Did as they

---

[7] For an account of the attack on the Island Battery see footnote 15 of *First Journal*. Lieut. Cols. Arthur Noble and John Gorham were in command, and they, together with other officers, were called before Pepperrell and his Council of War. The initial "D" used by the diarist is unexplained.

Thoug Fit they Cut his Throat Standing — 2 Night Goin upon Gard

Sabath Day the 26 Pleasant weather — this Day 169 of the Grand Battere Men went to A town Called Scattere [Scatarie] a Bout 15 Miles of it had 6 Houses In it this Day Preachd Salms the 7th Verss 11 Psalm the 50 Verse the 2 Smart firin to Day we Sopose to Tak the Iland Battery this Night and they went and they Landed A Bout 12 of the Clock at Night and the firin was as it ware a Continewall Blase for A Bou 2 hours and our Men that Was taken was 123 the french Say that they Kild 80 more

Mon-Day the 27 fogge — this Morning we Found a Great Many of our Men Ded Som with their Leggs of arms and heads of this Day our Men Came In from SCattere [Scatarie] with 8 men and one woman 10 of our Men got a Shore that was Wounded

Tuse Day the 28 Miste fogge — this Morning a Detachment Came to the Grand Battere for 241 men our Capt. Richardson Went with 20 of his Men and 19 of them Came Came [sic] hom 6 of them wounded the whole that went of all the Rigements was 5-0-0 the Iniagement Last a Bout 4 hours and the Nomber of all that was Kild of the Inglish was Eight about 15 wounded 30 of the french Kild 50 wound they got Nothing by this Bargin.

Weddens Day the 29 — General Electtion att Bostown — this Day General Election Is a Malloncolle — this Day 400 of our Men Is Gon to Bury the Dead 10 of our Company is Goan — A fine Pleasant Day this Is —

Thurs Day the 30 — this Day our Men Came In from Nor: East harbor and they Brougt In 7 french Men and 3 Wimin and by the Account they Gave there was 30 of them Kild and 40 Wounded and 4 Indians Kild and 7 Wounded of our men that was Kild was 8 — wounded 27 we Shot a way ther flegg Stafe smart firein this Day —

Fry-Day the 31 — this Day we fird 2 Gons to there one We haue 80 men sick and wounded In our hospittel fair Weather this Day

Satter Day the June the 1st — this Day we haue Taken one Shipp and one Brigge We fired a shot at Sitte and the shot fell Short and Struck a bote Ladend With men and Cut it In Two 200 of our Men is Gon to Noth East harbor

Sabbath Day the 2d — this Day Mr. [John] Newman Preach

SIXTH JOURNAL

and the Text was In Amos the 4 Chapt Verse the 12 the words Prepair to Meet thy God a genale Cold miste fogg weather a New Battere a Bildding —

Monday the 3 — this Day a Detachment Sent for 50 of the Grand Battery Men to go on Bord the Vigelence Six of Capt [Joseph] Richardson men But the all Returnd Back aGain Capt Donowh [David Donahew] hes Brought In 2 Morters from Bostown a Sloop Taken that Came from Canade LoD: [laden] with Prouision they Ran hur a Shore att Noth East Harbor and they all Maid their Esscape —

Tuseday the 4 — this Day Came In a man of war from Holland and a Brigg taken — to Day our Scout went out In Pursuit after them Men that Maid theire Esscap out of these Vessell att Noth East Harbor and Now they are Come in and they Taken 17 wimin and Children — But these that they went after was not to Be found

Weddes Day the 5 Pleasant Weather — this Morning a french Man Came to Us ouer the walls and he Giues us an account that 100 would Turne the first opertunity he says that they haue 123 of our men Prisners In the Sitty we fired Very Smart all Day att Eavning we tooke a Shipp of 200 Tons.

Thurs Day the 6 fair Weather — this Day the gons is Drawn for the Lite house Batter the Nomber of the Gon is 10 (6 Plased to the Iseland Bat erre 4 to the See) Very Smart firin one our Sid But Little one theires this Day Ariued heare from Nappeles [Annapolis Royal] the Injianeare [8] and he Says that the french and Indians that Beseeged them are Drawn off and are Soposed to Be Coming to Cap Brittion [Cape Breton] the Nombers of 800 —

Fry-Day the 7 — this Day Looks Likele for a Storme Very Smart firein one Both Sides — the Vegelence is fitted for Saile

Satter Day the 8 — this Day Comadore Warren is Goan In With a flegg of Truse the Reason why they went in was this to See

---

[8] The "Injianeare" is the British engineer John Henry Bastide. He was at Annapolis Royal when the siege there was raised May 24th. Pepperrell wrote him on June 2d at Annapolis, but he had left there May 27th for Cape Breton. Bastide was commissioned Principal Engineer at Cape Breton. He was later a Lieutenant General in the Royal Army.

weather they Would Sirrend and to haue them Mak Restituton for their Barbaras Treatment from theire Indians But they Say that they Know not of It [9] — Som Rain to Day But Know News

Sabath Day the 9 fair Weather a gain — this Day 2 Sermons Preachd to us By Mr. [John] Newman the Text: Amos the 4 Verse the 12 the werd Prepair to Meet they God o Irael the after Noon Luke the 19 Verse the 10 — for the Son of man is Com to Saue that which was Lost this Day a 60 Gon Shipp is Joynd to our forses and Says that there was 2 more with 3 Day a go.

Mon Day the 10 fair weather — this Day our Shipp in is Set Saile to New England for 1500 More Men But 9 Days is giuen for them to go and to Return the Lite house Plays Smartly att the Iland Battere which Damnifies them Very much

Tuse Day the 11 Good weather — this Day a Scout of 340 men went to a Town Called Sattere [Scatarie] at a farme Called Legraws farm went for to Take 400 Armes that was Soposed to Be Sent for a Number of Indians But we found None 4 Swesers [Swiss] came out and Gaue us this as a Count [10] But we Was Goan 2 Day and then Return it was Soposed to 15 —

Weddens Day the 12 Good weather — at 3 of the Clock we Returnd all of us this Day 2 Men of war Came In and Brought In 2 Twenty Gon Shipps the Lite Hous [Battery] Plays Smartly att the french —

Thurs Day the 13 — this Day 40 Gon Shipp Came In from Newfound Land and they Giues us an Account of 2 more Coming hears we are getting faggets for to Line the Sids of the Shipp for to Com in to the harbor they Design to Com in the first fair wind Very feirse firein one Both Sids a french Shipp Taken

Fry-Day the 14 fair weather — our Shipps are all drawn up in A line of Battle In order to Com in Very Smart firein one Both Sids att Night there was Soposed to Be matter of a thousand of Small

---

[9] There was sent in a letter from the Marquis de la Maisonfort, late Captain of the *Vigilant,* telling of the good treatment given him and the feeling against the French Indian allies. It was not a flag of truce and no demand for surrender was made.

[10] The Swiss deserters from the Karrer Regiment said that small arms, ammunition, and provisions had been sent to Mera (Miré) to supply a relief force of French and Indians.

SIXTH JOURNAL

armes fired In the Sitte in an hours Time which was Soposed to Be a Mutiane Betwen the Swesors [Swiss] and the french it was at 6 of the Clock in the after noone and at Night the french houe more Bomes that Night then they Did any night while the Place was Beseegd they Cept 4 Morters goin Constan

Satter Day the 15 fair weather — this Day one man Kild by a Bom that the french houe from Iland Batterre and this Day we got a morter of 14 Inches that Tore them to Peases Very Fast In So much that the french See It on the Battere Plaid and houe the Shipps was Reade to Weight upon them and hou the matter would Go with them So a Bout 4 of the Clock In the after None they Sent out a flegg of Truse But Nothing Don so they are to Com out att Eight of the Clock to morrow morning

Sabath Day the 16 — and att Eight the fagg Came out and Tarried till 3 and went In and Came out att 6 and they came to Termes for us to Enter the Sitte to morrow and Poore Termes they Be two [11] —

Mon Day the 17 Looks Like Rain — this Day a Bout Eight of the Clock, In the Morning the french flegg was Taken Down and the Inglish Put up all our Battere fired Grand Battery 17 Titcombs: 6: the Comandors Battere the 5 guns: the Iscland Batterre [12] 16 and Brooks Batter 5 Gons all these Batteries fird twise Round and a Bout 3 of the Clock the Comandore Came to an ancor in the harbor and our Shipps and all our Small Craft 50 Barrels of Poud [powder] was found att the Island Batre 20 in the Sitte and

Tues Day the 18 — a great Dealle of Rain fell — Last Night it Raind Very hard and this Morning ther Came a french Shipp to the mouth of the harbor and Struck with out firen But 2 gons She gives an a Count of 60 Gon Shipp one the Costs [Coast] — the Comander Came to the Grand Battere and gave a hogshead of Rum to Drink his health 2 men Came Into the Sitte with Letters that 1600 french and — Indians and they are to go Back — and

---

[11] The rank and file of the Army were indignant to learn that their hopes of booty were lost by the terms which protected the private property of the French.

[12] Under the terms of surrender the Island Battery was turned over as security before 6:00 P. M. on the 16th.

Tell when to Come and to fall one But as it happend these men Did not Return at Tall. —

Weddens Day the 19 fowle Weather — this Day our Men are Vere Unese and itt is Not without Case this Day the Solders of the french are to Be one Bord they Came out of the Sitte with there Collers and Armes and the french have Broot a great Number of there armes and Cutlashe this Day a Vessels is Set out to go to Bostown our Men are gitting there Artillery home —

Thurs Day the 20 fowle Weather to Day — this Day fowle and Som of our Men heard Sx Vessels and heard 7 Gons of att See a great Noys and hubbub a mungst the Solders a bout the Plonder Som will go out and Take it again Som one way Som a Nother —

Fry Day the 21 Bad weather — this Day we — Fowle weather and we Drawd 2 Gons to the Grand Battr I. B.[13] is Very Bise about his Bisnas and It will Be as well for him If he Would Not So much the french Keep Posession yet and we are forst to Stand att there Dores to gard them [14] —

Satter Day the 22 this Day Cloudy But no Rain — this Day a great [Touse?] in the Sitte Cloudy weather But no Rain No more of there Vessell to Be Sea Greate foggs B: is all the Talk — for he is as the Vest to be one Day one won Side and a Nother Day one the other Side.

Sabath Day the 23 fowle — this Day fowle and fogge and Som Gons heard off att See Som of the french are a gitting one Bord

Mond Day the 24 — fowle weather — this Day fogge and fowle one Schooner Bound to Newengland with Prisners his Complyment is 100 —

Tuse Day the 25 — this Day a Purtision [petition] Being Sent in But None Granted this Day 2 men Did Out of the Grand Batter No great News

Weddens Day the 26 — this Day about 9 of the Clock it Began to

---

[13] Possibly Col. John Bradstreet who had much to do with taking over the town and was Town Major Commandant. He was often a storm-center. The French claimed he had broken parole. Some of the Provincial officers questioned his loyalty and sincerity. He had a long and distinguished career in the British Army. See his own statement in *Tenth Journal.*

[14] The Provincial rank and file were annoyed at being required to guard the French property.

SIXTH JOURNAL

Brak a way and Cleard off Soone — at 12 of the Clock Capt [John] Rouse Came In and fird 17 Guns to Selute us — the Comandore fird 13 for Joy 2 french Shalaways [shallops] L: D. [laden] with sheep Cattle other Goods and —

Thursday the 27 Cloudy weather — this Day it Raind and one Man Did Nothing But a Tumult in the Sitte which I feare will a Rive to a Great heath [heat]

Fry Day the 28 — this Day Cloudy Not But a few of the french one Bord yet — No Great News this Day —

Satter Day the 29 — this Day fair Weather one Sloop Came Into the Harbor from Napelles [Annapolis] Royal But Brings no new at talle

Sabath Day the 30 — the french are not one Bord yet which Maks us Very Vnesee to Know What it all Means 10 Shallaway [Shallops] are Come In and 1 Schooner L: D. [laden] with Cows and other Loding —

Mon Day the 1 July fair Weather to Day — this Day I wen Into the Sitte and I found the Cannon 6 Brase Gons 85 Carrage 50 Swevil 5 Brase Morters one Iron one and the Height of the wall In genaral is 30 foots they Sell and By In the Sitte as they Do in other Plases Som Cursing som a Swarein

Tuse Day the 2d — this Day Severall Vessells Came to Caberose But the Vessells was Goan away and they Soposed we was all Taken But they Soone found to the Contarare they Never heard of the Sitte Being taken till they Cam to it —

Weddens Day the 3d fowle weather — this Day fowle weather there is one Shipp one Schooner Came Into the Harbor with Solders one Bord 2 Shipps is Goan to france with flegg of Truses it Thundered to Day and it hes not Ben herd before Sence we Came here

Thurs Day the 4d — this Day fair Weather 2 Shipp Gone out of the harbor one with Prisner the other to Porte Royal one Schooner Came from New England with Solders

fry Day the 5th — this Day 3 Schooners Came Into the Harbor with Solders one Bord-Doctor [John] Manning Came in with one of them Capt [Thomas] Sanders is Set Saile for New England one Schooner Bore him Company 2 men of war is goan out a Crusing on Costs —

Satter Day the 6 — Stephan [Iuial?] this Morning Capt. [John] Rouse Sat Saill for England Capt [Jonathan] Snelling Came Into the harbor with Solders one Bord and one Sloop one Schooner with 3 Came one Bord fair weather to Day — 15 Vessells is saild for wood to Scattere

Sabath Day the 7 — this Day Very Pleasant and Som thunder there Being a Rumor of a Vessells Seene off att the mouth of Cannade River 2 Men of war are Goan for 3 weeks Cruse —

Mon Day the 8th fair weather — this Day Came in Capt Donowhose [David Donahew] Sloop which Brings Bad News that he is Dead and 12 of his men the Comandore Is Set Shipp and one more is Set out for a Cruse this one man Married to a french Laid good —

Tuse Day the 9 Cloudy to Day — It has Ben South West Wind for Several Dayse Eight Schoners Set Saile for New England with Prisners this Day I went one Bord a Schooner Called the fish haugh [Fishhawk] Capt Newmarch Comander

Weddens Day the 10 — this Day Pleasant a while and then an East wind Brought In a fogg Seueral Gons hes Ben heard of at See one Schooner is Set Saill for france

Thurs Day the 11 — this Morning the wind Sprang up at South West and it Cleard of this Day the Rhodisland Shipp Set Saile for Bostown Just Came in a Schooner from Rhodisland 3 weeks Passage — this Eavaning there was a hot Talk about a mobbs Risin and they Say that they Did Rise So as to git what they wanted —

Fry Day the 12 faire weather — this Day 2 Sloops is Com to Saile to Go out of the Harbor one of them is Donowhos and 2 Schooners about 12 of the Clock 13 Shallaways [shallops] of french man and there goods —

Satter Day the 13 — this Day Capt. Newmarsh Receied his Orders for Sailin But the wind Being Contarare we Lay In the harbor one Sloope Came in from New York — 4 of ours wood Vessells Came In L:D: [laden] with the Same —

Sabath Day the 14 — this morning Sprang up a fair fresh gaile of North west Wind about 6 of the Clock In the Morning we Came to Saile and and [sic] we Lay Bey Calmd a Bout 3 Leegs of att Night the wind Sprang up and we Saild 5 Leggs

SIXTH JOURNAL 95

Monday the 15 — About 12 of the Clock we maid Canso and Saint Peters a Bout 5 Leegs off and a Contarare wind Sprang up and we Stod off —

Tuse Day the 16 South west — this Day we Stood in for Canso But the wind Being Contarare we Could Not git Into the Harbor Very Could this Night and Raine —

Weddens Day the 17 — this Day Very Could and Cloud and a Sma Breese of Nor West wind — Showere to Day —

Thurs Day the 18 South west — this Morning Very Could In Deede the wind Very high so that we was-forst to Lie two Vnder a Reefe fore Saill —

Fry Day the 19 South wind — Very high wind all Night and a bout 8 of the Clock we Sailed high South Weste Wind Very Could this Day —

Satter Day the 20 South West — this Day a fresh South west Wind and Rain utill a Bout 2 of the Clock then it was Calm and att night Cleard of Very Could —

Sabath Day the 21 — this Mor Ning it Raind But Cleard of Cold with a Nor: west Wind — But att 12 of the Clock the wind Sprang up a gainst us —

Monday the 22d — this Morning Pleasant and warme — this Day there was an obseruation taken But the Sun Did Not Shine Cleare So no Sertin Account Could be given of the Latitude —

Tuse Day the 23d — this Morning North East wind Sprang up But Cloudy and fogge and Raind — Som But Cleard of Calm and Pleasant and we ware within a Bout 4 Leegs off Cape Negrow —

Weddens Day the 24 — this Morning Calm and fogge Till a Bout 12 of the Clock then Sprang up a South East wind Blows up fresh and a Bout: 6: of the Clock we maid the Same Cape again —

Thurs Day the 25 — this Day att a Bout 3 of the Clock We Soposed to Be in the Bay of funday

fry Day the 26 — this Day a Small Breese of wind But Pritty faire and warme —

Satter Day the 27 — this Day an obseruation Being taken and we ware a Bout 3 Leegs to the Sothard of Cape Pan [Cape Ann] a Small wind But Warme —

Sabath Day the 28 South wind — this Day a Bout half an hour after 2 we Maid Cape Pan and a Bout 4 we Came up a Brest of it — and at 3 of the Clock we ancord att the Long Wharfe —

Mon: Day the 29 — this Day Very Raine and fogge But att Night I got Home

    Faire Well Cape: Britton
    faire well all you fases
    that Bread Such Dis: greases
    a gainst Solders that are True to their King
    for I Boldely Do Say
    If they once git a way
    You will Be hard Poot to it to Catch them agin.

SEVENTH JOURNAL

Privates George Mygate and Caleb Lamb

George Mygate of Springfield, Massachusetts, did not leave Boston for Louisbourg until after the fortress had fallen. He was an enlisted man in the Ninth Massachusetts Regiment in the company commanded by Captain Isaac Colton. His journal is free from any accounts of dangers or fears. The soldier tells of picking roses, hunting for foxes and trying to court a French girl. It is a cheerful story until his fatal sickness. The journal ends abruptly and is picked up by a friend, Caleb Lamb, who had held Mygate's hand as he died. Lamb, who belonged to the same company, made only a few entries. Later the journal became the property of Jonathan Mirick (Merrick) who used it as an account book.

A few years ago the journal was being thrown in a fire at Wilbraham, Massachusetts, when it was rescued. It is now owned by Charles L. Merrick of Wilbraham, to whom the Society of Colonial Wars is indebted for permission to publish the diary.

THE JOURNAL

A Jornal of the Travels of George Mygate from Springfield to Boston Day Began *Sat: June 15th* — Arived att David Shaws

Sab. 16 Ariv att Lad Richfor att Licester —

Mond 17 att Landlord

tusd 18 att Boston att the Lamb A Jornal of wether and fair Accounts

1745 Saturday June 22: 3: PM Sett from Springfield: Lay att David Shaws

Sabath Day 23: att Licester Monday att Marlborough

Tusd: 24 att Boston about: 4: PM

Wednesd 25 att Boston —

Thusd 26 att Boston

Frid 27 att Boston

Satt 28 about SunSet a Cannon Dischargd from a Snow Priveter Light upon a woman and Broke her thy mile ½ Distant from the vesel where it was Discharged from

Sab: 29 att Boston att meeting att the old South

Mond 30 att Boston —

Tusd: July: 1: Came on Board the Sloop Snow Commanded By Captain Edward Stow — Same day the News Came to Boston of the aken of Cape Briten and att night ther was Joy appeard in the face of Every one ther were Bonfires and firing of Guns and Candles in windows in all most Evry house in Boston

Wednesd: July 3: On Board

Thusd 4 on Board

Frid 5 on Board

Satd 6 on Board

Sab: 7 on Board

Mond 8 on Board and was Rousd oute of Sleep By the firing of ten Greate Guns from a Priveter I Prise then Brote in

Tusd 9 on Board [———— ?] and there were some French Prisoners and the Govenour and the Lady Brote into Boston —

Wed 10 Lay yet at anchor — aboute Sunset Recd orders — for sayling —

Thusd 11: About Sunrise Set Sail under moderate Brese west south west — and about 12: we was of against Cape an and had the Plesure of Seaing Several Water Spouts and aboute 4 PM Left the Sight of Land and Several of our men are Sick But I am as yet throw the mercy of God well the wind Continud all night very fresh we are Soposd to be 60 Legs from Boston

Frid: 12: the wind fare and the wether clare this Day we got throw the Bay Funday to Day I Saw Sevrl water Spouts one chasd a Parcel of Porpises — which Sight was very Diverting —

Sat: 13 — this morning the wether and wind Continues fair, and Plesant But I am Something Ill a bout 7 or 8 a fogg arose So that we could not See Scarcely half a not—afternoon Something Beter — as to my health Lay to and caught Some Codfish

Sabath: 14 the wind continued Fresh and fair for us but the whether Something Clouday mySelf in the fore Part of the Day very Ill a Sharp Pain in my head and neck wich was very troble-

som to me But after noon grew better and about 10 in A : M : Came
a cross Some Banks and the wind not very Smart Some of the
Ships crew : caught some Codfish —

Monday 15 the wind Shifts : in to the north East and is directly
a head of us the wether Continues Clouday and some rain about
12 : the wether cleard off and we made into a Harbour By what
name I cant tell and Go ashore upon a Desolate Island oute of
Cureosity and saw no living Creture save a squirel and Some
Pattridges there was fresh water as Red as the best of Claret and
very plesant to the tast we Saw the Signs of Indians — and
soposed they had Bin there —

Tusd: 16 This morning Set Sail about Sun Rise with a Brisk
gale Last night a fogg rose about 12 : and it was remarkable for it
dropt off from the 2d deck Like a Showr of Rain

Wednesd: 17 This morning the wether and wind fair and clear a
fair wind west nor-west and we came in sight of Cape Breton
Shore about 9 morning — aboute 2 PM : Came into the Harbour of
Luesburge [Louisbourg] Direct north from the City of Leois-
burge

Thusd: 18 the wether something dark and I went aShore att
Lusburg and viewed the city and saw many things that were very
satisfieng —

Tusd 23 this morning there was Tod [towed] oute of the Harbour 2 men of war in order to Persue this french Ship and aboute
ten of the Clock She struck to our forces they fird 2 BrodSide
the french fird never one to my certain knoledge — for I lay oute
Sid the City — to se the Play and about 3 PM I heard they set
after 3 more the wether I might have Said continues thick But
more warm than Late it has Bin to Day I went to the Kings Gate
to carry away Stores to the ComeSaries about a 100 Barrels of
Porke there was aboute 20 of us that were with Brigadear
[Joseph] Dwight 10 of Capt [Caleb] Jonsons men and 10 of Capt
[Isaac] Coltons — I should have mentioned a Priveteer that went
oute with them But forgot to till now —

Wed: 24 this morning I Saw the Sun Shine aboute 6 clock and
aboute 8 clouded up and Broke away again and about 12 I went
on Board the Rose In order to go to Saint Peter for wood and
in the afternoon I Saw the Princess Mary come in and the East

Indy Prise and they fird from the Prise ——— Guns and from the Comodoars ——— Guns

Thusd 25 this morning the wether Quite Clear and now I know — it is a Pleasant thing for the Eyes to Behold the Sun it is what I have not Seen Clear Scarsly Since I went a Shore at Lewisbourgh yesterday in the after Part of P M — I went along side all the men of war in the Harbour att Lewisbourgh Saving the vigilant the French man of war that was told in By the Commodore after the City was taken: 2 Smart Shours of Rain yestday P M —

Frid: 26 the wether Clear — I came a Shore and when I went aboard a Gain there was a Greate Disturbance conearning Iron — about ten clock Made Sail att night made Cabrowse [Gabarus] Bay Lay there all night.

Satt 27 went a Shore att Cabrowse Bay and got sevel Loads of Ballest Stones and about 2 P M came to ancor in the Bay —

Sab 28 Last night I wacht the fore Part of the night there Lay in the Bay 17 Sail this morning about 6 Set Sail oute of the Bay it Raind this morning Before I Got up but afternoon it cleared of and the wind — Norwest and we were forst to make tacks all Day —

Mund 29 Saild all Day and got to Saint Peters aboute 3 P M Began to Load wood — the wether Clear and fair —

Tusd: 30 to Day or this morning the Sun Rose Clear as Ever I Saw it and we all most finisht loding our Boat viz Sloop —

Wednesd. 31: this morning the wether thick and some Rain the most of our men went a Shore I stayd on Board — About 12 clock we finisht Loading the Sloop

Thusd Aug: 1 1745 [——— ?] Last night I wacht aboard the sloope Rose this morning the wether thick and the wind South sou: west and I and some more went a Shore about 1 A M Rise to Hunt foxes But found none But Plentifull Signs. I Pick Roses and wild Pease and Goose Berries in a Plentifull manner

Frid 2 about 6 this morning went to sea under a norwest gale we Left a 12 Sail in the harbour there was one Before us — and a Board her there was a Josiah dwight of Northampton and L. Hoar of Brinfield —

THE LOUISBOURG MONUMENT

Satt 3d Lay att the mouth of the Harbour all night By Reason as I conclude was the unskillfullness of the mariner they could not open the harbour and as Bright a moon Shine night as Ever I saw we Lay in sight of the Light House and Iland Batry and the Grand Batery — the Light and House the [——— ?] Note the Grand Batery as we Lay in the mouth of the Harbour was Right the Head of us the Island Batery att the Larboard Side the Light house att the Starboard Side of us the City att the Larboard of us —

Sat. 3d: aboute 10: came into the city a Clar Plasant Day and went Upon Duty to Gard Down att the Queenes Gate Dlie mor fevr or more Pang [1] there was for Persons buried to Day to of em buried in arms they was carried throw the Queens Gate

Sund: 4 I came of of the Gard and went to writing Letters and the Reason why I did was because the man that was to carry them was then a going on Board I Rote to the Reverend N M 2 to Mr. M. Burt 3 to Mr. S. Wm. 4 to mr. Geo master — 5 to Mr I Brower 6 to Mr. moses Cooley the 7 to mr David mirick the 8 to mr Joseph Ball the 9 to mr Saml Allin

Mond 5th: the foog is very thick it Began yesterday to Day it raind I card [carried] the letters to one castle of Sheffield to carry home

Tusd 6th the foog continues Heavy and Dark and very Rainy But I write some more viz T. Cooley Saml Terry — went to Commodore warren and got a Boate and in the afternoon I with 2 of my comerads went aboard the Cantebury and Brought the Boat a Shore — and P M went over to the Island Battery which was to my admiration for strength to the city is very Strong all most Beyond the conception of a Strainger that never se it

Wed: 7 the fogg continues thick and it Rains Still and in the afternoon I went aboard the Cantebury and got a whale Boat of the Commander's Bason first T. Coley went to the Commodore and gave us order to Go on Board the Cantebury under the command of Capt. John Lar Hoar and we Received the Boat and went over to the Island Batry

---

[1] Meaning doubtful. Possibly "daily more fever or more pain."

Thusd 8: this morning some thing Clare and I went in the forenoon to fishing and caug some. P M the wind Stiff-Norwest and we went not oute to fishing —

Frid 9th — this morning Clear and the wind Strong in the East [Rev.] Mr. [Stephen] Williams [2] was att our House and told us the sorofull news of Doctor [Charles] Pynchons Braking His Leg By a fall throw the Bridge att the Western Gate about 12 Clock went up to the Barraks and saw a man [Stanly] whipt 39 Stripes for Robbing the Grave of and Striping the corps of a Dead man of his linning

Sat 10 — this Day Clouday and a Strong East wind — So mighty and Stiff that a Schooner Intending for new England that Beteewn the Light house and the Island Batery She Stove against the Rocks But Whith the Loss of no man But only the vesel Some of the Cargo viz the Chests and other Small things Swam a Shore Withe oute much Damage — I went upon the Parade to train and we were Exersisd by Major Garner [Samuel Gardner?] of Boston — I was very Lame So that I could Hardly Stir —

Sunday 11th The wether Still continues Clouday and cold and the wind in the Same Corner — I Still continue Lame But I made Shift to go Down to the Hospital to Hear mr [Stephen] Williams Preach and to Se if I could find a Doctor But found none — P M I Lay Down on My Bead —

Mond: 12th the wind East Strong and Misty Small Rain I Still Continue Lame and Keepe my Bead —

Tusd 13 this morning Calm and Something Clar I Rose and went to the White horse with N. [Nathaniel] Chapin and C Lamb [3] and Abner hancocke and we Drank four Pints of wine — P M fair and Clam — and I had thots of matching with a young French Lady I went in to her Company — Had But Littel Discource for we could not understand one a nother —

Wed 14 this morning Cler and Calm — I went to Gard Downe att the Kings Gate no att the Queens Gate the wind was East North East and I was Something Ill and I came Home and Stayd 6 Hours about 6 P M there was 4 of our Army carried to the

---

[2] See *Ninth Journal.*
[3] Probably Caleb Lamb who concluded the journal.

SEVENTH JOURNAL

Grave and Some of them Persons of Honour and Buried in armes —

Thusd 15 this morning the wind Due Northe I sill on the Gard aboute 10 Clock the wind west and I Relievd of of the Gard and P M: the wind South

<pre>
           N: w   a
           B and I   w[ent?] to the
           Bar G   For [4]
</pre>

Frid 16 this morning the wind South and the wether Clouday after noon I went Round the Wall and Keept account of the Number of Carridge Guns Some 6 Pounders Some 12 Pounders: Some 18 Pounders Some 24 Pounders: Some 36 Pounders and all Some 42 — the Number amounts to — 200 — and Swifels Number: 48 — and Poart Hoals for Small-armes number 130 — and while I was upon the wall I Saw 2 Ships a coming in from the westerd which causd a Chearfull Countnance in all most Every Soulder Hopeing it was His-Exelency William Shirly Esq. was a Pasenger in Ether of em —

Sat: 17 this morning the wether Serene and Brite and the wind North West By West and aboute 9 A M we was all orderd to appear up on the Parrade in Half an Hour and accordingly we Did and about ten we waited or Garded His Exelency up to Generals Dwelling and this while the Drums Beat loudly for there was 24 of em and the Cannons — Roard Like thunder att Every Corner of the City and all over the Harbour I Believe there was not a minut Cesation Between Cannon and Small armes viz the Repoarts of em for the Space of 2 Hours the Commodore's Negro Played upon the trumpit Elevatingly

Sunday: 18 this morning Rain and So Held it all Day the wind — South West: about 3 P M I went to Bead Not well and in the — Night I was very ill insomuch that I Sweet Exceedingly with the feaver that was upon me — and a Pain in my Breast —

Mond: 19 this morning Clouday and some Rain and I by the Good Providence of God something Better P M Clear and I walkt upon the Parade —

Tusd: 20 this morning clear and the wind Strong in the South

---

[4] Thus in the manuscript.

about 10 I went upon the P[arade] over to the Grand Battery and it is very famos there is 33 ambuz [embrasures] for guns and was so many there Before tha Removed em in to the town they are 42 Pounders The magizens are 100 foot Round and about 60 feet High in the waul Boom is up to wards the top and it is viz floor is Layd with Hewn Stone there is 65 Poart Holes for Small arms to ward the Land which is the North Side

Wed: 21 Clear Day I was very Ill and I Kept House all Day — aboute 5 P M there were fird 19 Guns aboard Connectut cuntry Sloop I token of Honour of Person of Qality that was Burd that Day

Thusd 22 this morning Clear I very week and unable to Stir about any Duty — Aboute 6 P M thay fid 20 Guns 24 Pounders to Salute His Exelency the Govener and the Commodore and other gentlemen that went to Not[e] upon em —

Frid 23 Clar morning and I hope my Self Some thing Better as to my health the P M: thick —

Satt 24 this morning Clear and I Gon Gard In the afternoon [Rev.] mr [Stephen] Williams Came here and told us of the Death of — Job Colton —

Sund 25 Cloud. came of Gard and wery unwell mr [Stephen] Williams Preacht: att the Hopital Du Roy —

Mond 26 Clear and I no Better —

Tusd Cloud I toock a Portion of Ipecacuanha [ipecac] advised By Major [Charles] Pynchon it workt — upon me very hard I Sent for a nother Portion of Salt vitrol and took and that Set it a working 4 times —

Wednesday 28 Clear and I Some thing Better for which I Desire to Bless God

thusd 29 Clear and I more ill O wearisome Dayes and tiresome Nights I Endure

Fridy 30 in the morning Clear and I Some thing Beter But very week — about 12 Clock Cloudy —

Satt: 31 Clear and our Captain Set Sail for New England in a Ship [Edward] Ting Commander and about 2 P M Spyd a French man o war

Sab: Sept: 1: 1745 — Cloudy and the wind East — I no Better as to my illness —

Mond 2d: Last night Raind — this morning Clear and the wind North West: and I much Better as to my illness this afternoon walkt upon the wall —

Tusd 3d: this morning Clear the wind South: West: P M Donoho [David Donahew] Sloop Brote in a Prize Ship She took of the Gut of Canso and thay Say there is 5 French men of war on the Coast of Capertoon [5] Expected in Sight Every Hour with Six-English Prizes they have taken —

Wed: 4: this morning Clear the wind west —

thusd 5 this morning Cloudy and thick and So continues all Day

Frid 6 this morn clear and the North: West: By West: —

Satd 7 this morning Cloud; and fogge and we alarmd and ordred and orderd [sic] upon the Parade — in Expectation of a fleet Landing upon Cape Breton Shoar — But all vanisht away in the fogg and we all orderd to appear — and the alarm of war which was to Be Beat all Round the wall By 20 Drumers

Sund 8 I went and mounted Gard att the Barracks the wether Clear and the wind South: West: —

mond: 9 this morning Clear the wind North: West —

tusd: 10 this morning Clear and the wind North: West —

wed 11 this morning Clear the wind South —

thusd 12 this morning Clear — the wind North: West By West — and I yesterday was Blooded by By [sic] Docter [William] Hay in order to Cure me of a Cough I have — which causes me to Bring up all my Victuls: that I Eate aboute Haf an our after I Lay Down

Frid 13 I took Physick By Doctor [John] Manning' order and I was sorely Drencht of the morning Clear the wind in the South —

Sat 14 this morning Clear the wind South — and I Some thing Better

Sund: 15 this morne clear and I so as Leut Hitchcock thote me able to tend our Sick viz C L and P: S: [Philip Symons] and S: T: and P N: [6] and I B [Joseph Ball] and A [Asaph] Teal and

---

[5] Shirley called the Council of War together Sept. 10, 1745, to consider the intelligence that a French squadron was off Cape Sables.

[6] The roll of Capt. Colton's Company shows Caleb Lamb with the initials C. L., and Phineas Nash with the initials P. N., and no others with those initials.

So I Did Begin in Sunday afternon aforsd. I [Joseph] Ball was taken Sick yesterday —

Mond 16 Hase [hazy] and Something thick —

Tusd 17 Clear the wind west and the Governer and Comodore and there Ladyes and other Grete men and Ladyes went to the Grand Battery and Island Battery so Se it and there was Fired 17 40 Pounders fired att the Grand Battery and 17 — Att the Island Battere —

wed 18 Clear and the wind west — ove Leaf —

Thursd. 19 this morn thick and the wind South [——— ?] and his Excelency made a Speech to the Soulders and oferd em 40 Shillings Per Month those that are oblidgd to tarry hear Suspected to Be ocand [occasioned] : By the Solders talken of Risen and Laying Down there arems the which thay would undoubtedly have Done if he Had not have Done So —

———•———

[At this point George Mygate ceased to make entries and his friend Caleb Lamb took up the journal, telling of Mygate's death.]

———•———

Louisbourg Oct
18–1745 N : [Nathaniel] Chapin Deceased
Nov. 27: 1745 Abner Handcocks Deceased
Dec 9 1745 Gedion Warringer Deceased
26 Philip Symons Deceased
29 Joseph warriner Deceased
29 John Keep Deseased
31 Samll austine Deceased
Jan 6 174 / 56 Isaac meechan Deceased
7 Isaac Jillet Deseased
20 Josiah Kent Deseased
26 Daniel abbee Deseased
26 Benj Knowlton Deceased
30 Reubin Hitchcock Deceased
febrery ye 8th

Let [Lieut] Thomas Jones Decesd march the 18 Joseph Howland

Aprell the 2 George Mygate
Aprl the 3d James Peese
Wrote per me
Caleb Lamb at —
Louisborg it Being
George mygate Deser [desire]
Before he Deseased

>   He left the world not
>   in the least Dainted But
>   j thaught Contented
>   Having made his Pese with God
>   He had his Reson one minit
>   Before he Drew his last
>   Keeping his hand in mine
>   Caleb Lamb

November 19 1745 —
Yesterday I Came to Live with Mr. Sebaushan Toubbr [Sebastian Zouberbhuler] Comesairy to — Bregeeder Joseph Dwights Regiment

Joseph howland tended — ten Dayes Recon that with mine and It compleats 2 months

Asaph teal Did there for me
18 and 19 of Jan
I have payd J howland 5 Shile Boston money —
Nov 19 1745
Received of Comisarie S Toub [Sebastian Zouberbhuler] 4 Gallons ½ of Rum —
3 Gallons malloses More   47 Peices of Poark —
57 Weight of Bread I wot Not
a Barrell of flower
No 96 —
J Howland one Pair Soes   to delay
J Warriner one Pair Shoes
Abner Handcocks Shoes
Abner Handcocks Shoes
Jonathan Merrik Shoes

Morever to delay is danger delays are dangerous i Say therefor folow after charity which the lord of perfectness

———•———

[Lamb made no further entries and the journal subsequently passed into the hands of Jonathan Mirick who used the book for personal accounts.]

EIGHTH JOURNAL

ANONYMOUS

In the great collection of Louisbourg material presented to the Massachusetts Historical Society in 1834 by the heirs of the historian, Rev. Dr. Jeremy Belknap, were two accounts which have been considered separate journals. Photostats of both manuscripts were courteously sent by the owners to the Society of Colonial Wars where an examination showed that one journal was a rough outline of the second and that the second was apparently the draft for the journal sent by Governor William Shirley to London in 1745 as part of his official report. It is not known who prepared this journal. The writing does not resemble Shirley's or Pepperrell's. As the two drafts have historical importance and as the final version of the journal was last reprinted in 1748 it has been decided to give here the latter of the two drafts. There are slight differences in phrasing and in other minor matters between this document and the final report printed in 1746 and 1748.

The Council and House of Representatives of the Province of Massachusetts Bay had requested Shirley to prepare upon his arrival in Louisbourg in July, 1745, "a full Account of the Proceedings of the New England Forces" and this he sent to England in the form of a letter addressed to the Duke of Newcastle, Secretary of State for the Home Department, which bore the date October 28, 1745, and was accompanied by a journal of the siege. It is not known who compiled this journal but it was signed on October 20, 1745, by Pepperrell, General Waldo, Colonel Samuel Moore of New Hampshire, Lieutenant Colonel Simon Lothrop of Connecticut, and Lieutenant Colonel Richard Gridley of the train of artillery. Both letter and journal were published in London and Boston in 1746.

THE JOURNAL

March 24, 1744 / 5. The forces raised within the Province of the Massachusetts Bay being about three thousand two hundred and fifty men, — exclusive of Commission officers, embarked March 24th, 1744 / 5 in seven Weeks from the time of the Issuing Governor Shirley's Proclamation for raising them, under convoy of the Shirley Galley, then in the employ of that Government and now his Majesty's Frigate Shirley Captain [John] Rous Commander, and arrived the fourth of April at Canso, appointed by the Governor to be the place of Rendezvous for the Transports and Cruizers, and for a communication of Intelligence between himself at Boston Generall Pepperells Camp before the Town of Louisbourg and Mr. Warren from the Ships before Harbour, and for lodging all Stores not in immediate use in the Camp and Fleet; where they found the New Hampshire Forces, being three Hundred and four inclusive of Commission officers, arrived four days before them; and were joined the 25th of the same Month by the Connecticut Forces being Five Hundred and sixteen Men including Commisson officers [1] — Chappearouge Bay, which was the place appointed for landing the Troops, being so filled with Ice as to make their landing impracticable before, they were detained there till the latter end of the month, in which Time the General drew up and reviewed the Forces on Canso Hill and formed the several detachments ordered to be employed in the several attacks proposed to be made immediately after their landing at flat point Cove, within three Miles of the Town of Louisbourgh to the W : S : W : and four Miles distance from the Grand Battery to the S : W : according to the plan of Operation concerted at Boston, and there given him in charge by the Governors written orders.

[1] The figures given for the Massachusetts, New Hampshire and Connecticut contingents are the same as in the printed journal and are generally accepted as correct. New Hampshire also supplied 150 recruits for the Massachusetts units. Three of the Massachusetts regiments were from within the present State of Maine. Rhode Island sent the armed vessel *Tartar* with a crew of ninety and also dispatched three companies of soldiers, a total of 150 men, who, however, arrived after the fortress capitulated. New York sent ten 18 pound guns and some money privately subscribed. In July, 1745, Pennsylvania sent *li*4,000 in subsistence supplies to the Louisbourg garrison.

EIGHTH JOURNAL

During the Stay of the Troops there, a Block House was erected on Canso Hill and called Cumberland,[2] the Flag being hoisted on his Royal Highness's Birth Day picquetted without, and defended by Eight Cannon of 9 nine Pound, and to be garrisoned by two Companies of Soldiers of Forty men each besides officers. From thence two armed Sloops were sent to Bay Vert to take or destroy some Vessels that according to information were to carry Provisions from thence to Louisbourgh. And the 18th of April the Renomee [Renommée], a French Ship of War of 30 Guns nine Pounders with three hundred Seamen and Fifty Marines being charged with publick Dispatches, fell in with the armed vessels in the Service of the Massachusetts Government before Louisbourgh Harbour; where she maintained a running Fight with them, but got clear by outsailing them: This Ship afterwards fell in with the Connecticut Troops under the Convoy of their own Colony Sloop and the Rhode Island Colony Sloop the latter of which she attacked and damaged considerably, but finally the Sloop got off, as did the Troops with their other Convoy during the engagement and after having made two more attempts to push into the Harbour and been again hindered and chased by the Massachusetts Cruizers. returned to France without having delivered her Packetts. from whence she sailed again the beginning of July with six Ships more. being the Brest Squadron for Louisbourgh. The 22th of April Capt. [Philip] Durell in his Majesty's Ship Eltham of 40 Guns arrived at Canso Harbour from New England, having received orders from Mr. [Peter] Warren for that purpose, and on the 23rd Mr. Warren in his Majesty's Ship Superbe of 60 Guns with the Launceston of 40 Guns Capt. Kalmady [J. Calmady] and the Mermaid of 40 Guns, Capt [James] Douglas under his Command. And after staying there some Hours and conferred with the General by Letter, Mr. Warren with the rest of the King's Ships sailed to cruize off Louisbourgh.

On the 29th of April the Troops embarked in four divisions of Transports and sailed for Chappearouge Bay, under Convoy of one armed Snow, and two armed Sloops in the Service of the Massachusetts Government, under the Fire of whose Cannon they

[2] H. R. H. the Duke of Cumberland at that time commanded the Royal Army.

were to land. And at the same time a detachment of two hundred and Seventy men under the command of a Colonel [Jeremiah Moulton], and convoy of an armed Sloop in the pay of the New Hampshire Government, were sent to St. Peters, a small French settlement on Cape Breton with orders pursuant to the before-mentioned plan of Operations to take the Place burn the Houses and demolish the Fort which was accordingly effected. On the 30th of April between nine and ten in the Morning, the Fleet having the main body of the Troops on board came to an Anchor in Chappearouge Bay, at the distance of about two Miles from flat point Cove: upon the discovery of which the Enemy immediately fired some Cannon, and rang their Bells in the Town, to alarm and call in their people living in the Suburbs, and sent out of the Town a detachment of about 150 Men headed by Capt. Morepang [Morpain] and Mr. Boulerdrie [de la Boularderie] late an officer in the Duke of ——— [Richelieu's] Regiment in France to oppose the landing of our Troops upon the sight of which the General made a feint of landing a party of our men in Boats in Flat point Cove, in order to draw the French thither (which had its effect) and upon a signal from the Vessels the Boats returned and joined another party of Boats under his Stern, from whence under the Fire of our Cannon was landed, two Miles higher up the Bay, about 100 of our men before the Enemy could get up with them; and upon briskly attacking them, tho under the advantage of being covered with their Woods, after exchanging some shot killed six of them upon the Spot took as many prisoners (among whom was Mr. Boulerdrie) and wounded several other, forced the remainder to make a precipitate flight towards the Town, with the loss of some others, who were the next day taken prisoners before they recovered it; which was done with the damage on our part of only two Men's being slightly wounded. On the same day about two thousand of the Troops were landed without any farther opposition. And on the next day being the first of May the remainder landed, and began to get Provisions and Stores ashoar. The landing of Provisions Ammunition and heavy Artillery was attended with extreme difficulty and fatigue, there being no Harbour there, the Surf almost continually running very high so that frequently for some days there was no landing any thing at all, and when they did the Men were obliged to wade high into the Water, to save everything that would have been damaged by being wet, they had no Cloaths to shift themselves with, but poor defence from the Weather, at the same time the nights were very cold and generally attended with thick heavy fogs. By means whereof, it was near a fortnight before they could get all their Stores on shoar, and not withstanding all possible care to prevent it many Boats and some Stores were lost. — On May 2d a Detachment of four hundred men was sent round behind the Hills to the N: East Harbour, where they got about Midnight, and burnt the Enemy's Houses and stores about a Miles distance from the Grand Battery, and on the 3d of May we took possession of the Battery, which the Enemy had deserted, owing as it is supposed to the surprize they were in from the firing of the Houses in the Neighbour Towns [3] They had abandoned this Battery in so much hurry and confusion that they had only spiked up their Guns, without breaking off any of the Trunions, or much damaging any of the Carriages. There were found here twenty eight 42 lb Cannon and two of Eighteen Pounds, three hundred and fifty Shells of 13 Inches and thirty Shells of ten Inches, and a large Quantity of Shot. The same day a party of the Enemy in Boats attempted to regain the posession of it, but were beat off by about fifteen or sixteen of our men who had before taken possession of the Battery, and stood on the Beach, exposed to the Enemy's Musquetry from the Boats and Cannon from the Town which played continually upon them. The Distance from the Grand Battery to the Island Battery is 4800 Feet. This Battery commands the whole Harbour from the entrance between the Light House Point and the Island Battery. Two Flanks of two Guns each point from hence against the Town, and a Line of Ten Guns against the Island Battery, the remainder to the N: East part of the Harbour. By the fire from hence during the Siege, the Citadel and Houses in the Town suffered very much as also the Barracks at the Island Battery: The Towers of this Battery were something damaged one man killed, and a few wounded by the

---

[3] De Thierry, French commander of the Grand Battery, reported that it was untenable and the engineer officer confirmed this. The majority of the French Council wished to blow up the battery but their engineer (Verrier) prevented this, which proved a great mistake of judgment.

Enemy's Cannon, which fired very briskly upon it, as did also their Mortars, from the Town and Island Battery, especially at the beginning. In a few days the Camp was formed about half a mile from the place where they made a feint of landing but without throwing up lines, depending only upon their Scouts and Guards; but afterwards they encamped regularly and threw up lines nearer the place of landing their Stores. And Scouts during the whole Siege were constantly sent out, who seldom returned without bringing some prisoners, and very much confined the Enemy within their Walls, and prevented their making frequent Salies. May 4th We began to fire from the Grand Battery from three Cannon which had been cleared: as likewise to bombard the Town from Green Hill, being the place where the first Battery was planted (of one thirteen Inch Mortar one of eleven Inches and one of nine Inches, two Cannon nine Pounders and two Falconets) being two Miles distance from the Camp and fifteen hundred and fifty yards from the Citadel: Five Hundred Men were ordered to sustain this Battery; but finding the nine and eleven Inch Mortars would not reach the City they were removed the 7th of May, and planted with ten Coehorns at the distance of nine hundred Yards from the Citadel, where a Battery was erected the 10th of May of four 22 Pounders The thirteenth two of them burst, owing to their not being sound The fifteenth of May four 22 Pounders more were brought to this Battery as also the two nine Pounders and thirteen Inch Mortar from Green Hill: From this Battery the City was bombarded, and as the Shot from this Battery ranged through the Center of the City, it damaged not only the West Flank of the King's Bastion which it flanked; but also the Citadel and the greatest part of the houses in the Town and even Port Maurepas in the eastermost part of the City. This Battery was sustained by the same Forces that sustained the Battery at Green Hill. The damage received at this Battery was breaking the Trunion of one of the Coehorns and bursting another; six men wounded of whom one died, by the bursting of two 22: lb Cannon, one man killed and two wounded by the Enemy the same day. The 25th of May the thirteen Inch Mortar was burst and a Bombardier wounded, occasioned by some flaw in the Shell which broke in the Mortar. Another 13 Inch Mortar from Boston was mounted in the same place, and played the eighth day after the other was burst. The transporting the Cannon was with almost incredible labour and fatigue. For all the roads over which they were drawn, saving here and there small patches of rocky Hills, was a deep Morass, in which whilst the Cannon were upon Wheels, they several times sunk, so as to bury not only the Carriages, but the whole Body of the Cannon likewise. Horses and oxen could not be employed in this Service, but the whole was to be done by the Men. themselves up to the knees in Mud at the same time; the nights in which the Work was done cold and for the most part foggy; their Tents bad, there being no proper materials for Tents to be had in New England, at the time the Forces were raised. But notwithstanding all these difficulties, and the people's being taken down with Fluxes, so that at one time there was no less than 1500 Men incapable of duty, occasioned by their fatigue, they went on cheerfully without being discouraged or murmuring, and by the help of Sledges of about sixteen feet in length, and five feet in Width, and twelve Inches thick they transported the Cannon over these ways, which the French had always thought impassable for such heavy Bodies; and was indeed impracticable by any people of less resolution and perseverance, or less experience in removing heavy Weights; and besides this they had all the Provisions, Powder Shot and Shells, that they daily made use of, to transport over the same Ways, upon their Backs. During this time the French erected two Cavaliers of two Guns each, upon the Rampart of one of the Faces of the Kings Bastion; planted a great number of Swivel Guns upon the Wall facing the Harbour; and to secure the low Wall at the South East part of the Town, added to the top of it a Plank Work picketted, to raise it to the same height with the rest of the Wall, and a range of Pallisadoes at a little distance within the Wall, and raised a little Battery of three small Guns upon the Parapet of the lower South Bastion fronting Cape Noir, a small Hill which very much commands the Town. May 7th a Flag of truce was sent into the Town with a Summons to deliver it up to his Brittanick Majesty to which an Answer was returned by Mr. [Louis] Du Chambon, Commander in chief, that the King his Master having intrusted him with the defence of the Island, he could not hearken to any such proposal, till after the most vigorous Attack, and that he had no Answer to make but by the Mouth of their Cannon. May 8th. The Enemy made a Sally, but were soon repulsed — The 13th. Notwithstanding all the Care and Vigilance of the Men of War and the Colony Cruizers, a Snow from Bourdeaux got in, which they attempted to fire by a Fireship from the Grand Battery, but in vain. May 16 The Coehorns and nine and eleven Inch Mortars were removed to a hill within 440 Yards of the West Gate, from whence they annoyed the Enemy very much and received no damage at all. — A Party of a hundred men came out of the Town in the night, and landed near the Light House Point, and the next day attempted to surprize a party, that was posted at the Light House, who first discovered the Enemy from an Eminence, where they were on Guard; forty only of our men advanced towards them; the Partys met in a Wood, and the Enemy was routed, five of them killed, and a Sixth the Lieutenant wounded and taken Prisoner; The rest that escaped joined some others and 80 Indians about Mera [Miré], and were attacked two days after by another Party of our Forces that were out on a Scout, this dispute lasted a considerable time, and several of our men made thirty discharges each on the enemy, who were again routed. In this Action there was but one Prisoner taken. Upon the return of this Party another Scout was sent out the next day, who returned in two days and brought ten Prisoners, who reported that many of their People were killed and wounded in the last skirmish. Our Scouts and Cruizers at different times took and burnt most of their small settlements near and took about 300 Prisoners. — The 17th of May the Advanced Battery was raised bearing W : b : N : ½ N 230 Yards distance from the West Gate, and one Eighteen Pounder mounted and the next night another Eighteen Pounder and two 42 Pounders were mounted; these were all brought from the Grand Battery upwards of two Miles as the Road goes, over a very rough rocky hilly way from hence not only the West Gate was beat down, but a breach made in the Wall adjoining, and the North East Battery was damaged and rendered almost useless, their Guns lying entirely open to the Fire from this Battery. This Battery being so near the Town, there was no safety in loading the Cannon but under the Fire of the Musquetry, which was very smart on both sides. The Enemy

EIGHTH JOURNAL

generally opened the Action in the Morning, with the Fire of their small Arms which we returned with Advantage, We were likewise warmly entertained by the Enemy from a Flank of their North East Battery, from the West Gate Battery and the West Flank of the King's Bastion, which had flanked this Battery and therefore on the 20th [May] a trench being dug on the South End, one Eighteen Pounder and two nine Pounders were brought from the Eight Gun Battery and mounted upon the South Line against this Flank, which with the remainder of the Guns at the Eight Gun Battery, dismounted some of the Enemy's Cannon, and annoyed them so much, that they were silent the rest of that day which was often the Case afterwards, particularly May 22d. The Fire was very hot on both sides till 12 a Clock at noon when the French were beat from their Guns, The 23d of May the Enemy mounted two new Guns at the West Flank of the King's Bastion but in four hours were forced to leave them. The 6th of June They had two Guns run out of new Embrazures cut thro the Parapet near the West Gate, which soon began to play with great fury, and we were obliged to turn three Guns against them, and in three hours we dismounted one and silenced the other for that day. The nine and eleven Inch Mortars with constant use straining their Beds, occasioned their being removed to this Battery, which was nearer the Enemy, as were also the Coehorns. The Bombs in great number fell all round, but did very little damage. There were ten Men killed and fifteen or sixteen wounded several of them with Musquet Balls. In the meantime the Enemy worked constantly in the night to barricade the Gate way where a Breach was made; they also made a retrenchment across the Circular Battery, and raised another work to cover their Magazine, and laid a Boom before the Town to hinder Boats from landing under the Walls. At the same time our Men of War and Cruizers were very diligent, and took several Prizes and on the 19th of May there was an Engagement off the Harbour in sight of the Camp between some of our Ships and a French Man of War. The 21st a letter came to the General from Commodore Warren, acquainting him that he had taken the Vigilant a French Ship of 64 Guns, Besides the Superbe the Mermaid, Eltham, Massachusetts Frigate and Shirley Galley were all in the Engagement and at the taking of her Three days after the taking of the Vigilant Captain Edwards in the Princess Mary of 60 Guns joined the Commodore, and the next day Capt. [Frederick] Cornwall in the Hector of 40 Guns. The 20th of May the N: West Battery commonly called Titcombs Battery was erected, bearing N: W: b: W: about Eight Hundred Yards distant from the West Gate, and two 42 Pounders mounted, which were brought from the Grand Battery, and about a fortnight after were brought three 42 Pounders more. This Battery did great Execution against the Circular Battery. By means of this Battery and the Advanced Battery, not only the West Gate was demolished, but a large breach was made in the Wall to within ten feet of the Bottom of the Ditch, the Circular Battery was almost entirely demolished but three Guns out of Sixteen being left standing, and these so exposed to the N: West Battery that nobody could keep the Platform. The West Flank of the King's Bastion was almost entirely ruined, but in some Measure repaired with Timber This Battery the advanced Battery and the Eight Gun Battery were sustained by thirteen hundred and fifty Men. After many fruitless preparations for an Attack on the Island Battery, it was attempted on the 26th of May at night by a party of 400 Men, but from the Strength of the Place, and the advantage the Enemy had of being under cover and our men exposed in open Boats, which a Musquett Ball would sink, the Surf running very high, and their not being thoroughly acquainted with the best place of landing, they were repulsed, with the loss of about Sixty killed and drowned and a hundred and Sixteen taken prisoners. The 10th of June the Chester arrived from England, and joined the Comodore, and on the 12th the Canterbury and Sunderland, as did likewise the Lark with a Store Ship under her Convoy bound to Annapolis Royal. It being of the utmost consequence to be Masters of the Island Battery (The Island Battery is a strong Fort at the entrance into the Harbour, mounted with thirty twenty eight Pounders, and seven Swivels, having two Brass ten Inch Mortars, and garrisoned with 180 Men) and after the last Attempt thought impracticable to reduce it by Boats, it was determined to erect a Battery near the Light House opposite to it which would be 3400 feet distant and in such a manner, as to be opposed to the Fire of but Four of the Enemy's Guns, and at the same time to Flank a line of above twenty of their Guns, which, notwithstanding the almost insuperable difficulties that attended it, was happily effected, and two Eighteen Pounders mounted the 11th of June and by the 14th four more sustained by three hundred and twenty Men. (The difficulties were the transporting of the Cannon in Boats from Chappeaurouge Bay to the Eastward of the Light House, the getting them up the Bank of the Shoar, which was a Steep craggy Rock, the haling them a Mile and a quarter over an incredible bad way of Hills and Rocks and Morasses.) Powder growing short, the Fire had for some days been very much slackened, and the French began to creep a little out of the Cazmates of Cover, where they had hid themselves during the greatest fierceness of it. But this being the Anniversary of His Majesty's happy Accession to the throne it was determined to celebrate it as became loyal Subjects and brave Soldiers, and Orders were given for a discharge of all the Cannon from every Battery at twelve a Clock, which was accordingly done and followed by an incessant fire all the rest of the day, which much disheartened the Enemy, especially as they were sensible, what must necessarily be the consequence of this New Battery. It was now determined as soon as possible after the Arrival of the Canterbury and Sunderland, to make a general Attack by Sea and Land, accordingly, they arriving the next day all the transports were ordered off to take out the Spare Masts Yards and other Lumber of the Men of War: the Soldiers were employed in gathering Moss to barricade their Nettings, and Six Hundred Men were sent on board the King's Ships at the Commodore's request, the Large Mortar was ordered to the Light House Battery; and a new supply of Powder arriving the fire was more fierce from this time to the fifteenth than ever; when the Mortar began to play from the Light House Battery upon the Island Battery, out of nineteen Shells seventeen fell within the Fort and one of them upon the Magazine, which together with the Fire from the Cannon, to which the Enemy was very much exposed, they having but little to shelter them from the Shot that ranged quite thro' their Barracks, so terrified them that many of them left the post and run into the water for refuge.

 The Grand Battery being in our possession, the Island Battery being so much annoyed by the Light House Battery, the North East Battery so open to our Advanced Battery, that it was not possible for the Enemy to stand to their Guns, all the Guns in the circular Battery, except three, being dismounted, and the Wall almost wholly broke down, the West Gate demolished, and a large Breach in the Wall adjoining, the West Flank of the King's Bastion almost ruined, all the Houses and other Buildings almost tore to pieces, but one house in the Town being left unhurt, and the Enemy's Stock of Ammunition growing short, they sent out a Flag of Truce to the Camp, desiring time to consider upon Articles of Capitulation, this was granted till the next morning, when they brought out Articles, which were refused; and others sent in by the General and Commodore, and agreed to by the Enemy: Hostages were exchanged and on the seventeenth of June the City and Fortresses were surrendered and the Garrison and all the Inhabitants, to the number of two thousand capable of bearing Arms, made Prisoners, to be transported to France with all their personal Effects. During the whole Siege we had not more than a hundred and one Men killed by the Enemy and all other Accidents, and about thirty died of Sickness. And according to the best Accounts there were killed of the Enemy within the Walls about three Hundred, besides numbers that died by being confined within the Cazmates.

NINTH JOURNAL

Chaplain Stephen Williams

This distinguished Colonial minister was long in charge of the parish of Longmeadow, Massachusetts. He was born on May 14, 1693, and died on June 10, 1782. At Louisbourg he was a chaplain at large to the land army, although certainly attached to Col. John Choate's Eighth Massachusetts Regiment, and he arrived there on Saturday, July 6, 1745, in the frigate *Massachusetts*.

The diary of Mr. Williams presents a picture of the expedition unlike that given by any other of the participants. It is a dreary and gloomy record filled with notes of the ceaseless demands upon him by the sick and dying. McLennan in his *Louisbourg From Its Foundation to its Fall* writes of the trying period which followed the excitement and glamour of the attack and the victory, "the garrison settled down to what to them would have seemed a dreary winter, with their only occupation the repair of the fortifications and buildings. It proved more than a dreary autumn and winter. Louisbourg at its best was a town of narrow streets and lanes. The interruption to ordinary life of the siege had resulted in an accumulation of filth that turned the town into a midden. The change from sleeping in the open, to infected barracks and houses was unwholesome, and the entries in the diaries of these months is a dreary repetition of sickness and burials. Warren, in addition to the 'scorbutick disorder' which afflicted him, had a touch of the prevailing disease from which he recovered. The Rev. Stephen Williams was at death's door for weeks with sufferings which he bore with fortitude, ceasing his ministrations to the men only when his strength was completely spent."

Stephen Williams kept journals for much of his life and many of these records are preserved. The one used here is owned by the Massachusetts Historical Society and lent by them to the Society of Colonial Wars. The manuscript has never been published but is noted by several writers. Francis Parkman refers to it but found the handwriting too "detestable" to read. The difficulty is that Williams's hand was not only careless but that he used many private shorthand symbols which have made the transcription of his journal a slow and difficult task. These symbols have been translated or expanded in the following text.

THE JOURNAL

Louisburg july 18, 1745. this morning capt: [Isaac] Colton, and his officers, visitd — me — to whom, I comunicatd my thots, of going home, wth Colenell [John] Choate [1] — but they all declard against it, and told me they came upon the encouragement of my being in the army — but — after prayer at the chapple I pceivd the notion of the collenell going Home, was over —. this day — was to be observd as a day of publick thanksgiveing my Kinsman Mr E. W. [Elisha Williams] preachd a very suitable Sermon — in the Audience, of the Generall Comodore [2] officers and soldiers — I dind with the Generall and Severall french Gentlemen and ladies were present — we are in a tumult and hurry — it does not seem, to be a thanksgiveing day — at the Evening prayer — I was desird to go, and See a young man (whose name is Miller) who is very Sick — he appears to be a Serious young man — I hope is prepard for death — I prayd with him — in the Evening Collonell Choate informd me that they had Some news of a French Fleet of men of warr and transports — Some where off from Nantuckett — where they are designd I know not.[3] The Lord be pleasd to preserve for his pleasure — Guard, and defend or Sea Coast. I learn from capt. [Isaac] Colton that a man is Killd by the in-

---

[1] Capt. Isaac Colton of the 9th Mass. Regt. (Dwight's) had arrived at Louisbourg the day before this entry. Col. John Choate and his 8th Mass. Regt. arrived on July 5-6, finding the fortress already taken. As his regiment had been raised for the specific purpose of reducing Louisbourg, Choate and his field officers sent a formal petition to Pepperrell asking whether his regiment was to be considered part of the Army. The Council of War on July 9th decided that the 8th Mass. was "part of the army." Choate remained.

[2] The General is always Pepperrell and the Commodore is Warren.

[3] De Salvert, the new Governor of Isle Royal (Cape Breton) with a French squadron which turned back to France on hearing of the capitulation.

dians at Numbr 2[4] about the Great Meadow — thus an indian warr is begun — where it will issue — I know not — I pray God, to preserve his people —

19 I offered prayers in the chappell in the morning and after prayers visited the young man [Miller] — I Saw Last night found him Speechless — yet — was able to Give me some signalls — visited another Sick Man — and two companies — belonging to or regiment — this day — many of the French — movd of (Even four vessels) designd to France — I wish there were more of them Gone. in Evening Brigadier d [Dwight] was here — I am concerned to See what a State we are in with little prospect of a comfutoble Settlement — of Good order —

20 in morning prayd at the chapple, and in the Hospitall and then visitd capt: [Isaac] Colton and company — dind —with the Generall and there understood we were to march in the two chappells all ter nately with the Episcopall clergy. Mr W and J [Elisha Williams and I] waitd on the Comodore and capt: [John] Hoar — and Setled the point — at what part of the day — we were to preach — Went to See capt: [Isaac] Colton, and prayd with his company — and prayd in the Hospitall —

21 the Sabbath. I went to the chapple in the Hospitall — Expecting to preach — but found the Comodores chaplin had begun the service — capt Bret,[5] and Mr. B [Bernard?] — seemd much concernd that there was Such a mistake and Blundr — this blunder — occasiond another, at the chapple, in the Citadell — twas all occasiond (I supose) by the mistake of the comodores Chapline. Mr. W and J [Elisha Williams and I] dind at the comodores (2 chaplins [of 40 men were there?]) in the afternoon, I preachd in the chappell, at the Hospitall — and had for my Auditors — the comodore, capt: Bret. — and a crowdd Auditory of or own people — this day, a young man dyd — in the Hospitall (belonging to capt [William] Fletcher) another dyd — last night belonging to Connecticutt — and mr Williams Attendd his funerall — which made it necessary for me to attend prayers in the citadell — as well as Hospitall —

22 in the morning I prayd — at the citadell — as well, as Hos-

---

[4] A military post on the Massachusetts frontier.
[5] Commanding H. B. M. S. *Sunderland.*

pitall — the weather is pleasant — I went to See — a young man [Mallett] — belonging to capt [Charles] Biles his company — who appears to be near his end — I prayd with him — he has the character of a Serious youth — among the company — he belongs to — I visitd others — this afternoon a Ship appeard off the Harbour, and fird a Gun — tis Soposd to be a French Ship — the men of war, are prepareing to go out after her — when I prayd at the Hospitall there was Great complaint — for want of Good attendance — no victualls being prepard for the Sick — in the Evening the men of warr — towd out of the Harbour —

23 in the morning I attendd prayers — at the citadell and Hospitall — the men of warr came up with the Ship — that appeard in Sight Last night — and after a Broad Side — She struck to them — but we dont know what ship it is — this day — the Gunner of our castle, who had attendd the Expedition — was Burid in Arms — his name was Rolla — a Swiss by nation. in the Evening I visitd capt [John] Harmon, who appears to be an Excellent Xtian [Christian] ; we prayd and Sang together —

24 prayd at the Citadell, and Hospitall — The young man, belonging to capt Byles' company is dead this morning — his name — was Mallett things are managd strangely at the Hospitall yet, I pray God, to direct me, what to do — in this affair — went to Mr [Elisha] Williams and walkd in the city — dind — at Home — capt [Jonathan] prescot being with me — . after dinr vistd capt [Jeremiah] Foster — and capt: [John] Baker — prayd with capt Baker — this afternoon the ships came in, with their prize, which proves to be a very rich ship — from the East — Indies — the Lord keep us humble — under such repeatd Smiles —

25 this morning prayd in the citadell — returnd home prayd and Breakffastd after Breakfast — 15 Gunns fird at the prize ship and 15 from the Town — prayd — at the Hospitall — walkd to the citadell, dind at Home. Mr W [Elisha Williams] with us — afternoon I rode (with collonell [Sylvester] Richmond) to the Grand Battery a strong place — and capable of being made Stronger — Saw and prayd with a Sick man there named Sergeant — Night prayd at the Hospitall —

26 this morning in Hospitall, and citadell — heard the complaints of Some of the Sick — went — to colenell [John] Storer — who says that he will take speciall care. two jesuits came into Town — out of the Country —. [Rev.] Mr. [Joseph] Hawley here and dind with me. Afternoon walked abroad, with Mr. H and dr P [Charles Pyncheon] as I passd by the comodores he invitd me in, to drink — a dish of coffee — I Saw the French merchant, and his daughter, that came from the indies — who were Gay, and Easy — the comodore, and his officers treatd me with civility, and respect, as did — Capt: Bret, whom I met in the Street — I was something Griped — and inclineing to the flux — prayd in the Hospitall the people — Gave account they were better tendd: after prayer, in the Hospitall — I went to See capt: [John] Baker, and his company and prayd with them. —

27 The Bell rung Early — I went up — to the citadell and prayd there but few attendd — being Early and Some mistake about the Signall. prayd — at the Hospitall — where they are better tendd —. but Some are very ill —. Pale and Heavy — I laid me down to Sleep — in fore noon awakd refreshd — Note that I need — prudence and discretion — as to my conduct that I dont offend those — I am nearly concernd with — as to liberality — I pceive more companys of men come down — and vessels from n England with live Stock as cattle — Sheep — fowls — but I dont See how the poor people — are able to buy — I mean the Soldiers — who want such things very much. — I rode out on Colonell [Sylvester] Richmonds horse — to See Lieutent M ——— and company — as I came home Saw — the two men of warr — belonging to the comodore — endeavouring to get into the Harbour, but they were obligd to ly by — beyond the island Battery — after I returned home and prayd at the Hospitall — I was calld to See one Twitchell belonging to Capt: [Ebenezer] Edmunds company, who is very Sick — I prayd with him — he is an old man and is very low —. I find it difficult managing with those that I am such a pfect stranger to —. Oh Lord make me faithfull. in the Evening — Coll R— [Sylvester Richmond] and capt: E— were discoursing about their dly [daily] affairs — but colenell C— [John Choate] and I So far discountenancd — it — as that they laid aside the discourse —

28 Sabbath — this morning a Ship appeard — at a distance — and the men of warr — made out after her — and came up with her — and the people: from the wall — Saw the smoak of their Guns — and conclude she struck to them but they quickly went out of Sight — I preachd in the forenoon at the Hospitall chappell. dind at Home — then road to the Grand Battery — preachd there — and then prayd with a Sick man — namd Sergeant belonging to Braintree: he dyd and returnd — home — and then went to the Hospitall and prayd there with one Warrington — who was dyeing. he dyd Soon after — I came Home prayd with the family. Was weary and went to bed — and restd comfortably

July 29, 1745. prayd at the chappell — and Hospitall —. the Town is in a tumult — being Muster day. Last night a man [Stanly] took the sheets from a dead corps that lay in the vault — he is prisoner, what punishment — will be inflictd on him — I know not — this day the men of warr, returnd — with the Ship, they had taken which proves an India man — thus — or Enemies Substance, is putt into or hands — oh that it might be improved aright —.

this afternoon there was an unhappy fray in the city — one of the captains of the men of war — caind [caned] a Soldier who — struck the capt: again — a Great tumult was occasiond — Swords were drawn — but no life Lost — but Great uneasiness, is causd — I pray God — to calm the minds of all in the Army and fleet — and Give prudence — to the officers — I vistd — Colonell [Samuel] more — and Capt [Isaac] Colton. the capt: is considerably indisposd — with a flux — I pray God to help him. — I went and prayd with the man [Twitchell] belonging to capt: [Ebenezer] Edmunds company — who was dyeing — he Soon dyd. and Then vistd Collonell [John] Choates company, where are two men Sick — and prayd with them they appear religious men, but I fear run into the extreams of the present day. I prayd in the Hospitall —

30 prayd in the citadell and Hospitall. — a vessel or two are come in, from Boston and piscatua. bring more men — what they intend — I know not — same day — I vistd Mr W [Elisha Williams] forenoon — dind and afternoon went to capt: Edmunds — prayd with them that were Gatherd together on occasion of the funerall —. went to See capt: Colton — but he was gone abroad

— vistd capt: [John] Baker and company — I hope they are better — Evening — prayd in the Hospitall — and observed one man in Great distress — oh that God would help him — and oh that God would help me to do my duty — in the Evening — capt: [Robert] deninson and others, were in Colonell Richmonds chamber — occasionally — we went into some conversation — that I hope may be for profit and advantage. this day — a Court martiall, has been held — I know not what has been done — I wish there was more of order —

31 in morning chappell and Hospitall — I have Something of a cold — Mr. W. and H. [Williams and Hawley] came to visit me — we walkd abroad — and met Mr. [Charles?] pynchon who informd us that by a letter from Londondery [New Hampshire] there was an acct of fourteen men, kild at deerfield, [Mass.] by the indians and 4 at number 4 — an affecting account indeed — or people — must need, be greatly destressd — thus we are caled to Sing of judgment as well as mercy — The Lord help us — to do — both aright — oh that the Lord, would prepare for what tideings we may hear further — oh that God, would humble us and bring to depend upon him — . Mr. W. [Williams], Collnll W. [Williams] and Mr H — [Hawley] dind with us — aftr dinr one Lt. [Daniel] Giddins — Sent to me to come and See him — I went — to him — he is Sick — he appears to be a serious man, resignd to the will of God — I hope God, will raise him up — and make him yet serviceable — in the Evening — I took pains to get a pticular acct of the story, that comes from London — derry — but cant — learn the certainty of anything but hope — things are not So bad — as we feard — the Lord be pleasd to prepare for his holy pleasure — for what tideings So ever — we may be calld — to hear — .

Aug. 1, 1745. prayd in the citadell and Hospitall — one Ebenezer Smith of Taunton — dyd last night in the Hospitall — . the Lord be pleasd to affect us suitably with his dealings. — dind with Collonell [Richard] Gridley a number of merry men — together — the Lord bless them and bring them to see the Salver [Saviour] afternoon prayd with the company — that were going to Bury — the man, that dyd last night — preachd at the Hospitall : — and prayd at the Citadell — (mr W being Gone to the island Battery)

— was weary at night Some of the officers of the men of war, were here — (haveing business with Colenell Choate —) kept us up late —

2 attendd prayers, at the citadell — . and after prayers went with Colenell [Nathaniel] Thomas to See a man, that is very Sick — and prayd with him — . this morning — a Ship appears — what She is — I know not — I went to the Hospitall to pray there and found two men were dead there, (that dyd last night) one was a marine, the other, was one Bidwell that belongd to Capt: Heustons [John Huston] company — oh Lord be pleasd to pity and Spare — the residue of thy people — oh Lord — we are but dust — a french man dyd last night in the Hospitall — the young man I prayd with in the morning dyd soon after — I visitd capt: [Isaac] Colton, who is much indisposd — visited Collonell Choates people — dind with Collonell [Nathaniel] Thomas. walkd upon the wall. pceivd that the Ship — mentiond above — was taken by the man of warr, she proves a rich Ship — from Buenos Ayres — thus the wealth of or Enemies falls into or Hands — I road out to See — capt; [Ebenezer] Alexander, who is Sick. visitd Lieutenant [Daniel] Giddins, and prayd with him. vistd capt: [John] Baker. prayd in the Hospitall — where one Weston is apprehendd to be very near his end. he dyd soon after — : he livd at plymton —

3 attendd prayers at the citadell — and Hospital — . visitd capt: [Isaac] Colton, who is indisposed and discouragd — but I hope not dangerously ill — a dull day — I am dull and Weary — but able to keep about — the Lord be pleasd to prepare for his own holy day. — night at the Hospitall — this day one munson of New Haven dyd —

4 Sabbath — prayd in the citadell and Hospitall. preachd in the Hospitall chappell — in the forenoon and in the afternoon at the Grand Battery — many Sick — visitd capt: [Ebenezer] Aexander as I returnd — prayd at the Hospitall at night in the Evening — was calld to See a poor man — (in distress or worse) but I found him — distractd — raving — I prayd with him — his name is Bradish — one of capt: [Estes] Hatch' company was burid — who dyd yesterday.

5 morning prayd at the citadell and Hospitall. visitd and prayd with some of the Collonells men — that were going Home. visitd capt: [Isaac] Colton who is not well — found him better — dind with capt: [Robert] denison — afternoon visitd capt: [John] Baker — prayd there. visitd Lt [Daniel] Giddins and prayd with him. prayd at Hospitall — evening — visitd one Stanchfield [Standifield?] and prayd with him —

Augt. 6: prayd at the citadell, and Hospitall — one Converse dyd in the Hospitall — he belongd to Collonell [Sylvester] Richmonds regiment. and to capt. [Benjamin?] Williams company —. [Rev.] mr [Joseph] Hawley Breakfastd and prayd with us — rainy dark day —. after dinr — one Sleeper came to me and desird me to write a letter to his minister, which I did. — Lt. [Ebenezer] Hitchcock — came and desird me to visitt capt: Colton, who (he says) is worse —. I went to see him, and found him poorly — being followd with flux and vomiting — prayd with him. I beg of God to spare and help. — this day I hear one John pollard (of Ipswich) was killd by his fellow Soldier — at Canso. tis soposd twas accidentall — tis a dark rainy day — I have not visitd many Sick. Evening prayd in the Hospitall — Some of the woundd Speak — of Going Home — I know not what to advise to — the Lord be pleasd — to direct and help. — in the Evening capt: [Robert] deninson sat with us —

7 morning prayd at the citadell and hospitall. one John Kent of Collonell [Samuel] Willard's regiment — dyd last night in the Hospitall. the weather is wet — abundance of rain — many not well — went and prayd with one of Major [Ezekiel] Gillman's men ["Roundbtt"] — and with capt: [John] Baker — who is much amiss and with Lt. [Daniel] Giddins who I hope is better. visitd Stanchfield [Standifield?] — came Home — and dind — alone — afternoon visitd capt: [Isaac] Colton [Rev.] mr [Samuel] Mooday and the Generall — very rainy day — people amiss — with colds — very dull and Heavy — my Self —

8 morning in citadell — and with major Gillmans man, that I Saw yesterday. his name is Roundbtt — I apprehend he is near his End — prayd at the hospitall — the people there complain of the removing as disturbing — they quarrell and complain — [Rev.] Mr. [Elisha] Williams went to see Mr. Moodey dind with the Generall — where we saw an irish clergyman — with whom Mr Williams had a dispute — about religion — after dinr walkd abroad — with Mr W and towards night walkd abroad on the walls — with Colonll C[Choate] and went out of the city — when I returnd — I heard dr [Charles] Pynchin — was hurt — I went to the Hospitall and prayd there — and went to see the dr. found he had fallen thro the Bridge with his horse — had Broke his leg — and was bruisd in his face — the leg — was set by the man of warr's doctor — whose name is Graves — I hope he may do well — N B I this day heard of a Say that Morepang [6] had viz: that he thot the n England men were Cowards — but now he thot that if they had a pick ax and Spade — they would dig their way to Hell and Storm it which they had done.

9 morning col. citadell — hospitall — saw dr p. [Charles Pyncheon] capt [Isaac] Colton and then rode out to See Josh. Geary. and one [John] Taylor of S: Hadley, who are very sick — returnd — this day capt: Shearbarns scoonr run ashore, on the island Battery point — the men were Savd — but the scooner like to be lost — the Schonr carid 6 Swivell Gunns — after dinr visitd dr. Pynchin, and prayd with him. walkd abroad — prayd at Hospitall — visited capt [William] Allen and the company there — . in the Evening heard, that a son of Waltr Hubbard Esq — of Bristol dyd — at one of the houses, west of the city he had been aboard one of the men of war — but was dismist — : — the scooner above mentioned was stove to pieces — . nothing savd —

10 in the citadell — and Hospitall — visitd dr p [Charles Pyncheon] and capt: Colton — found them better — but E. Bliss is poorly. visitd — Lt [Daniel] Giddens — and found him better — visitd Stanchfield [Standifield?] — who is Sick a raw day — wind — N — E and windy: a good wind for those gone Home — the Lord be pleasd to be with them and prosper them — Some vessels from Connecticutt, and Rhodeisland — and one from Charlestown, in N. England but I dont know there is any news — Last night one Searl of Roxbury dyd — he belongd now to Collonell Molton [Jeremiah Moulton] regiment — Note — this day one Stanly the man that took the sheets from the dead corps — (mentiond — july 29) was whipd at the parade, at the Head of the Army. 39 Lashes were Giuen him — this day the man belonging

---

[6] Morpain, port captain of Louisbourg under the French.

NINTH JOURNAL 131

to major [Ezekiel] Gillman's company, named Roundbtt — dyd — Evening prayd in the Hospitall — and was calld to See one Porter (at the House capt: [John] Baker livd in) who is in a distressd — case — deprivd of his reason, — and convulsd — there was an old namd judd (belonging to Salem) very sick in the same House.

11 Sabbath, at the citadell and Hospitall — saw dr [Charles] pynchon — preachd in the forenoon at the Hospitall chapple, dind at Home — and afternoon — went to the Grand Battery and preachd there — and prayd with a Sick man there — came Home prayd at Hospitall, — went to the House where capt: [John] Baker livd — and found, mr Judd dead, prayd with porter (— who is of wenham) who dyd Some time after — Evening — pceivd an uneasiness — in many respecting the State we are in. N. B. one Blake (belonging to capt: Nathaniell Williams company) dyd in the Hospitall in the forenoon.

12 citadell, and Hospitall, visitd — dr p [Pyncheon] who is comfitably of it; capt: [Isaac] Colton and company: found Eb: Bliss poorly of it — prayd with him — then went to see 2 sick men, at Collonell [Samuel] Willards and prayd with them — dind at Home. — went to the funerall of our two men — when at the Grave. — Blake was burd there. and as we came to the Lane — we met another corpse — belonging — to capt: [Estes] Hatch' company, went to the Hospitall — prayd — there — and found — some very bad — went to See one [H.] Barker that is Sick — prayd with him — and about 10 a clock was calld to see a poor man, at the Barracks who is very Sick — prayd — with him — he belongs to Bridg-water —

13 citadell, and with Barker (above mentiond) who appears to be near his End — went to See dr p — who appears comfortably of it — prayd in the Hospitall — where many are poorly of it — and seem near their End — to see capt: Colton, and company — E. B. [Ebenezer Bliss] is poorly of it — I prayd there. visitd — Bradish (mentiond Aug: 4) he is Soposd to be better — visitd the 2 Sick men, at Collonell Willards, and prayd with them — dind with capt: [Andrew] Ward, after dinr rode out, to see capt: [Ebenezer] Alexander — and prayd there — one [John] Taylor is there — very dangerously Sick, went to Lt. Moors — and prayd there — J. [Joshua] Geary is I hope better — and the rest — able to move — tho some poorly of it. returnd to the city prayd in the Hospitall, and with dr pynchon, H. Barker, above mentiond — dyd — this day — as did one James Stuart belonging to capt: [Jonathan] prescots company — who was Sick but a few days — N. B. this day the Generall has Given Collonell [John] Choat order under his Hand, to Send — away the French inhabitants he has been to notify them of it — they Seem to be much affectd and are very Loath to go —

14 citadell, and Hospitall — where one Gambell, of capt: [William] Warners' company, dyd, capt: Warner belongs to Boston — visitd — capt: Colton — saw — Ebenezer Bliss — who is poorly; prayd there — dind at Home — afternoon walkd out of the city wth mr [Elisha] Williams returnd and had — company at Home drank tea — N. B. poor m— fall Sent for me this day but to my surprise — his concern was about a worldly affair — yet I thot his Soul — was taken up, with the things of another world — but — he discovers a resigndness — to the will of God — . — I prayd at Hospitall — had something of a restless night —

15 citadell — and Hospitall — visitd E. B. [Ebenezer Bliss] — who I hope is better — then rode out to See [John] Taylor at capt: Alexanders — who is (I apprehend) near his End — prayd with him — visitd Lt. Mun [John Man] — they are poorly of it — but I hope none dangerously ill, returnd home, before noon. poor mack fall dyd — this morning — and the last night — the Bridgwater man — (mentioned (Aug: 12) dyd in the Hospitall — he was brot there last night. and one xtne [Christian] Connecticutt man (he livd at Fairfield) that belongd to Capt: [Daniel] Chapman of Tland [Tolland] dyd — last night — allso — and a French man, dyd in the Hospitall so that 4 psons, were burid — this Evening. I dind at the Generalls and afternoon — there were men in arms — to get the French people aboard — . and an uneasiness in many — prayd with the people that attendd Mack — falls funerall — prayd in the upper Entry in the Hospitall — . in the Evening was calld to See one Hunt (in Capt: [William] Allens — company) — who is very sick — Greatly distressd — what pain — accts him-Self — not fit to dye — a dark cold — prayd with him — .

16 Citadell, and Hospitall — saw dr [Charles] pynchon, he is

A View of LOUISBURG, in NORTH AMERICA, taken from the Light House when that City was besieged in 1758.

From the Society's Collection.

comfortably of it. I am somewhat indisposd. visitd capt: [Charles] dolittle who is not well — dind at Home. prceive Great uneasiness — among people upon diverse accts — some upon acct of the french people — that are indeed aboard — I have the head ach —. one of capt: Swans men dead this day. toward night 2 ships — seen, Sopost to be from Boston — and that the Gouvernor [7] — is aboard — the ships provd to be the Hector from Boston — the Governour, on board — and the comodores Lady — and the other was the Superbe — returnd — from her cruise. they came Safe into the Harbour — I had the Head ach in the Evening and Something of a restless night — But I apprehend tis my vshall Head ach — the Lord be gracious to me, pity and favre —

Aug: 17. Something restless — So that I Sent and desird — mr [Elisha] Williams would attend — prayers in the citadell — which he did. I got Home, and felt better — attendd — prayers — in the family — and Hospitall. this morning — the Generall — Sent for Collonell [John] Choat — and had discourse — with him — I hope — that Good may come —. the army were in arms — to receive the Governour — who — came a Shore about 11 of the clock — went thro the ranks to the citadell — mr Williams and I went and waitd upon him, and congratulated him — I dind with Collonell [Andrew] Burr — and mr Williams then walkd on the walls — but felt poorly — returnd — home, Lay down, and Slept. and woke considerably refreshed freer from pain — went, and prayd at the Hospitall, capt: [Isaac] Colton came to see me, and tell me, that Roger Cooley — is Sick — as well — as E. B. [Ebenezer Bliss] — I pray to God, to help them to spare them in mercy — the Sabbath is approaching — I pray God, to prepare me for the duties — and Services of his — own — holy day —. I saw dr [Charles] pynchon in the morning who seems to be comfortably of it — this day — one of capt: [Benjamin] Jves men dyd —.

18 and Sabbath. I am more comfortably of it — than I was, prayd in the citadell and Hospitall — preachd — in the forenoon in the Hospitall chapple —. afternoon went to the Grand Battery and preachd — there —. John Taylor of S. Hadly dyd last night I — prayd — with the company at capt: [Ebenezer] Alexanders —

---

[7] Governor and Mrs. Shirley, Mrs. Peter Warren, and others.

when they were going to bury the man, this the first man, that belongd to or county, that has dyd Since they came from Home — a Signall and remarkable providence — but a holy and righteous God — has begun with us — oh Lord be pleasd to prepare for thy holy and Sovereign will and pleasure. as I came Home I calld at Collonell [Andrew] Burrs were I found Collonell [Sylvester] Richmonds son, who came in captain [Edward] Tyng [8] — who tells me that — dr [Joseph] pynchon is come hither: I hope he will be of service — to us that are here —. he belongd to capt: [John] Harmon

19 at the Hospitall — and citadell, — one Garretson dyd in the Hospitall — and one math peters very Sick — that I discoursd with — he belongd to the Rhodeisland recrvits — severall others — are very bad in the Hospitall — one of the men of warrs men, told me, they had four men, dyd within 48 hours — some of them — ly dead, in the Hospitall — tis dull weather — I feel dull, and Heavy — this day dr [Joseph] pynchon — came on shore and brot me some letters from Home — informing me — my family are in walking Health — I bless God — the Lord is or preserver, at Home, and abroad — I visitd — capt. [Isaac] Coltons company E. B. [Ebenezer Bliss] I hope is better — R [Roger] Cooly is ill — the Lord be or helper this day one dakin dyd in the Hospitall. as did Lt Gross — of Hartford, belonging to the Connecticutt colony Sloop. I dind at Home, visitd capt [Charles] doolittle — the men, are concernd — about their Homes — I walkd — on the walls, wth dr p, and mr Russell — prayd in the Hospitall, in Evening collonell [John] Choat — was much amiss, he took — Some herb-drink — at night — and Sweat kindly. [Loring? Lowry?] sat up with him, and — I lay on my own bed, with Woodberry — was much distressd by the fleas — but Slept — Some. — last night stayd — up Stairs with Collonell R [Sylvester Richmond] — we were visitd in the Evening by Collonell Burry [Andrew Burr]

Aug: 20 the collonell seems Easy as to his pain this morning. — I bless God, — and pray the indisposition may pass off — lightly. — the collonell comfutably all day — I attendd: — prayers — at

---

[8] *i. e.,* in Tyng's ship.

citadell and Hospitall — visitd dr p — kept House — . — Evening at Hospitall — saw poor march — who Seemd to be somewhat encouragd — . in morning — one judah West desird — prayers that his sons death — may be saue to him — on his passage — to N — England. he dyd

21 Citadell and Hospitall — visitd dr p — [Charles Pyncheon] who is not so well — in Some time — visitd capt. [Isaac] Colton, — Roger Cooley poorly — prayd there — J [Joseph] pynchon Esq — expressd desire to discourse with me and [Rev.] mr. w [Elisha Williams] — dind — at — Home — concern, in the men, and officers about going Home — . mr W. came in disappointd — as to intendd walk, went out of the city, with [Rev.] mr Hauley [Joseph Hawley] — went to the Hill and so to the East Gate — came Home — mr w — and J. p. Esq. [Mr Williams and Joseph Pyncheon] came in — a man card out — to be burid — without a coffin — two dyd in the Hospitall — one very suddenly — was able to walk to the Hospitall — a few hours before. one Quimbey dyd: of capt: Baglies [Jonathan Bagly] — company dyd — at his Lodgeings. night — I prayd at the Hospitall — one of the Rhodeisland-men — appeard to be dyeing — his name was m. [math.] peters — he was a Sergt. he dyd — Soon after; one of the above mentiond men was a Rhode island man — in the Evening a number at or House — discoursing — Great concern among them —

22 citadell and Hospitall — . dind — at Home — mr W — and collonell W — [William Williams] dind — with us. — afternoon walkd — with mr Williams on the walls — measurd — Evening at Hospitall — and visitd — a young man of capt: N — [Nathaniel] Williams company — discoursd and prayd — with him —

23 citadell, and Hospitall, a proposall for a Generall muster — But — deferd — till the morow. or Field officers — are about — to prefer a memoriall to the Governor: on behalf of the regiment — I visitd — a poor young man — that is Sick — and not baptized. he is in — distress and desires Baptism — I discoursd him — and Examind him as to his Know ledge — . — and prayd with him — and left him; for the present — . visitd capt: [Charles] doolittle — and returnd — home — . dind — at Home — with Fair-weather and capt: N [Nathaniel] Williams with us — after dinr — visitd mr Williams — and capt: [Andrew] Ward and then went to See the man — mentiond above — discoursd — with him. — and Enquird — of his capt: (whose name is [John] Light) about him —. then — major [Ezekiel] Gill-man was calld in —. and the people being calld together — I propoundd — a confession of faith — and covent to the man — which he assentd and consentd to — and I proceedd to Baptize him —. his name is Joseph Crowell he is of Exeter — Evening at the Hospitall — where two of the twenty are taken Sick —

24 citadell, and Hospitall —. a Generall muster of the Soldiers — and the Gouvernor made a Speech to them — at which they Gave 3 Huzzas — But I prceive there is Great uneasiness — and concern — among the army — I pray God to Guide and direct — and lead to proper measures — toward night — visitd — capt: [Isaac] Colton — found them — not worse — I receivd a letter from my Son John datd Aug: 5 and learn the family are well I do pray to God — to Give me a thankfull heart —. I learn Job Colton is dead — the Lord Sanctifie his Hand to his bereavd parants — prayd in the Hospitall —

25 citadell, and Hospitall —. Last night Lt Root of Farmington dyd — as did — one or two of the marines at the Hospitall — I preachd — in the forenoon — in the Hospitall chappell — and afternoon went to the Grand Battery, — where mr Fairweather met me and preachd for me — a Good Sermon, returnd Home prayd at the Hospitall — mr williams visitd me and told me of a design he had — I pray God to give him courage and prudence to prosecute it —

26 — citadell, and Hospitall, Last night dyd one varnum — and an Indian belonging to collonell [Nathaniel] Thomas' company, and this morning, one Scammon dyd — belonging to Brigadier [Samuel] Waldos regiment. he had been Sick but a little while —. and Sergt Newcome belonging to Collonell [Samuel] Pitts company dyd this day. as did 4 of the men of warrs men, out of the Hospitall —.

27 morning citadell, and Hospitall — and then Sat down, to write to the colonell but was calld — away — to see, Joseph Crowell above mentioned, who was soposd to be dyeing — he is very poorly of it — I returnd Home and began to write again —

but was calld to See a man very Sick — near the West Gate — belonging to capt: Harvey. I prayd with him — returnd Home and finishd the collonells letter — dind at Home, and then visitd — the men, at the House where capt: [John] Baker livd —. 2 of them are poorly and are going Home — I prayd — with them then visitd capt: [Charles] doolittle, and found him better — but Sergeant Smead — is ill — the Lord help him — I visitd Collonell [Robert] Hale who is going Home — this day dyd one West of Salem —. and one was burid from the Hospitall belonging to the man of warr — Evening visitd — dr C [Charles] — pynchon — found capt: [Isaac] Colton with him — he is poorly of it — I pray God — to direct him — and Show him his duty —

28 morning citadell, and Hospitall. last night one Wardwell of Bristoll dyd — visitd — capt: Colton, who continues poorly — found R. C [Roger Cooley] better — but p [Phineas] — Nash — Sick — I am poorly my Self but I am able to walk about the Lord be pleasd to help me — and Enable me to cast all my cares and Burdens upon him — I hear this day that Capt: [Nathaniel] Bosworth — of Bristoll dyd after he got to N-E- got as far as Attleborough and dyd there — the Lord is Holy in all his ways, and righteous in all his works — I dind with the Governor and — walkd — the walls, and saw a man carrd out to the Grave — and went and found it was one Varnum of Andover, belonging to capt: [James?] Fry — Evening — visitd — capt: Nathaniell Williams not well — but I hope better at night was visitd — by mr wms dr p — and collonell Wms — discoursd — in a pplexity — the Lord be pleasd to deliver and help us — Show us or duty — Note capt: williams told me of a man preservd at st peters who was preservd from a shott by corks in his pocket —

Aug: 29, 1745. morning citadell and Hospitall — one of the men of warrs men dead there — visitd — Collonell [Joseph] Thatcher who is not well — prayd with him — dr pynchon — saw us — as did mr Wms — heard News — as if Some French men of warr — were comeing this way — the Lord prepare for his pleasure. N. B. — omittd — on Aug: 24, when a French priviteer Sloop came just to the island Battery — but seeing English colours — stood of — and made to the East and took — one of our wood sloops, shipd the men — and let them pass — with the Sloop — capt: [William] Fletcher went after her — but I fear-whether-hell be able to find her — dind at major [Ezekiel] Gillmans —. with some French Gentle folks — who were modest — and Handsome — after dinr visitd — capt: [Seth] Hathoway who is Sick and prayd with him. visitd Sergt Smead, and mr dodgett walkd — the walls — Joseph Crowell dyd this afternoon.

30 citadell, and Hospitall, one clap of Connecticutt dyd this morning visitd dr c. p [Dr. Charles Pyncheon] capt: [Isaac] Colton's company, he is determind to go — Home, and has Got leave, visitd capt: [Ebenezer] Edmunds — Sick and very desirous to go Home — dind at Home — visitd Brigadier [Joseph] dwight who is poorly of it — took leave of the Gentlemen — going Home in capt: [Edward] Ting. I pceive Capt: Colton — is gone Home with Ting allso — his going was So Sudden — that I had not opportunity — to See him — before he went aboard — we seem to be disquietd — and disheartnd — Greatly — oh Lord — I desire to cast all my cares, and Burdens upon thee — and pray that thou wouldst Sustain me —

31. citadell, and Hospitall —. visitd dr C— pynchon, who is not quite so well — walkd upon the walls — and went to see — the men that came with capt: Colton — and prayd with them. Collnll C [Choate] — poorly — I am concernd — this day one dyke of capt: [John] Heustons company dyd — this day — a Ship — appeard — of — soposd to be a French vessell — but made of — and none psud [pursued] — them — she went to the West —

Sept 1 citadall — and Hospitall — forenoon preachd in the Hospitall chappell and mr [Elisha] wms being ill — I preachd in the afternoon — at the citadell chappell — Governor [and] comodore being present. visitd dr [Alexander] Bollman who is ill — one Carver of capt: [Jonathan] Cary's company dyd — or Sick in crease — oh that God would help us — a French captain [John Le Croix] (taken by capt: [William] Fletcher) belonging to Canada — has made his Escape and I pceive — Casteen and two clergy men — are put under custody — being as is supped — privy to it [9] — this day one [Jonathan] Fox of capt: [John]

[9] Cf. *Third Journal,* September 7th.

NINTH JOURNAL 139

Heustons company dyd This was a man belongd to Suffd [Suffield] in our county. the Lord affect us with his Hand —

2 citadell and Hospitall. this day one Lakin of capt: [John] Warners company dyd —. he was in the Hospitall — as did one Joseph Fuller of capt: [Daniel] Chapman' company of Toland — Colonell [John] Choat is poorly — I am concerned about him — after prayers in the Hospitall — I went, and visitd — capt: [John] warner (who livd Somewhere near meromack River) who is very Sick, and prayd with him. and at Collonell Choats house — and prayd with one Hovey and others Sick — and visitd — E. Choat, and other Sick there, and prayd with them — and with Some of capt [Benjamin] Jves men, in another room. then — I visited capt: [Isaac] Coltons company, and prayd with them. and visitd young Joshua Maxfield — who is very Sick, and prayd — with him — dind at Home — the collonel was able to walk abroad —. after dinr went to See — one Burbanks of capt: Chhs [James Church] company and prayd with him — and with one [Onisimus] Nash of capt: Heustons company — and with Mr Hodge: visitd Sergt Smead — capt: [Seth] Hatheway — Brigadier [Joseph] dwight, and dr [Alexander] Bollman — prayd — at citadell, and Hospitall — prayd with capt: Chapmans company — night they were going to bury jos: Fuller — and at citadell and Hospitall — and then visited one Young-man at the Barracks — who was Sick — and prayd with him — this day dyd one david Brown of capt: [William] Warner of Bostons company

3 citadell, Hospitall, and with capt: [John] Warner — who is very bad, Last night Youngman — that I prayd with (Last night), dyd — as did one of capt: [Daniel] Fones men — in the Hospitall. capt: Fones comandd the Rhode-island sloop. I have some Headach — Burbank, above mentiond dyd this morning. about 1 clock — a sloop and ship — appeard — at the west — comeing down which provd, the sloop — to be one of or cruisers — the ship — an English Ship that had been taken by the French — going from Carolina to England — they Give an acct of a Number of french men of warr comeing to this place. this day [Onisimus] Nash of Sheffield dyd — as did one [Thomas] Wheelwright of Wells — belonging to Colonell [John] Storers company — and one [Zac] Gould — of Collonell [Samuel] Willards regiment — that went aboard the transport, Sick — dyd this day in the Harbour. in the Evening I had the Head ach — was restless and feverish — had an uncomfortable night —

4 citadell, and Hospitall — am able to keep about tho but poorly — visitd dr [Charles] pynchon — . then Lay down, and slept. was able to Eat Some dinr after dinr visitd capt [Isaac] Coltons company, found them poorly — but I hope not worse — this day visitd capt: [John] Baker very poorly — this day we hear that — the King of prussia and the Queen of Hungary — have comprimisd matters and that the duke of Tuscany — is chosen Emperour — great News — if true as I hope it is — we hear also that a ship was seen off — and we are concernd — not knowing but, they are french — night I prayd — in the citadell — saw Brigadeer d [Dwight] and dr [Alexander] Bullman in the Evening — visitd mr S [Samuel] Winslow — who is very Sick, and prayd with him — at his Brothers [William Winslow] — the commissary —

Sept: 5. this morning at the Bell ringing at 8 a clock — I went up to the citadell — but just then — the drumms — were beating, to call to arms so that — no body attendd — so that I returnd — and went to the Hospitall and prayd there — and from thence to capt. [John] warner and prayd — with him. there are 2 other men, very Sick, in the Same House — I went to See mr [Samuel] Winslow — and prayd with him — he is very Sick this forenoon we had an Alarm — a report, being Spread — that two Large Ships appeard in the offing. — the companys were calld to arms — But the fog came on — that we could see nothing from the walls. tis reportd 3 french men, ran away last night — and that [John] Shaw is sent after them. Last night Josh: Maxfield dyd — and one ———— at the Hospitall — that was caryd — thither yesterday — dind at Home — afternoon Saw mr [Elisha] Williams — and then visitd — capt: [Isaac] Coltons company and prayd — with them Neighbour Crowfoot and others, are Gone Home — visitd — capt: [Ebenezer] Edmunds company and prayd with them — and returnd Home — weary, and tird — but recruitd — a little, and went and visitd one Tufts — that is Sick — belonging to Charles-Town — and prayd with him. visitd dr [Alexander] Bollman and prayd with him; found him — in a Sweet frame — prayd

— at the citadell, and Hospitall — sat up late by reason of company — had a restless night — had the cramp —

6 citadell and Hospitall — and visitd Hovey of the collonell company and prayd with him, visitd mr [Samuel] Winslow and prayd with him — he appears to be near his end — capt: [John] Warner who livd on miromick [Merrimac] River dyd — this morning — one of the men of w: warr men, dyd in the Hospitall — in the morning and another was sd to be dyeing when I attendd — prayers — . Sergt Walker of capt [John] Heustons company dyd this day — after dinr I was calld to see two men in the Barracks — that belongd to capt: [William?] Smith of providence — and prayd with them — to ward night visitd dr Bullman — who is very Low, prayd at citadell, and Hospitall, when at the Hospitall — one of the marines told me, they had burid three men this day and had 3 more Lay dead — in the Evening prayd with mr [Samuel] Winslow — had a comfutoble night.

7 citadell — Hospitall. and with mr winslow — and one Wms at the house where doctor morrison lives — and with Winchell, clerk, of capt: Heustons company — and with mr dodge. visitd Sergt Smead — yesterday one Campbell of capt: [John] prentices Sloop — dyd — Suddenly. Last night Capt: [James] Stevens dyd — at the island Battery — a valuable man belongd — to Salisbury — this day mr Samuel Winslow dyd — as did one Tarbell of Woodstock — belonging to capt: [Palmer] Golding — night citadell and Hospitall — this day — capt: [Thomas] perkins, returnd — with a Number of french men that had obscondd — a brave Exploit —

8 and Sabbath: citadell, and Hospitall. preachd — in the forenoon in the Hospitall chappell — in the afternoon at the citadell chappell — doctor Bullman, is very bad — this Evening mr Winslow was burid — Evening — citadell and chappell Evening — a visitt —

Sept: 9, morning citadell — and Hospitall. — forenoon visitd at capt: Coltons and prayd with them; visitd capt: Mountfort [Richard Mumford] — and saw mr Ebenezer Raynolds — saw mr Wms he is Better — dind at Home, and mr [Joseph] Hawley with us — Note — in the forenoon I visitd capt: [Peter] Hunt, and one of major [Richard] Cutts men who is Sick — prayd — at

Both — houses. afternoon rode out to Lt [John] Man's and prayd — with them — . Jonothan Warriner is Sick — saw dr Harvey — and visitd him — went to see dr Bull-man, who is still very low. this day dyd — one littlejohn — of capt: Warners company. and a Sergeant of collonell [Samuel] Willards company. night — citadell. and hospitall — this day — capt: [William] Fletcher made me a present of a fine french Gun. Evening was calld to see one Nicolls of Amesbury, in the Barracks, he belongs to capt: Johnson' — company, I prayd with him —

10 morning citadell, and Hospitall. Last night dyd one mr [Capt. Robert] Glover, who was the Adjutant Generall — a foreigner — came from the West indies. visitd dr Bullman, who I fear is near his End — visitd the Sick at Collonell [Samuel] Willards house — and prayd with them — visitd — Winchell, clerk to capt: Heuston — and mr dodge, who I hope, are better — went to See mr Wms and there found capt: miles of New-Haven, who informs me, that my uncle Mather is dead, — this Seems to be a call to me to hasten home — dind at Home — visitd capt: [Isaac] Coltons company — and prayd there — [Caleb] Lamb is low. toward night we heard, that twas thot a french fleet — was seen off cape Sables — and therefore, twas agreed the Fleet should go — out. night citadell and Hospitall — at night the men that had listd — were orderd — to be in a readiness to go aboard the Kings ships Early — in the morning, this Evening, I was Greatly disquietd — by capt: p — who was here —

11 the men, were mustering Early — to go aboard — . I prayd in the citadell and then went in to See dr Bull-man, who I apprehend is dying — prayd at Hospitall — and then visitd dr Swet and dr [Charles] pynchon and prayd with them — dr S — not being well, and dr p — designing Home. visitd Corp: Ellis, at major [Nathaniel] Twing's — and a young man — that was Sick there and prayd with them — then — went to the Generalls — and found dear dr Bullman dead.[10] a Great power upon us — Last night one Lt Bullock of Rehoboth dyd. as did one Thomas, who was clerk of capt: [Jonathan?] Lawrence' company, and capt: [Ebenezer] Eastman' Negro London, dyd this morning, thus or dead

[10] Dr. Alexander Bulman of York, Maine, was Pepperrell's personal physician.

NINTH JOURNAL 143

— are multiplyd —. one of capt: Warners men whose name, was procter dyd he had tendd at the Hospitall. yesterday one of capt: [Jonathan] Baglies men dyd toward, night the men returnd from the on board the men of warr — the comodore hauing heard that the news they had about french ships — was not to be relyd Upon. The comodore was Generous to the men, and Gave them — Brandy and wine — note that this day one Sergeant Millet of Capt: [Charles] Byles company was burid — that dyd Last night.

12 morning citadell, and Hospitall, forenoon visitd — the people at capt: [Seth] Hathaway and prayd with them, visitd — one Hodges — of capt: [George?] moreys company — and prayd with him — he Gave me acct of his being awaknd — and comfertd — by mr Wheelocks preaching at Taunton — visitd 2 others of capt: Morey' company — and prayd with them. visitd capt: [Charles] doolittles people, and found them better — dind at Home. afternoon went to See Lt. [John] Mans company — found Jonathan Warriner, and one Larkin sick — and prayd — with them —. this day dyd one Youngs and one Tufts of capt: [Bartholomew] Trows company. and one david Williams, and one chester, of capt: [John] prentices Sloop — about noon — one march of New-Berry that was woundd at the island Battery dyd —. this day two of major [Moses] Titcombs men dyd —. in the Evening I was calld — to pray with one Town of capt: [Ebenezer] Edmunds company who is apprehendd — to be near his end, on this day past — philip Negro (formerly servant to the Revd mr devotion of Suffd) dyd he was of collonell [John] Storers company.

13 morning citadell, and Hospitall — and with one Barnard of capt: [Samuel] Rhodes — company — and with the Sick, at major [Nathaniel] Twings —. dind with colonell Broad-Street [John Bradstreet] — where I saw two men from Annapolis who say all is Still and quiet there. this day one Sergt — West that belongd to capt: [William] Warner of Bostons company, dyd, as did 2 of the comodores men, and one of capt: [Daniel] Fones. who dyd in the Hospitall — his name was Alexander Brower. this day dyd also one Ephraim Barker of capt: [James?] Frys company, as did one of capt: [Richard] Mumfords men of Rhode-island.

14 morning citadel and hospital. with the Sick of capt: [Isaac] Coltons company and with the Sick of capt: [Ebenezer] Edmunds company — after dinr went to Grand Battery — and saw capt: [Andrew] Watkins who is very Sick. prayd with him and with two others that are Sick there — Jonothan Warner of Lt [John] Mans company dyd —. I attendd his funerall —

15 Sabbath. Citadel and Hospital — preachd in the forenoon at Hospitall — chappell — afternoon at Grand Battery — and prayd with the Sick in two Barracks — there — and with the Sick at Lt mans and with the Sick at capt: [David] Melvins — returnd home — tird and did not go to the Hospitall — this day one Sergt Barnard of capt: [Samuel] Rhodes company — was Burid —

16 citadel and hospital —, Last night Lt [Samuel] Torey of connecticutt, and one Town of Capt: [Ebenezer] Edmunds company dyd, and one Go[— ?]n of Collonell [Samuel] Moores regiment — saw mr Wms in forenoon — he and mr H. [Hawley] dind with us — after dinr collnll C [Choate] mr W [Williams] and collonell W [Williams] — had discourse together — I attendd the funerall of Town above mentiond — and prayd at the house — another man there is very Sick — visitd capt Coltons company — I hope they are better — this day 2 of the men of warrs men, were burid and a french man, in the Evening a councill of warr was called[11] — I pceive the army are very uneasy — indeed — what the consequence — will be I know not — I pceive — that severall things were votd in the councill — to make the army Easy; as that all but 2000 should be releasd — and the wages of those that tarry be advancd — and they promisd to be dismissd by the 1st of June — that the Guns should be devidd — I hope things will be made Easy.

17 morning citadel and Hospital, visitd capt: [Seth] Hathaway and company — and prayd with them. Sergt Cummins seems near his End — I pceive things — appear difficult — the Lord Give the wisdom that is profitable to direct — forenoon the doctors were here, to consult with the collonell about the Sick — dind at Home — after dinr went, with mr Wms and mr [James] Monk — aboard the Canterbury man of warr: were kindly Entertaind by mr Bernard — the chaplin, after I returnd — I visitd — mr Hodges — at

---

[11] This Council Meeting was on the 17th. The reference to guns means that the Provincial soldiers wanted the small arms of the French. (6 *Mass. Hist. Soc. Coll.* 10: 45.)

capt [George?] Moreys, and prayd with them — and visitd — capt: [Peter] Hunt and prayd with him. this day, and Last night, dyd two men, at the Grand Battery; one of capt: [Benjamin or Joseph] Goldthawits company and one of capt: [Andrew] Watkins company. Sergt Cummins dyd also — and one ——— of capt: Chaplins [Joshua Champlin] company, two of the men of warrs men dyd — one was a surgeons mate — the Guns were deliverd out, and dividd — among the men — the councill met again — and votd Severall things —

18 morning Citadel and Hospital — the regiments met — and the Govrnour — made a Speech — to them — containing severall comfutable things — which I hope has made things more Easy — I desire to have my Eyes to the Great keeper of israel — I visitd a young man, at major [Moses] Titcombs — who is Sick — and prayd with him — and prayd at the funerall of Sergt Cummins: went to see Capt: Warner and visitd mr Hodges — toward night two of the men of warrs men — dyd — and of our forces 3 dyd. one was of capt: [Jonathan] Snellings men, — left here — another was one Edward, of capt: [Jonathan] Baglies company; another an indian man of capt: chaplins [Joshua Champlin] company of Rhodeisland —

19 Citadel and Hospital visitd dr [John] manning and [William] Hays — and capt: [George?] moreys men, in two companies — and prayd with them. — dind at Home; afternoon visitd major [Moses] Titcombs kinsman and prayd with him — went aboard capt: Kingberrys Sloop to See him he being Sick — and prayd with him — visitd capt: [Isaac] Coltons people, and prayd with them — Joseph Ball is very Sick. visitd — philip — moran of capt: [Ebenezer] Edmunds — company and prayd with him — he being very Sick — and I fear near his End. prayd at the Hospitall — where I hope they are Better —. Evening visitd — capt: Wm Warner, where 5 persons are Sick — his Son, I apprehend is in a dangerous Condition. I prayd with them. — I pceive Some men, were upon Examination, by a committee — this Evening — respecting Some combination — the Lord. Give wisdom —

20 morning citadell and Hospital and with capt [Ebenezer] Eastmans Kinsman — and with the doctors morning and Hospital Last night moran of capt: [Ebenezer] Edmunds company (mentiond above) dyd. — as did Hodges mentioned — Sept 12. afternoon visitd — and prayd with a Sick man of collonell [Shubael] Gorhams regiment — who is very Sick — attendd the funerall of moran. prayd with the company. found a man in that House very Sick — with whom I discoursd — visitd — capt: [Isaac] Coltons company, and prayd with them — officers Speak of going Home and leaveing their men — I am concernd — I pray God — to direct — . I was indisposd — at night — was obligd to get up — by reason of a Gripeing and flux — but I hope — it is only the carying of — Some indisposition — by bad Smell —

Sept 21 notwithstanding my indisposition Last night I was able to attend prayers in the morning — at citadel and hospital — I kept house the greatest part of the day — Lay on the bed — but to ward night went to the Hospitall — and prayd. this day deacon Holey, one of the carpenters dyd —

Sept 22 and Sabbath — Last night I was restless and obligd to get up — in the morning did not attend prayers at the citadell — Got mr W [Elisha Williams] to preach for me — unable to attend the Exercise — but — tarryd — at Home, in the afternoon — was visitd — by Brigadier d [Dwight] and mr W — at night — had a comfutable night — thru Gods Good-ness —

23 citadel and Hospital — . this day dyd Lt collonell Nathaniell Thomas — a verey worthy man — I visitd dr [John] manning, and [William] hays — very sick and prayd with them and so — I did at capt: [Seth] Hathaways — where one Thurrell dyd — . and one of capt: [Philip] dumerisque company dyd at the Grand Battery — after dinr — visitd — the part of the company, where capt: [John] Baker livd. prayd with 2 Sick men there and with Some of collonell [Shubael] Gorehams regiment and with dr Swet — at night — capt: [John] Rouse came from England with accounts from the king — Great joy at Home — upon the account of the reduction of this place the Goveneur, Generall, and comodore (tis sd) are knighted. this day one of capt: [Jacob] Tiltons company — belonging to N — Hampshire, dyd — he livd between the city, and the Grand Battery, this day a man was Burid in the forenoon — but as yet I cant learn who he was — he did not belong to the Hospitall —

24 morning citadel and Hospitall — forenoon — prayd — with

NINTH JOURNAL

dr [John] manning — who is bad and with Joseph Ball — who is bad — the discourse is about the news from England — things I fear Go bad in Flanders. — but the Lord reigns let the Earth rejoyce. I have a bad Head ach. — yet was able to walk about and attendd the funeral of collonell Thomas. this day one of capt: chaplins [Joshua Champlin] men dyd in the Evening — I prayd — with dr manning — . who I fear is near his End — . many men are taken Sick especially of collonell [John] Choats own company —

25. I am more comfortably of it this morning and prayd at citadel and Hospital this morning dear doctor [John] manning dyd — I visitd capt: [Isaac] Coltons company and prayd with them J. B. [Joseph Ball] — is dangerously ill — visitd — capt: [Charles] doolittles company and prayd with them one Morgan is very bad — visitd — the part of the company that belongd to capt: [John] Baker — . and prayd with them. visitd one of the rooms in the collonel house and prayd with some sick — then attendd the drs funerall and prayd — there. the Guard at the East Gate — told me that 2 psons were carid out — at the Gate with coffins (which I supose — belong to the army) and 2 without (that I sopose belong to the marines)

26 morning Hospital and Citadel visitd — dr Swet — who I hope is better and the company belonging to capt: [Isaac] Colton and prayd — there and at the collonells House — and at capt: [Charles] doolittles — this day — dyed — in the Hospital one Wormwood belonging to the sloop dow [Dove or Doe] one Rackwood master — and one wheatin of capt: smiths company — and one of collonell [Shubael] gorehams regiment murtherd Sept: 20. Evening I went to the Hospitall — but the smell was so Nauseous, that I could not tarry — toward Evening I went to see collonell [Nathaniel] Donnells Brother [Capt. James Donnell] and prayd with him. —

27 morning citadel but not at Hospitall — because of the [Raison?] [nausea?] afternoon prayd — visitd Lt [Eleazer] Ellis and prayd with him — visitd the people at the collonells House — and prayd with them. — went to mr [Elisha] Wms and did some thing toward a Sermon — in the little study there: dind at Home with Some company — after dinr visitd — Morgan at capt:

[Charles] doolittles — and prayd with him — and alnight prayd with dr Swet. this day — one of capt: [William] Fletchers men dyd being a Shore in one of the Houses betwixt the city, and the Grand Battery — capt: [James] donnell dyd this day and one Cutting of collonell [Samuel] Willard company; and capt: [William] warners Son of Boston.

28 morning citadel visitd — mr W [Elisha Williams] — and the people at the collonells House, and prayd in 3 rooms — this morning Lt [Eleazer] Ellis dyd of major [Nathaniel] Twings — regiment [company?] and one man, at the Grand Battery — dind at Home, afternoon — visitd — Morgan at capt: [Charles] doolittles and prayd with him. prayd also with men, at the House, where capt: [John] Baker livd — and atendd capt: [James] donnells funerall — mr — Wms went aboard, to go Home — thus all the ministers are Gone, but I — oh that God, would favor me with — his gracious presence, that he would preserve and teach me, prayd at the citadell at night

29 and Sabbath — last night I was followd, with the flux was obligd — to get up 3 times — but thru favour, am Better this morning — prayd — at the citadell — preachd — at both chapples — this day one Joseph Geary of capt: Chhs [James Church] company dyd: and one indian namd John mommopuit of collonell [Sylvester] Richmonds company dyd — allso — and two men, at the Grand Battery, as capt: [Benjamin or Joseph] Goldthawit told me and one of capt: [Jonathan] Baglies company — who dyd Suddenly —

30 morning citadel and with one Howard of capt: [Samuel] Rhodes company, visitd, and prayd — with the people that are Sick, at the collonells House, and at capt: [Charles] doolittles and where capt: [John] Baker livd — and with — mr [Ebenezer] prout, a commissary — this in the town. we have news, of a French Squadron off New Found Land — the Lord be pleasd to prepare for what his pleasure — may be — Give wisdom, and courage, to or — men of war — . afternoon — visitd collonell [Nathaniel] donnell, and capt: Warner — this day a man dyd — at the Grand Battery, and one Richardson, of capt: [John] Heustons company — Evening — receivd — letters from Home: they — tell me, with Joy and with Grief — my family — wants me at Home — I pray

NINTH JOURNAL 149

to God, to show me what my duty is — just, as I was Going to bed — I was called to visitt a man Sick in the Barracks but I did not think it my duty — to go —

Octobr 1: 1745. morning Citadel and visitd — one Stevens in the Barracks — and prayd — with him — and two others Sick there. visitd mr Shore: visitd at the Collonell House — and prayd —. and at capt: [Isaac] Coltons — and prayd Some are Better, and Some worse —. this day — a vessell — came in from N. — York — who brings acct Gov: Clinton is to visitt the indians at Allbany. Some of the Gentlemen — came from Allbany — one Cutbridge of capt: Goldens [Palmer Goulding] company. visitd — with capt: [Charles] doolittle — and [Capt. John] Baker — and prayd — visitd — the Generall in the Evening —

2 morning Citadel and Spent the day i e the Greatest part of it in waiting for the collonell 2 of capt: [William] Fletchers men dyd and 2 more a few days ago — one of capt: [James?] Frys men dyd — this day — and the Guards at the East Gate tell me there was another dyd — after prayers — I visitd — one capt: davis — and prayd with him — and prayd at capt: doolittles

3 morning citadel — visitd — collonell [William] Wms and visitd and prayd — at capt: [Isaac] Coltons — capt: [Ebenezer] Edmunds — and at the collonells house —. Last night dyd — an indian of capt: [Joshua] Champlins — company — and one of capt: [Edward] Tings men, and one of capt: mountfords [Richard Mumford] — and one of capt: [Isaac] Coltons — namd — Gamaliell Ghent —. and sd man, of capt: mountfords — or Smiths company dyd — afternoon at capt: [Charles] doolittles capt: [John] Baker — with mr [Samuel, Jr?] Waldo and mr [Ebenezer] Prout — Spent the Evening at collonell Williams —

4 morning citadell — and with — one mr Stephens and 2 indians at the Barracks, and with — mr Waldo — and at capt: doolittles — afternoon visitd the Houses — out of the city — and Saw — some in Great distress — in the Evening — visitd the Semtary —, this day Josiah Clark of capt: [Peter] Hunts company, dyd — and may-thy. Richard [Mathias Richards] of capt: [William] Smiths company; an indian of Rhodeisland dyd —. and 4 of the men of warrs men —

5 morning citadell —, with Collonell [Samuel] Willard — mr

Waldo, major Hodges — two rooms — in the collonells House — capt: [Isaac] Coltons and capt: [Ebenezer] Edmunds company — dind with collonell [William] Wms — and did something — towards a sermon, in the study there — this day dyd one Totman, of Brigadier [Joseph] dwights — regiment — he belongd — to plimouth, and two men from the island Battery. and one at the Grand Battery. two of the men of warrs men, and 2 French men from the Hospitall —

6 and Sabboth, morning citadell — preachd at the Hospital chappell. afternoon — at the citadell. Last night Capt: Mountford [Richard Mumford] dyd. and a Sergeant of capt: Marshalls — company, and one Thomas Collins of the Superbe and one Sergt churchill of capt: [Sylvanus] Cobbs — one of capt: [Estes] Hatchs — men, and one of major [Moses] Titcombs. this day capt: [Edward] Tyng came in and the Wger [Wager?] man of war. one david Smith — Born at dedham, but in the service of the men of war dyd

7 morning citadell, and at capt [Charles] doolittles — [Capt John] — Baker, and at the collonells House — afternoon — at capt: [Isaac] Coltons and capt: [Ebenezer] Edmunds — . was visitd by mr Fair-weather — receivd — letters from dr Colman and dr Sewall — about Chaplian — Collonell [Sylvester] Rich-mond and his son, went on Board capt: Coffin with design to go Home — this day were Burid — Joshua Wakes, of capt: [Stephen] Lees company of connceticutt and John Hedding, of capt: Witherbys company. and two men, belonging to the Superbe man of warr, whose names were Morrison Jones, and Thos — Jones.

8 Last night I was restless — had the Head ach — but was able to attend prayers at the citadell — visitd and prayd with mr Waldo. collonell Richmond, and son came on Shore, and took leave of us. — I visitd none that were Sick saveing mr Waldo — because of my indisposition — was able to attend prayers at the citadell — had — a comfutable night. this day four of the men of warr. viz: the princess mary, capt: [Richard] Edwards the Sunderland, capt: Bret, the Centerbury capt: [John] Hoar — the Superbe — capt. ———— [Durell?] with the two india Ships, saild — from Home — to New foundland, and so for England — and in the Evening a packet Boat — went out, designed — for England directly. a man near Lt Barnes dyd I think his name was Temple. but dont know. this day dyd Lt Barnes [Isaac Barran?] of Chelmsford — of capt: [David] Melvins company and one of capt: [John] Heustons company namd Joseph Rowsden, and one Abraham Sherman, of Lt. [Edward] Coles company of Rhodeisland.

9 I am comfortably of it this morning I bless God, I prayd at the citadell, and with Collonell [Samuel] Willard, and with Collonell [Nathaniel] donnell, and with the people at the Collonells House; and with them at capt: [Isaac] Coltons, and with them at capt: [Ebenezer] Edmunds — this in the forenoon — was visitd by Capt: [Jonathan] Snelling — from Boston — afternoon vistd — capt: [Charles] doolittles company — and capt: [John] Bakers, — and capt: [John] Heustons company — then waitd upon the Generall, and the Governour — and petitiond them to dismiss — p. N. and S. T. —. after Evening prayer — visitd — dr Swet — and went with dr morrison — to visit — Some — men at the collonells House this day Sergt: Howard of capt: [Samuel] Rhodes company was burid — and towards night one White, a Lieutent — of New Shire dyd — and a negro of capt: [Jeremiah] Westons company and in the Evening one Burnhill of capt: Edmunds company dyd —

10 morning dull and listless — prayd at citadell — visitd major Hodges and prayd there — saw — dr [Robert] Keith and dr Swet — was dull, and indisposed — did not visitt the Sick — as usuall — but was able to go to the citadell — with mr Fairweather who prayd — at my desire — kept in in the Evening — and had — a comfutable night — toward night one Easty of the Collonells company dyd and daniel drake that had Long Lain-by a wound — and one of capt: [Estes] Hatchs company, and one John Brown and one of the man of warrs men, and a french man

11 I am comfutably of it — prayd at the citadell — waitd on the Admirall congratulated — him, on the approbation, his services, had met, with, from his majesty — and the Honours the king had conferd — upon him — and I told him, that as Some of the New England people, would be obligd — to tarry here — I trusted — that or Chaplins, would, be protected — and Encouragd by him — he told me they should — and — that — he had the Greatest charity for us — and believd — or people, were more Examplary than theirs — and Rapeatd many kind things to me and told me he desird presbiterianism might be Established here — I visitd — capt: [Charles] doolittles company, and prayd with them — severall are Sick — mr Fairweather came on Shore, and invited me on Board capt: [Edward] Tings where I dind — with — capt: Tyng; capt: [Jonathan] Snelling — was handsomely Entertaind — mr Fairweather made me a present, of a pair of Hand Some Stockings — after dinr I returnd home, and attendd the funerall of — Easty of or company — .I attendd prayers at the citadell — and then came home, and was calld to go the the Barracks and prayd with — one Francis Brown, of Standford, — who seems to be a dyeing — he has a good reputation among his companions — this Evening — there is Great fireing of Small arms, and illuminations. the day past, being the kings coronation — Some houses are illuminated — rockets playd — the Lord — Give us truly thankfull hearts for or civill, and religious privileges — this day dyd — or at least where burid capt: [Gershom] davis, and his Lieutnt: [James] Hildrick and one Joseph Cogsall of the Generalls regiment, and John Woodward, of Bd [Brigadier Joseph] dwights and one of capt: davis' company above mentiond — and Ezekiel crossman, and Samuel Cook — who were I think both of Rhodeisland, and palatiah Long of Boston. and one of the Superbes men

12 had a Good night, prayd — in the citadell, and with one of capt: [Bartholomew] Trow men — and with capt: [Charles] doolittles men — and twice with the men, at, the Collonells House. Francis Brown, I prayd — with Last night dyd soon after as did one Williston of capt: [Seth] Hathaways company. and two of the Rhodeisland men, of capt mountfords [Richard Mumford] company — and Smith's — and two capt [Gershom] davis — company. and corporall Wait. of Northampton. of collonell [William] Williams' company.

13. and Sabbath — morning citadell and with one of collonell [Richard] Gridleys — men; preachd in the forenoon at the Hospitall — chapple dind with the Admirall; afternoon went to the Grand Battery, and preachd — there — mr Fair-weather preachd in the forenoon at the Grand — Battery. and in the afternoon at the citadell and prayd — at night. in the citadell — . Capt: [Samuel] Curwin, fell down, as he came from the chapple — in a fitt —

NINTH JOURNAL 153

and was taken up. and carid into the House — and bloodd — and came to again — the people are Greatly destressd and discouragd — oh that God would help them and comfort them. and lead them —

14. morning citadell, and with dear dr [Gillam] Taylor — at — capt: [Charles] doolittles and [Capt. John] Bakers — visitd — capt: [Samuel] curwin, who is Siting up — attendd the funerall of Lt. [Nathaniel] Harriman, of the collonells [Choate's] company — a very desirable man. this day one of capt: Baglies [Jonathan Bagly] — men was burid — and one of capt: [Estes] Hatchs — and five others two were of the men of warrs — men; as for the others — I cant, learn — who they were as yet — a warm Evening — one of the men, was of capt [Christopher] marshalls company

15. at citadell, and, twice at the Barracks att which — visitd — dr — [Gillam] Taylor — and capt: [Isaac] Coltons — company — and capt: [Ebenezer] Edmunds — company. visitd — capt: [Samuel] curwin. Last night — or yesterday an indian of capt: John-sons — company dyd and one Samuel manning of capt [Ebenezer] Edmunds company, and one chamberlain of the same company, one mr charly of Boston, that came down atradeing, dyd this day. 3 of the men of warrs men were burid — this day. and the Guards — at the East Gate — tell me, 3 others psons were burid — but I cant learn their names — I dind at the Governours — visitd — capt: [Peter] Staples — who is Sick — Sat at the Generalls — in the Evening — with — a Gentleman from Virginia — Nathaniell Wood of Collonell [William] Williams company dyd — this afternoon — in the Evening one of the men of warrs lieutenant — that is Sick in the Hospitall — Sent for me — and I went and visitd him

Octobr 16 — morning — citadell — and visitd at capt. [John] Baker — [Charles] doolittle — and at the collonells — House — capt: [Isaac] Coltons — and [Ebenezer] Edmunds and prayd — with them — dind at Home. visitd the man of warrs Lt. and visitd and prayd with dr [Gillam] Taylor — I passd — by the dead House in the Hospitall and observd — a French man, and an English man. — lay — quietly together in their — winding Sheets —

17. morning citadell — . the regiment being — calld — to gether — have Signifyd their desire that the collonell Should go Home — to Endeavour to Serve them — at the Generall Court — visitd —

capt: [Charles] doolittles [Isaac] coltons — major [Moses] Titcombs — capt: [Peter] Staples. this day Nathaniell Chapin of capt: Coltons company and one Spaulding of capt: [Ebenezer] Nicolls company. and two of the men of warrs men — were burid — and one Robert Bryant, of capt: [Thomas] Stanfords company.

18. citadell dr [Gillam] Taylor — at capt: [John] Bakers, and with capt: [George?] Moreys men, and at the collonells House — visitd capt: [Samuel] Curwin — after prayers, in the Evening — visitd the Generall — the Generall, has receivd — a letter from the Secretary, who informs him, they are takeing care, — to send — some Chaplins — I rejoyce, and hope, they will soon — be here — this day one merrill a mosheto indian or melatto, of the Generalls regiment — dyd — and one Grainger. one of the man of warrs — men — and one daniell FitzGerald — of Brigadier [Samuel] Waldos regiment

19. morning citadel with capt: [George?] morey — and capt: [John] Bakers men, capt: [Isaac] Coltons and twice in the House — where capt: [Ebenezer] Edmunds men are — Last night Sergt Chattuck of the collonells company, and one Barlow, of capt: [Seth] Hathaways — company, and an indian of capt: [Jonathan?] Lawrences company dyd the army were musterd — this day — and Govrenour Shirley, and the Admirall — made a Speach to them — I attendd the funerall of Sergt Chattuck — one of capt: [Jonathan] Baglies men, dyd — and one of the men of warrs men. I perceive the Admirall, in his speach — that he made to the Army — cautiond — them against — swearing, and cursing and profaining the Sabbath — I bless God — that putt it into his Heart — thus to caution, and wish, it may prove beneficiall — to the army — in the Evening Sergt drown sent to me, to pray with him — I went, and prayd —

20 and Sabbath — morning citadel, mr Fair weather — preachd for me, in the forenoon in the Hospitall chapple — I preachd at the citadell in the afternoon — after service the Governour invitd me to drink tea — as I came from prayer — I went in, and prayd with Sergt drown. the Govrnour — spoke favourably to me, about p. N. and S. T. I desire to put my trust in the Lord — this day one of capt Ephraim Bakers men dyd — he was woundd in the Siege, and John Holms of capt: [Thomas] Stanfords company

21 morning — visitd — capt: [John] Bakers company — prayd in both rooms — and at the collonells House — capt: [Isaac] Coltons — major [Nathaniel] Twings — and with mr metcalf — dind with the Governour — who Give me a dismission for p. N. and S. T. this day one of the men of warrs — men was Burid —

October 21 1741 [sic]. this day — Severall psons, were burid — belonging the army viz: one of capt: mountforts [Richard Mumford] men, and one of capt: [William] Smiths, of Rhodeisland and one of capt: kings of Salem — and the Guards, tell me there was another, which they think — belongd — to capt: kins-lough [John Kinselagh] —

octbr. 22. morning Citadel and at capt: Coltons — at Lt. Cheneys. — p. N. and S. T. went aboard — to go Home — but the wind is not fair — and the Sea is — very rough — the Lord — be pleasd to go with them, when they Go — N. B. that the Generall informd — me, that the Admirall told him, that he had receivd — a letter from dr Mac-Sparran — wherein he desird — him, to take care of the chh [church] interest — but the Admirall made light of it — and declard — he would readily — Encourage — pres-biterianism — and said — he would make no difference — this day or the Last night dyd — one of capt: [John] Kinsloughs men, and one of capt Witherby. and 2 of capt: Johnsons, and 1 of capt Smiths, and the Guards told me of another — but the name they could not tell. Evening — Brigadier W [Waldo] was here, and kept us up Late — and prayer was omittd in the family — the only time twas omittd — the Lord pardon us. in the Evening I visitd Collonell [Simon] Lothrop — and prayd with in his House where are many Sick —

23. morning Citadel — after Breakfast — I walkd — out of the East Gate — and took the inscription — there — and then visitd — at the collonells and at major Hodges — and returnd — home —. afternoon with mr drown and at capt: [Isaac] Colton, and with one Baker of capt: Grants company. and with major [Nathaniel] Twings — men, and with mr metcalf I pceivd — a bad Smell — and afterwards — was taken with a Gripeing, and and

[sic] followd with a flux — which I believe Savd me — Evening visitd Lt millar and Some Sick and prayd — there — was at mr Greens and drank tea. this day one of capt: Smiths — men, and one Tilton of New Hampshire — dyd — 2 of the man of warr men, and a french child

24 morning citadell — at capt: [John] Heustons — and twice at Capt: [John] Bakers — with a man at capt: [Moses?] pearsons, with Baker above mentiond — at capt: Coltons and at the collonells House — visitd the Admirall, who offerd — me *li*200 New-England old tenor to tary — a year — dind with the Admirall — after dinr visitd collonell [Samuel] pitts and dr delboude and prayd with them — this day one of collonell [Sylvester] Richmonds men, one of collonell [Samuel] pits men one of major Hodges men one of capt: Witherleys men, were burid — and one of the men of warrs men. — in the Evening — I went up to the House — capt: [John] Baker — livd in — and prayd — with the distressd — company —

25 morning citadell, twice at the House Last above mentiond — and with capt [John] Heustons men, major [Moses] Titcomb — capt: [Isaac] Coltons — and with a Sergeant belonging to collonell [Nathaniel] donnell — and then went upon the Ramparts — and met the Admirall, who desird me to walk with him — which I did — and then returnd — home — and went to dine with the Admirall again — afternoon — went and prayd — at the House where capt: Jon [John] Baker livd —. where they are very Sick — attendd — at the funerall of Lt. Collonell [Samuel] pitts — mr Fair-weather — attendd — the citadell prayers —. this day four men, burid at the Grand Battery — Lt. collonell [Samuel] pits — Sergeant Herrick, and one of capt: Chaplins [Joshua Champlin] men and four more, as the Guards at the East Gate told me, but their names — I cant yet learn — but learnt afterwards that one of them — was namd Isaac Cutter — and another was one of capt: [Jonathan] Baglies men —. this day two of capt [David] melvins men, that live between the city and Grand Battery were burid.

26 morning Citadel — after prayers, and Breakfast, I visitd — deacon Shaw — and Severall others that were Sick — and prayd — with them — and then walkd out to Lt. [John] mans company — who is Sick — and Severall others with him; viz: Lt. [Benajah]

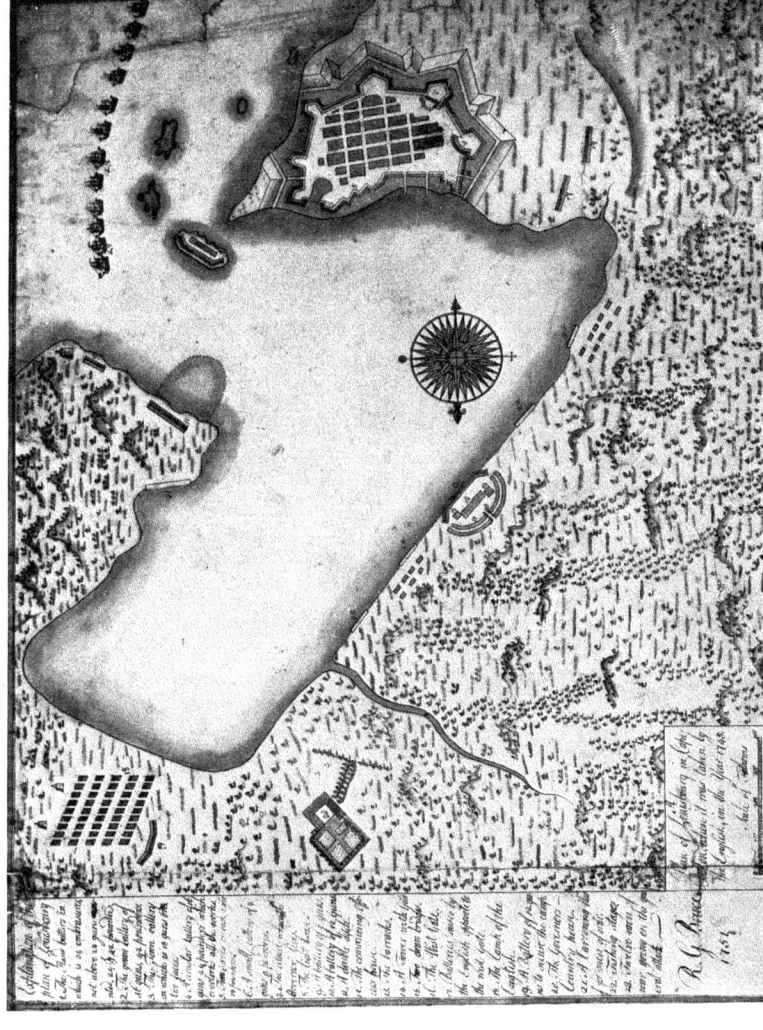

From the Society's Collection.

Austin — Thos Stebbins — and Benjamin Ball son — and John Ashley — (who is delirious) I prayd with them, and took leave of them. dind at Home with mr Fairweather — and then walkd — on the wall with him — and then visitd at the collonells House and prayd twice there — and at capt: [Isaac] Coltons House — the Admirall Sent me a Number of pamphlets — Last night two men dyd — at the Grand — Battery — and — one maxey of the collonells company, and a Negro of capt [Samuel] Rhodes company, and one Blanchard of capt: [Jonathan] Hubbards company, and one mather of capt: Gales company.

27 and Sabbath. morning citadel preachd A. m. at the Hospitall chapple — p. m. at the citadell chapple — Admirall, and Generall present — and a Great Assembly — I took my leave of the Assembly (as Soposing I should — not have another opportunity with them) many seemd affectd — the Lord Grant they — may be benefitd — oh that God would take care of them — and graciously teach His people — . this day dyd — one Sergt Cutler of capt: [John] Heustons — company, and a man of capt: Ephraim Bakers company — and one of capt: [William] Smiths — company of Rhodeisland —

28 morning citadell — and at capt: [Charles] doolittles — and twice at the House where capt: [John] Baker — livd — Ensign [Joshua?] Inslie — dyd — just as I Got to the House — . and with capt: [Isaac] Coltons — company. I dind at the Admiralls and after dinr capt: Spry and mr Wood and mr Fairweather, went aboard, the Viligant, and Chester, was handsomely treatd by the officers — when I came on Shore — I attendd — the funerall of Ens: Inslie — kept at Home in the Evening. this day a Sergt of capt [Samuel] Rhodes company dyd and another man — whose name I dont know

29. morning Citadel and with Sergt Shaw, and company — at major [Nathaniel] Twings — and capt: [Isaac] Coltons — twice at the collonells House — where many are Sick 17 of his company in that House — not well — . when I returnd — Home — I found the collonell himself not well — but I hope tis only from a cold — . the day is foggy — severall Gunns, have been heard of in the offing, which have been answerd — from the island Battery — the collonell — better in the Evening — . I visitd — the Generall, in the Evening — . and collonell [Samuel] More and [William] Williams Suppd — with us — . this day one of the company of Artillery, was burid — and one of capt: [William] Warner of Bostons men, and two more of the Army and one of the men of warrs men. the two Last men of the army I dont know the names but had the acct from the Guard at the East-Gate — . the Collonell had a comfortable night — I desire to bless God — . one or two men dyd — at the Grand Battery — as capt: Noble told me —

Octobr 30. 1745. morning citadel — the collonell better — I visitd a poor Sick — man, at capt: [John] Lights and prayd — with him: waitd — upon the Governor — had a word with him. and visitd — mr Shore — and at one of the Barracks — and prayd. and accidently Wait — into another Barrack — where I found poor mr E— [Ebenezer] Raynolds — very Sick — I discoursd with him — and prayd — with him — I am much concernd for him — returnd home — and heard that Lt Mun [John Man] was poorly of it — had a strong invitation from the Admirall to dine with — him — I went — there was the Governour — and we had a Splendid Entertainment indeed — it is the kings Birthday — the company very modest — and decent — . I took leave Early — and went and visitd — one [Preserved] Smith — at collonell [William] Williams who is very ill — indeed — and prayd — went to capt: [Isaac] Coltons — and prayd with them — after prayer — went into the Barracks — and prayd with Severall Sick men, of capt: [Bartholomew] Trows company — and then visitd — Joseph Cooley and James Wood — and prayd with them — I hope Joseph Cooleys indisposition is only a cold — visitd dr [Gillam] Taylor — who I hope is Better —the Lord, be praisd — for his Good,ness to me — who or what am I, that I Should be preservd — and kept — in health — when others are in destress — . this day two men dyd at the Grand Battery. and an indian of capt: Lawrences company. and a man of capt: [Peter] Hunts company — and one of capt: [Ammi Ruammah] Cutters — men

31 morning Citadel and then — went and Baptizd — a child of one Sanders of Methuen — the child — being not like to live — as was apprehendd — namd john then visitd — Lt Mun — etc. and prayd with them. the Lt — and John Ashley — are Speach-less and I think Senseless — oh Lord God be pleasd to help them — . when

I returnd — to the city, I visitd at the collonells and prayd in two rooms — and then went and prayd with one [Preserved] Smith — at collonell [William] Williams — who I sopose is dying — dind with the Governor — visitd mr [Ebenezer] Raynolds and prayd with him — and with Charly Whiteing — after Evening prayer — visitd — collonell [Simon] Lothrops Kinsman prayd — with him this day John Barry, Roland Flood, John Clark, John Lite, William Crow, Joseph Nible, and a Sergt of collonell [Joseph] dwights company — and John Moses — were burid, and one of the men of warrs men. and a french man —

Nov: 1. morning citadel and after prayers visitd — Charles Colton in one of the rooms in the Hospitall, who is amiss — and visitd at capt: [Isaac] Coltons and prayd with them — J peas is taken anew there. visitd and prayd with mr metcalf visitd — dr pearse [Joseph Pierce] — . visitd at major [Nathaniel] Twings. and prayd — old mr puffer of Wrentham is dead in that house; visitd at the colonells — House — and prayd — in two Rooms — Sergt Wait, and one Kimberly are very bad. visitd at Collonell [William] Williams and prayd — with [Preserved] Smith who is yet alive — dind at Home — . afternoon visitd and prayd — at capt: [Charles] doolittles — and — in both rooms in the House, where capt: [John] Baker livd — with Joseph Cooley, and with mr [Ebenezer] Raynolds — and with mr osborn — . visitd — in the Evening at dr [Gillam] Taylors — Lt [Samuel?] Morgan of cape Ann dyd — and a Lieuetnant of capt: [John] Lights company, and another of N— Hampshire men, one durham, and mr Thos Sewall, of collonell [John] Storers company, one of Lt. [William] Throops men, and one of capt: [Adonijah] Fitchs men and 2 at Grand Battery and one of Capt: [James?] Frys men — and one of capt: [Samuel] Rhodes men

Nov: 2 morning citadel and then in 3 Barracks — visitd dr [Gillam] Taylor and prayd with him — and got some physick for Lt — Jones — visitd and prayd — with him and those of his company — . visitd dr morrison, who is better — saw Charles Colton. Collonell [William] Williams dind with us — as did — mr comissary [William] Rogers — mr F [Fairweather?] — visitd — me — seemd to me to desire to preach at the citadell — but I thot twas best for me to preach there — I — would pswade him, to preach at the Batteries, or at the Hospitall chapple — oh the pride of our Hearts — Last night mr Ebenezer Raynolds dyd in one of the Barracks — and this morning — Lt John mun [Man], dyd at one of the Houses out of the city — and preservd [Preserved] Smith — one of coll [William] Williams company dyd last night and one at the Grand Battery — and Sergt Hoit of capt: [Thomas] Chenys company chas Allens — and the capt: of the Guard told me there two more, but d— not tell their names —

3 morning citadel — a. m. preachd — at Hospitall chapple. p. m. preachd at citadell chapple — was So Late that we had no Bell for Evening prayers — but went to See a young man, in capt: [Edward] Williams company of New Hampshire — who appears near his End — I prayd with him — tis a very cold blustering day — this dyd one Abbot of capt: [Ebenezer] Eastmans company and Joseph Jonis, belonging to collonell [John] Broadstreet, and phineas page of capt: [Robert] dinnisons company, and Isaac Fox of major [Nathaniel] Twings company. were burid

4 morning citadel and went and prayd with mr Haywood — (who kept the Tavern at Brookfield) who I think is dying and with capt: [Jeremiah] Weston — who lyes in the same room — who appears bad — and with joseph Cooley — and at capt: [Ebenezer] Eastmans-house — where one man is in a very destressd case — all the rest — comfutably of it — Collonell [Jeremiah] moulton told me one of his neighbours was dead (his name was Thos Barry) — and I heard that John Ashley of Springfield — was dead — I visitd at the collonells house and prayd in two rooms — and at capt: [Isaac] Coltons — and at capt: [Thomas] Chenys — dind — with — the Governour — and visitd — the Gennerall who is not well — in the Evening — was hurt — by Collonell [William] Williams — discourse — with Collonell [John] Choate — I dislike the conduct, of my Kinsman — this day one Sergt Rhodes of collonell [Sylvester] Richmonds regiment — and one William [Worth? March?] of the same Regiment — and one Nathaniell Brays were burid —

5 morning citadell — walkd abroad — and saw mr Wood, and took my leave of him — then waitd — upon the Admirall — who treatd — me with Great — respect — I took my leave of him — yet — said — I might again wait — upon him — dind with collonell [John] Broadstreet — visitd capt: [John] Heuston — who is very ill — the Admiralls Sloop returnd from N-Found-Land — Brings — nothing — very remarkable — the Burialls this day were of William Conant, of [Shubael] Gorhams regiment and Nehemiah Coolidge, of [Joseph] dwights regiment — Benjamin Hodges of [Sylvester] Richmonds. Thos Stark ditto Ebenezer — Hodge of [Jeremiah] Molton, and one of the men of warrs men and mr Haywood of Brookfield —

Nov: 6. 1745. morning citadel after prayer — visitd and prayd — with — capt: [John] Heuston — who is yet very ill — and with Joseph Cooley — and hope they are all better — and with daniel Fuller, and others in the Hospital; — and with C. [Charles] Colton, who is not well — capt: [Edward] Tyng and mr Fair-weather dind with us — after dinr I went and visitd — in the Hospitall — took — some acct of the people, as to their State — tendance — discoursd with the Generall — about affairs of the Sick — Spent the Evening at collonell [William] Williams — Burialls — 2, at the Grand Battery, one of capt: [William] Smiths of Rhodeisland in the forenoon —. one of those at Grand Battery was capt: [Abraham] Edwards one of capt: Momford [Richard Mumford] company — the names were Morgan murphy and Thos Jeffs — and philip pratt of capt: Bakers a free Negro of capt: [John] Heustons company dyd this day

7. morning citadel and at the collonels House — capt: [Isaac] Coltons — capt: [Thomas] Chenys, and with mr [Holeys?] of providence, and with dr [Gillam] Taylor — visitd dr [Joseph] pierce — Jothull Mose of capt: cheneys — company and one Rollins of the collonells company — and 6 others — were burid — one of them was an Hartford man whose name was Charties — he came with the Rhodeisland man — and one Haywood of Brookfield — and another — was capt: Ephraim Bakers man — Supd with Collonell [William] Williams

8. morning citadel and heard that capt [Bray] deering of the Generalls regiment was dead and one of collonell [Jeremiah] — Moultons — men, and one John Staples of capt: [Ebenezer] Eastmans company —. this day Benjamin Ball of Springfield — dyd — I got dr Whitworth — to go and see the men, at capt: [Isaac] Coltons house — he speaks comfortably of them all — . visitd — the Generall — in Evening — receivd Some letters from Home — visitd some Sick people in the Barracks, where mr [OSenr?] lives

9. morning citadell — walkd — the walls — . visitd — capt: [John] Heuston, who was asleep — visitd — Charles Colton — visitd — Joseph Cooley — I hope they are Better — but israel Warner — is New — taken — I prayd — with them — visitd the House — where deacon Shaw — lies Sick — and prayd — with them. Some in that House are very Low — an indian of collonell [Sylvester] Richmonds company dyd — . I went this afternoon to monsieur — Costeens and Bought — some cuffs in the Evening I was calld to See mr Commissary [William] Rogers — who is in Great destress and trouble of mind — the Lord — Grant it may issue well — one of the man of warrs men was burid —

10 and Sabbath. morning citadel mr Fairweather — preachd for me, both in the forenoon and afternoon — . I preachd — an Evening Lecture — to a great Auditory — the Lord Grant Good — may be done thereby — . I dind at the Admiralls — . I went to See — Hancock (at capt: [Isaac] Coltons house) who is much Amiss — is relapsd — this day were burid — one Ebenezer Stevens. and Amos Hovey both of Collonell [Jeremiah] Moltons company, and one mudget, of capt: [John] Lights company of New-Hampshire; and one Slate an indian of collonell [John] Broadstreets company — and a Lt ——— of capt. [Benjamin or Joseph] Goldthwaits company.

11 morning citadel at the collonells House — at capt: [Isaac] Coltons, with old mr Goodhue, in the forenoon—afternoon at the House where capt: [John] Baker dwelt and with capt: [John] Heuston, and with ISrael warner — and with one Caule of capt: [Jonathan] Hubbards company this day were burid capt: Jeremiah Weston, of collonell [Sylvester] Richmonds company, and Samuell durton of collonell [Jeremiah] Moltons regiment. William Ripley of Brigadier [Joseph] dwights regiment. Thomas Robins, of Brigadier [Samuel] Waldos — and Roger Mather belonging to a transport of New-Hampshire. and a Lad belonging to the Ships —

12 morning Citadel — visitd — collonell [William] Williams company — capt: [Isaac] Coltons, and capt: [Thomas] chenys and visitd — capt: [Daniel] mac-gregory, who is very Sick — . dind at

Home — had collonell [Samuel] Moor collonell [William] Williams and mr m — . — at dinr — after dinr —visitd— the Revd — mr — Wood — who gave me a fine pair of Stockings — this day were burid — Nathaniell magiston, and Joseph dodge — of capt: William: Smiths — company and of the Generalls regiment — and Joseph Squire of collonell [Samuel] Willards — regiment

13 morning citadel — visitd — capt: [Isaac] Coltons — men — and capt: [Thomas] Chenys — and capt: [Adonijah] Fitchs men in Evening, — and prayd — with them. dind with the Generall in the Evening — was calld to see capt: mac-gregory — who is Soposd to be dyeing. I visitd. allso — the poor men in the Barracks — where mr [Ebenezer] Raynolds — Lay — who are in a destressd case, and complain they are neglectd — and I fear tis the case. this day were Burid Capt: [Robert] Glovers negro, peter, and Newport Cofew a free Negro, of capt: Mountfords [Richard Mumford] company. and one Thos: Groton of capt: [Jeremiah] Fosters company and Francis deal, and Amos Goodsal, these two of capt: [James?] Frys company and one John procter of capt: Kings company, and one daniel Call.

14. morning Citadel. visitd — at capt: [Charles] doolittles he is Sick and severall of the men, visitd — at the House where capt: Baker lived — and at the collonell House — went in to see dr [Gillam] Taylor — who is I hope, upon the Recruit — then, I went into the Hospitall, and prayd with them and I found six men dead there. two of the men of warrs men, and the other four were. one Kelly of capt: [Jonathan] prescots — company, one Coreh of Rhodeisland one of capt: J [John] Warners — men, or capt: [Oliver?] Howards — and one of collonell [Sylvester] Richmonds men, his name I could not learn this morning were burid — Thos parry clark of capt: [Thomas] Chenys company, and one Nathaniell Richmond. Last night capt: [Daniel] mac, gregory abovd mentiond dyd, as did one Little of major [Moses] Titcombs company — and one of collonell [Sylvester] Richmonds men, namd Robert Browning. afternoon — visitd — dr Morrison, and at the House where Joseph Cooley — lives, and found Severall of them much amiss. as I went from there, I met two men, carying to the Grave that belongd — to capt: [William] Smith of Rhodeisland — the name of one, was — Grondy, and the other

Joseph Mason. and William Martin of Brigadier [Joseph] dwights regiment. and Gideon Sanders of Brig: [Samuel] Waldos and Bildad Moses, of capt: [Adonijah] Fitchs company.

15 morning citadel — one of capt: [Jonathan] Careys men was Burid visitd — at — capt: [Charles] doolittles — capt: [Thomas] Chenys — capt: [Isaac] Coltons —. dind — with collonell [Samuel] More —. visitd — the Generall, who is not very well —. this day were burid — one matthew Slarrow of collonell [Samuel] Willards regiment and capt: [Jonathan] Hubbards company. one jeremiah Hall, of capt: [Samuel] Rhodes company, and collonell [Jeremiah] Moltons regiment, and one of capt [Jonathan] prescots — men of the same regiment. his name I could not learn and one John mackdonell of capt: [William] Smiths company of Rhode-island

16 of Nov: morning Citadel — after prayers, and Breakfast. visitd — at capt [Charles] doolittles and prayd — I hope — he is better, at capt: [John] Heustons, who is still Low, and visitd capt: [James] pierpont — who I hope is like to do well — and visitd — the House where joseph Cooley — they are very ill — and I fear — how it will go — with some of them —. as Joseph Cooley, and israel Warner pticular Joseph Sexton (who has Nursd them —) is not well — oh that God would arouse and help us —. a Sloop appears in Sight — but could not get in — the Generall is not well —, John durham dyd this day, he was of capt: [Thomas] doties company — this day one Richard Thomas — of the collonells company dyd. as did one Enos that came from Windsor Since the Siege dyd. and Joshua prat, and John Reed of capt: marshalls company and Benjamin Stanton and John Coreah of capt: [Richard] Mumford company N. B. capt: [Andrew] Watkins told me 3 psons were buryd at the Grand Battery this week

Nov: 17 and Sabbath. morning Citadel and preachd in the forenoon at the Hospitall chapple — dind with the Admirall — preachd in the afternoon at the citadell — visitd — the Generall — who I hope is better — this day the Sloop — above — mentiond got near the island Battery and Anchord — the men of warrs — boats went to them; they came from New-England — Eighteen days passage — but I dont hear any news — this day one of capt: Mountfords [Richard Mumford] men was burid — namd Stephen Trays and

NINTH JOURNAL 165

one Joseph: goodhue of ipswich dyd — and one John Brown of the Generalls regiment — and one Robert Reed of capt: Kirslough [John Kinselagh] men and George Horan of capt: Champion [Joshua Champlin] of Rhodeisland and one obadiah Boin of capt: [George?] Moreys company — N. B. that some time Last week, one of the men of warrs men — in drink — went upon the ramparts, and being askd by the centinell (who was a youth) where he was Going, he replyd to Hell — and went upon the wall — near the South Gate, and fell of into the ditch — broke his Back — and has Lost the use of all his Limbs — and one Joseph Wait of ipswich — being upon the Guard, and in drink, fell of the wall — at the Admiralls — (where he was set centinell) and fracturd — his scull (as is Soposd) and hurt one of his Eyes, he is carid to the Hospitall — but is dilirious — in a Sorrowfull case —

Nov: 18 morning citadel and pceivd — dr [William] Rand was come down — and mr [John] Newman, from New-England — and Brot Some news — mr N [John Newman] dind with us the collonell had Some discourse with him — I went aboard — capt: [Edward] Tyng, to See mr Fair-weather — who is not very well but I apprehend is better. the Generall is better, than, he was, yesterday — I rejoyce. I was deeply affectd with the case of israel warner, Joseph: Cooley — whom I visitd — Last night — who are in want, of Every thing — bed, physick — oh that God would help them — . this morning, John Sassiman, an indian of capt: [Seth] Hathaways company — was found dead, in the street, he went out tis thot in a distraction — haveing been ill — an awfull providence. this day were burid jacob cummins of capt: [Thomas] Chenys company, and one Hall of capt: [Daniel] Chap-mans company of Toland

Nov: 19, 1745. morning Citadel — came Home and wrote for the collnell and then visitd capt: [Charles] doolittle — who is very bad — after dinr visitd — Joseph — Cooley — they are very poorly of it —, prayd in two rooms — in that house — prayd — at the citadell — visitd — and prayd with a man in the Barracks — and with mr Greens nurse who is ill — visitd — the Generall — and was at Collnell [William] Williams — but was taken with an ague fit there and more of one in the night — went to bed, took some Herb drink — and Sweat, was restless — What God will be pleasd to do with me I know not, I desire to be Entirely resignd — to the will of God — oh that God would wash — cleanse, and purifie me — this day three men were burid as the Guards send me word but they have not sent their names.

20 I am amiss this morning but yet thro Gods goodness am able to set up — I desire to cast all my cares upon the Lord — this day I hear that mr Spears is come down as a chaplin, with capt: [Elisha] doan. — and mr [John] Newman came a day or two ago — the Lord be pleasd to be with them and make them faithful in the work. this day or Last night dyd one ——— of the Generalls company, and 2 of collnell [Jeremiah] Moltons men and 2 of capt: King, and one of capt: [Peter] Hunts I had a comfortable night — considering my indisposition — restd considerably — Sweat Some — but have nothing of pain considerable —. I am in the Hands of an Holy and merciful Sovereign — and there I desire to be —

21 I feel more comfortably this morning Breakfastd upon Tea and toast — and feel — more lively — but before noon felt more dull and Heavy — at noon Eat a little fresh pork, and Butterd Turnip — dr Whitworth came in, when I was setting down, to dinr — and says he will call again, towards night — the Lord be pleasd to direct him, to what is proper to be done — this day fourty year ago, I arrivd at Boston, from Canada, where I had been a prisoner — thus the Lord has waitd upon me fourty year — but alas, how often howe I have Grievd him, and badly abusd his Goodness — the Lord be pleasd graciously to pardon and accept me, for the Sake of j x [Jesus Christ]; amen. John Stevens in capt: [Jonathan] Baglies company, and collonell [Robert] Hales regiment — and Michael Bently of capt: marshalls company, in collonell [Jeremiah] Moltons Regment were burid the doctor visitd me in the Evening, and told me the Symptoms were Such with me, that he thot a vomitt — was necessary — I took a vomitt, it workd — well — I went to bed, and Sweat a great deal, voidd much urine — the colonell Went and Lodgd with collonell [William] Williams, and Woodberry, Lay in the room — I have no distressing racking pain — but very Heavey oh Lord — I am thine, save me I beseech thee with Everlasting Salvation — this is my desire.

22 this morning — I feel free from pain — the collonell came Home and prayd with us before I got up, after I got up — I felt

NINTH JOURNAL 167

dull — and Lay down again — but was able to drink some Fresh Broth brot from the Admiralls — the dr thinks my pulse is more calm —

Nov: 22. Last dyd two of capt: [Seth] Hathaways men viz oliver Gwinsey and Jacob Allen. and one Symonds of capt: [Thomas] Chenys company and two out of the Hospitall, and [Joseph] wait above mentiond that fell from the Admiralls wall dyd — as did israel warner of Springfield: the acct of the men — of warrs men is wrong. the two men were daniell Fuller, and James Hirstock of capt: [Edward] Coles company of Rhodesisland and one Robert Anable of capt: [Charles] Kings company and joseph Cowell of major [Plats?] company and Nicholas Street of capt: [Cornelius] Soles company and matthew Way of capt: Ephraim: Bakers company. in the Evening — I feel more comfortably — the dr thinks — I need hot blister — if it be Gods pleasure to allow to return to my own house — I hope he will Enable me to show what Great things he has done for me — I had comfortable night tho somewhat restless — and was concernd — because: the collonell lay by The fire upon my acct —

23 very calm pleasent morning I got — up — I hope, I am not worse I desire to leave my Self with the Lord — the Admirall has Sent to Enquire of my welfare — and direct me Send to him for any thing I want — I bless God, that raises me up friends — all favours come from him — I desire to look to the Lord — but would thankfully — acknowledge the Kindness of God toward night I am more dull and Heavy — what God will please to do I know not — I desire to baire my Self with him: this day capt: [Charles] doolittle was burid — and one Webb of capt: [Thomas] Chenys men and one of major [Nathaniel] Twings company his name was Walter Hicks — and one Commins of capt [Thomas] Chenys company. and James Withevin of capt: [Sylvanus] Cobbs company and philip Tracy under capt: [Joseph] Faibanks.

24 Sabbath had something of a restless night — but comfortably of it I have this day been kept from the publick wor Ship — Lord affect me with thy dealing this day were burid James Sanson, of capt: [Edward] Coles company, Generalls R[egiment] Ebenezer Wait of capt: [Thomas] doties company. Brigadier [Joseph] dwights R[egiment] Hunphry pain, in capt: pains company John

Bacchus belonging to mr Bastied [John Henry Bastide] — an ingineer William Thornton of Collonell [Richard] Gridleys company an Enginer John Nichols under capt: [James?] Fry, in collonell [Jeremiah] Moltons Regiment.

25 Some thing restless night but I hope am really better this morning — some better in Generall — this day were Burid

mens names	capts	Regiment
Richard Root	[Charles] King	Coll [Jeremiah] Molton
peter Brown	Gold	Col [William] Williams
Jonathan Bowman	[Caleb] Johnson	[Joseph] dwight

Lt [William] Reddington in the independaint company — capt: [Daniel] Hill — restless in Evening and had a more restless night — my Sleep, was not sweet — but full of dreams —

26 I feel Sore and Heavy — but the doctors in Sist upon it that they my fever — does not increase. but all tho phySicians may be of value — and I would apply to them — yet to the Great Jehovah, would I apply and depend upon him alone — the covenant of the Great Jehovah is orderd in all things — and this I would have be all my Expection and desire —

27 went aboard the Massachusetts Frigate — was carid — in a chair — coverd — but was so ill on the voyage that I can Give little or no acct of any thing that passd on the whole voyage — my Fever increasd — till about three days — before we got to Boston, when the dr soposd it Broke — we arrivd at castle William decembr 8 being Sabbath — on monday the Governor went aShore — but the wind and weather, were Such that I was not brot aShore till Wednesday, when I was putt into a cradle and coverd-over, and brot to the House of my most kind Generous, and obligeing Friend: A Walley Esq — my circumstances dificcult, on Some accts — but I am taken care of in the most tender manr — and thro Gods Goodness — Gain strength

[Matter omitted by editor.]

9 [*January 1745/6*] some head ach, in the morning — but after I got up, was comfortably of it — prayd with the family — but breakfastd — in the chamber — stormy day of Snow and rain,

NINTH JOURNAL

which prevents my going abroad — had a comfortable day —. N.B. this day it was reported that mr B— that went to France, in the flag of Truce — had — all his papers Seizd —

10 this day I hear that mr Spear dyd at Louisbourg, and the captains marshall and [Ammi Ruammah] Cutter — oh the Sovereignty — oh that distinguishing Goodness of God I rode out in the afternoon — as far as the White Horse — towards night — I was visitd by mr Secretary — and in the Evening by Collonell [John] Stoddard, capt: partridge, and my Brother Elijah — my Nurse left me this Evening — but all the family Seem ready to minister to me — I slept well

[Matter omitted by editor.]

14 [*January, 1745/6*] was this morning visitd by mr Nabby — and capt: Bernard — I went over to Roxbury — had a pleasant — ride — got no cold — Evening — capt: p— came hither — and brot me acct — that the Generall Court — had Grantd me 28 *li* Lawfull money — for my Extraordinary Service — at Louisburg — the Lord be pleasd — to make me thankfull and fruitfull — I had a comfortable night

15 this morning Collonell [John] Choat came hither, and Brot a letter from collonel [William] Williams — at Louisburg — that Gave acct of the Sickness, and that they had burid — 20 in one day — Since we came from thence — oh that God would be pleasd — to help — and pity and spare, and Sanctifie his Hand — this day I walkd — abroad and made a visitt or two — but the afternoon — was sloppy — and I kept house. I receivd — some letters from Home, I bless God that my Family are So comfortably of it — Lord pity and bless the Flock — that I pceive are Sick and weak —

16 — comfortable in the morning forenoon — waitd upon the Governour — who receivd — me, very kindly — then went to the committee of warr — who paid me, my wages — the Lord Grant, I may aright, improve my daily Good things. this day my Brother came from Waltham — to carry me thither in his chaise — but the weather is Heavy — dear collonell C [Choate] — dind with us — when he took leave of me, he Sent a present to Some of my family —

[The journal continues with matter unrelated to Louisbourg]

TENTH JOURNAL

Colonel John Bradstreet

This manuscript is not properly a journal but it is a valuable and hitherto unpublished account of the siege by a leading participant. The original, supposedly in Bradstreet's hand, is in the possession of the New York Historical Society which has kindly permitted its use here. Francis Parkman noted in the Public Record Office in London a letter from Bradstreet, written in 1753, without address, (as is the following letter), in which that officer declared that he not only planned the siege but "was the Principal Person in conducting it." The two manuscripts are probably not the same.

John Bradstreet was a brilliant officer with a notable career, too long to be more than noted here. He was a man of unlimited self-confidence and of great ambitions as the letter here given tends to show. As he was not born until about the year 1711 he was quite youthful at the time of the 1745 expedition but he enjoyed the confidence of Shirley, Pepperrell and Warren. His letter does not fail to note all the details of his service that were to his advantage but a few other events may profitably be considered.

Bradstreet entered the British Army in 1735 in the usual way for a young man of good standing by buying an ensign's commission. This commission was in a foot regiment commanded by Lieutenant General Richard Philips, the absentee Governor of Nova Scotia. Bradstreet visited Louisbourg in 1736 and in 1738 and, after his capture by du Vivier in 1744, was a prisoner in Louisbourg fortress until exchanged at Boston. His knowledge of the city and of the French, his training as a British officer, and his experience in Nova Scotia with irregular troops, all made him valuable on the expedition of 1745. He claimed, as he states below, that he was promised the supreme command by Shirley. His actual commission, dated in February, 1744, was as Second Colonel and Captain of the Second Company in the First Massachusetts Regi-

TENTH JOURNAL 171

ment, of which Pepperrell was Colonel. When the town capitulated, Bradstreet commanded the first troops to enter and he was made the Town Major Commandant considerably to the indignation of the French, who claimed he had broken his parole. Bradstreet was never popular in the Provincial Army. On May 11, 1745, Commodore Warren wrote to Pepperrell, "For God's sake, Sir, put a stop to that disagreeable and ill-grounded suspicion that some unthinking people have pretended (for I can think it no other) to conceive of Collonel Bradstreet." That same day Pepperrell called the Council of War together solely to consider the reports that Bradstreet was disloyal to the expedition and the meeting ended with an apology made to Bradstreet by Lieutenant Colonel Thomas Chandler. Shirley, writing to Pepperrell on May 22d, refers to the "villainous surmizes" concerning Bradstreet.

After the siege Bradstreet was rewarded by England with a commission as fifth captain and adjutant of Pepperrell's new regiment, although he had been urgently proposed as lieutenant colonel. His subsequent military career was distinguished and he reached the rank of major general in 1772. He died at his home in New York City on September 25, 1774.

THE JOURNAL

Sir

Agreeable to your desire I send you the following brief account how far I was concern'd in the Reduction of Louisbourg. Viz.

That I was an Officer in the late Lieut. General Philipps's Regiment, taken by the French at Canso in June 1744, and carry'd to Louisbourg, where I had an opportunity of informing my self of the State and Condition of the Said Place, and of Laying a Plan for the attacking thereof; which I communicated to Governor Shirley at Boston in December following, and was by him referr'd to a Committee of the Council and Assembly of that Province, who greatly approv'd of my Information and Plan; and upon which the Expedition was undertaken, and the Command agree'd upon with Mr. Shirley to be given to me, but he finding it would be difficult to raise a Sufficient Number of Men Unless under the Command of one of their own Country Men, appointed Sir William Pepperrell;

upon which I declin'd going, or having any thing further to say in the Affair; till it was agree'd Sir William Pepperrell should be advis'd by Me, well knowing how impossible it was to Succeed under the Conduct of People totally Ignorent of the least Military Branch necessary in such an undertaking, notwithstanding the disadvantage the French were under. That the True Motives which Induced me to hope the Said place might be taken by the people of his Majesty's Colonies only was as follows; (tho I must acknowlidge I did represent the Strength of the place and every other circumstance relating thereto in a worse condition then they realy were, by reason I found the people in General were greatly against undertaking any Expeditions, from the bad Success they always had in them which conduct I thought Iustifiable in me, as so favourable an Opportunity for attacking that Place could never be Expected, Viz, That from the necessity the ffrench Governor was under of Supplying Six East India Ships which put into Louisbourg in August 1744, with provisions and Ammunition; and Sail'd for France in October following, the Garrison and Jnhabitants would be under the greatest distress for want of provisions, if not Supplyd by the latter end of May next; and that the quantity of powder remaining in their Magazine was very inconsiderable for a Fortified Town of that kind.

That their Establishment of Troops was but Six Companys of Marines of Seventy Men each, with one of Swiss of one hundred Men; all Short of Compliment, and badly disciplined, the whole greatly discontented, and that the Company of Swiss had Mutined; — The Governor Old and infirm, and intirely unacquainted with the Difence of a Fortification; — The Engineer absent, and the other Officers in General Jgnorent of Military disciplin; and few of the Inhabitants well acquainted with the use of Fire Armes. —

The Fortifications round the Town of large Extent, greatly out of repair, and Lyable to be Attack'd at Several different places with Advantage; and from its Situation every part thereof could be Enfiladed — The Grand — Battery on the North Side of the Harbour in such a Situation from som works not being finish'd, — together with its being over look'd by a high Hill clost to it, that they must be under the necessity of deserting it immediately on the approach of an Enemy by Land, to avoid being taken — And their

THE LOUISBOURG FLAG
(*From the copy owned by the Society*)

TENTH JOURNAL

Jsland Battery at the Entrence of the Harbour laid them under the disadvantage of taking one whole Company to defend it.

That by the possession of the Said Grand Battery, together with Fascine Batteries which might be Erected near the Light House and other convenient places, it would be difficult, if not impracticable, for any ships to Enter the Harbour, but if any should be so hardy as to attempt getting in and Succeed with provisions and Ammunition (which was much to be doubted when Seeing the British Flag flying at the Grand Battery and several other places) it would be impossible for the people of the Town to aVail themselves of it, as no Boats could pass and repass from the Shore to the Ship, admitting her to be run a Ground; and that if we Sail'd in March we Should certainly be there before any French Ships would be on the Coast; But abstracted from that, such Privateers as could be Collected in the Colonies (if they did their Duty) would be Sufficient to Jntercept the Merchant Ships expected from ffrance and Canada with provisions in April and May.

That there was two exceeding good Coves in Gabarouse Bay, but Two Miles from the Town, to Land the Troops, Cannon and Baggage, and that the upper part of The Said Bay was a good Harbour, where the Transports could remain safe; and by which we were always Secure of a Retreat in Case of Necessity. — That Canso was a proper place to Rendevous, as we could from thence take the Advantage of the first North West Winds Driving the Ice from the Louisbourg Shore, and being but Twenty Leagues distant from thence, there could be no Doubt if we manag'd properly, we Should all arrive at the above Coves together, which was a Meterial circumstance.

That we need be under no apprehension from its being known in France, that the People of New England intended an Expedition against Louisbourg, as the French King and his Ministers have a great Opinion of the Strength of that Place, and will certainly dispise such an Attempt, as they have not forgot Sir William Phips's Expedition from Boston in 1691, against Quebeck, where they no Soonner Landed their Cannon and Baggage, but Stole off in the Night to their respective Ships, leaving the whole behind them, tho the place was in a defenceless Situation; Together with their Expedition against the ffort of Annapolis Royal, in which they

Acted much the same part — But for our further Security we might rest Assur'd, the Moment our Royal Master was inform'd that an Expedition was on Foot, and that we should Actually sail in March with about 4000 Men with every thing necessary for such an undertaking, orders would be Jssued for a proper Number of Ships of War to follow Us, which was the Case, for upon the first Notice thereof, an Express was sent from England to Sir Peter Warren at Antigua, ordering him forthwith to Ioin us with all the Ships he could; which he did at Canso with one 60 and three 40 Gun Ships; and Several others were likewise ordered from England to Ioin him off Louisbourg, who accordingly did in very good time.

And in Iustice to the Captains I must Say, they all kept their Stations as well as if it had been in one of the best Climates and Navigations in the world; which did require great Iudgment and Indifatigableness, in as much as they were Jntire Strangers to the Coast, and had for the greatest part of the time they crus'd of the Harbour Excessive thick Fogs, Strong and unconstant Currents, and some Gales of Wind.

As a full and exact account of the Siege and every other thing Relative thereto would be excessive long, and put You out of all manner of Patience; I shall therefore beg leave only to Set forth a few of the principal facts, namely,

That 4017 Effective Men Saild from the Different parts of New England about the Midle of March, and Ioin'd at Canso the first of April, where we were detain'd till the last of the Month before the Ice Separated from the Louisbourg Shore, when we Saild in the Morning of the 31st. and by Eight next morning Landed above half our Men with Little or no opposition; and as so much depended on having possession of the Grand Battery directly on Landing, I was to have Attack'd it with 500 Chosen Men the Night following, but the French thought proper to save me that Trouble, by deserting it, and contented themselves only with Nailing the Cannon: But as I did expect that would be the Case, care was taken before we left New England to have proper Workmen and Tools for Drilling them out; which was soon Effected: And I further advis'd a Number of 42 pound Shott to be Cast before we Saild for More Cannon, which was accordingly done, and was of great use, as they not only Served for Battering in Breach, but also on Several other Occasions.

That with as much dispatch as could be expected, all the Troops, Cannon, and Baggage were Landed and properly Jncamp'd, and the Town as Closely Invested, as could be expected from our Numbers, and considering the unavoidable difficulty which arose from the Little or no Subordination Subsisting between the Officers and Common Soldiers; and the necessity of immediately Erecting four Batteries of Cannon besides Mortars. — With one of these we Enfiladed that part of the Town which was not expos'd to the Shot of the Grand Battery — With a Second we Beat down the Mertons and parapet Wall of the North West end of a Circular Battery to the Sea of 16 Twenty Seven pounders, and by that means we had the whole Platform open, part of which Guns we dismounted and oblig'd the French to withdraw the rest — With a third, which was within two hundred Yards of the West Gate Bastion, we not only distroy'd part of the Said Bastion, and made a practicable Breach therein, but likewise dismounted all the Guns on the North West flank of the Citadel; and from its Situation one of their principal Sea Batteries of 15 Forty Two Pounders were so expos'd to the fire of Eight pieces of Cannon, that it could be of no use to them whatsoever — The forth was at the Light-house, and properly Situated in Case any Ships might attempt coming into the Harbour; and with which we could always bring between 40, and 50 Guns to bear against such as were fairly enter'd.

There was one addition only to my Plan, to which I did object before we Saild from New England, and us'd all the means in my power to desswade them from it; but to no purpose, they were determin'd to attack the Jsland Battery by night with Boats, and accordingly did, by which 130 Men were made prisoners and 81 kill'd, with no other advantage on our Side, but the wounding one French Officer and Two Soldiers.

That a General attack by Land and Sea had been agree'd upon, so soon as the Distruction of the Circular Battery was Compleat, and the Breach at the West Gate Bastion made, as that Battery was the only one which could Rake the Ships.

That on the 16th. Iune every thing was Compleatly finish'd for a General Attack; and we then only waited the first fair Wind for the Ships to enter the Harbour, and I was to Command the Attack by Land;— But in the after Noon of that Day, the French Governor sent out an Officer to Signify his Intentions of Capitulating, to which we had no objection; and thereupon the fire on both Sides Ceas'd, which had been kept up from about the 7th May to the above mention'd 16th June, in a Constant and Regular manner; and every thing was so Compleatly finish'd the Same Night, that the Ships of War, and all the Transports got into the Harbour next Day, and the Marines enter'd the Town on the Harbour Side, and I march'd in on the Land Side with 800 of our best Men; where we found the Garrison and Jnhabitants in a Distress'd Condition by fatigue and want of Provisions; and no powder left, but what they said the Ruls of War oblig'd them to have when they Capitulated, Viz, Three Rounds for each Great Gun.

That nothwithstanding the Troops in the Town seem'd to do their Duty well, Still the Governor did not think it prudent, from the discontent they had shewn, to Trust any of them on any Service out of the Town; and therefore what few Sallies were made, were by the Jnhabitants, and of Little consequence.

If I had Copys of the Letters Sir William Pepperrell and Sir Peter Warren wrote the Duke of NewCastle immediately on the Surrender of the Place relating to me, You would thereby be better able to Judge of my whole Conduct during the Siege, which Letters are in His Graces Office — But such paragraphes of Letters and other papers as I have now by me relative to my Self, I shall hereunto annex, as they may serve to give You some further Light — And it was in the Intermediate time of Sir William Pepperrells being appointed to the Command, and its being agree'd he Should be advis'd by me, that the following Vote was past and sent me, Viz:

"At a Council held at the Council Chamber in Boston upon "Thursday the 14 of March 1744.

"Whereas the Council apprehend it of great, Importance to the "Success of the Expedition against Cape Breton that Mr. John "Bradstreet should proceed with the Forces, and that this was the "Expectation of the Government when they — undertook this Af- "fair; and Whereas the Board are inform'd that the Said Mr.

"Bradstreet declines this Service. — Unanimously Voted that his "Excellency. be desir'd to offer him all Suitable Encouragement for "his engaging therein.
"Copy examined   J Willard Secretary."

An Abstract of a Letter from Governor Shirley to me —

"Boston June 22d. 1745
"The Accounts which the General and the Commodore have "given of Your Servicableness upon the Expedition are answerable "to my Expectation from You, and do You much honour — I Think "we have now a fine prospect of Success, and You may depend upon "my representation of Your Services in so advantageous a light to "The Ministry, as I hope will not fail of procuring a just recom-"pence of them by his Majestys favour"
Wm. Shirley.

Abstract of a Letter from Govr. Shirley to his Grace the Duke of New Castle — "Louisbourg 1745 — Mr. Bradstreet late an Officer "in General Philipps's Regiment; to whose Jntelligence and advice "it is very much owing that I set The Expedition on ffoot, has so "recommended — himself by his Extraordinary Activity and good "Conduct in his Majestys Service during the Siege to Sir William "and mySelf that we are both Exceeding desirous to have his good "Services Rewarded with his being Sir Williams Lieut. Colonel in "the Regiment design'd to be Establish'd, for which purpose I take "the Liberty also to mention him to your Grace; he has likewise been "very Servisable here in the Post of Town Major Commandant, and "has in every thing Exerted himself for his Majestys Service."
William Shirley.

Now, Sir, in answer to the last part of Your desire; and that it may no longer be a Mystery to you that I was taken out of an Old Regiment and put into a New one which was soon reduced, and from which I have nothing left but the same Rank in the Army, I should have had, if I remain'd where I was; and why I was not by his Majestys favour appointed Lieut. Colonel to the Regiment of which Sir William Pepperrell obtain'd the Command (in consideration of this Service to my Country) especially when it had been so fully represented by Sir William Pepperrell, Sir Peter Warren and Governor Shirley — I am to acquaint You, that it was thought absolutely necessary for his Majestys Service, that I should remain at Louisbourg after its Reduction, to Assist in putting it into a posture of Diffence, and to carry on some other Services, which prevented my coming to England to Sollicet for his Majestys favour in the Said appointment of Lt. Colonel, to which I attribute my being forgot, and only appointed fifth Captain and Adjutant in Said Regiment — Tis true some time after, when Mr. Fox (to whome I shall ever think my self under the greatest obligation) was inform'd of my Services, did move the King for my being appointed Lieut. Governor of St. John's in Newfoundland, which his Majesty was Graciously pleas'd to grant — But as the pay is but Ten Shillings per Day, it has Cost me very handsomly out of my private fortune every Year to kep up that Character; as a proper appearence is necessary for the Kings honour, and good of the Service, in the Colonies in particular. But I assure You the Money Matter is not what gives me the greatest concern; my Trouble is for the loss of Rank, which I flatter'd myself my Services had Intitled me to, and in as much as I am Sensible what a Stumbling Block it will be in my way in the Colonies in case of a French War, where I have the Vanity to think I could be usefull. — The Commissions I had for this Expedition and other Services, were two of Colonel, and one of Town Major Commandant of the Town and Fortifications of Louisbourg for either of which I never received more then one Months Pay as Colonel.

APPENDICES

APPENDIX I

THE FLEET

Comparatively little attention has been paid to the subject of the use of naval forces in the Colonial wars. The editor for some time has collected notes bearing on the vessels in service during the course of the Louisbourg expedition of 1745. He was anticipated in publication by Howard M. Chapin, Librarian of the Rhode Island Historical Society, who in 1923 issued a valuable study with the title *New England Vessels in the Expedition against Louisbourg, 1745*. Despite the appearance of that article the editor presents his own notes which differ in some details as well as in arrangement from Mr. Chapin's. He acknowledges indebtedness to Mr. Chapin for several important items, and for confirmation of some of his own tentative conclusions.

BRITISH SHIPS OF THE LINE

	Men	*Guns*	*Commander*
Superbe	415	60	Flagship of Commodore Peter Warren / Captain Richard Tiddeman [1]
Eltham	250	40	Captain Philip Durell [1]
Mermaid	250	40	Captain James Douglas succeeded by Captain W. Montague
Launceston	250	40	Captain J. Calmady
Princess Mary	450	60	Capt. Richard Edwards
Sunderland	450	60	Capt. ——— Britt
Canterbury	450	60	Capt. John Hore (Hoar)
Chester	350	50	Capt. ——— Kemp / Capt. ——— Geary
Hector	300	40	Capt. Frederick Cornwall
Lark		40	

[1] At some date before June 20, 1745, Captains Tiddeman and Durell exchanged commands.

French Prizes Used as Men-of-War

	Men	Guns	Commander
Bien Aimé	140	30	Capt. Clark Gayton
Vigilant	450	64	Capt. James Douglas (see the *Mermaid*)

Provincial Vessels (Armed)

	Men	Guns	Commander
Shirley	150	24	Capt. John Rouse (Acting Commodore)
Massachusetts (frigate)	150	24 (or 20)	Capt. Edward Tyng (Senior Provincial Naval Officer)
Molineux	150	20	Capt. Jonathan Snelling
Prince of Orange	80	14	Capt. Joseph Smithers (or Smithurst)
Caesar	70	14	Capt. John Griffith
Fame	150	20	Capt. Thomas Thompson
Boston Packet	90	16 (or 12)	Capt. William Fletcher
Tartar	90	14	Capt. Daniel Fones
Resolution (or Resolute)		12	Capt. David Donahew (Killed in action. Succeeded by Capt. Joseph Richardson)
Defence		16	Capt. John Prentice
Abigail		10	Capt. John Fernald (or Furnell)
Bonetta		6	Capt. Moses Bennett (succeeded by Robert Becket or Beckwith)
Massachusetts (sloop)		10 (or 8)	Capt. Thomas Sanders
————		8	———— Swan
Lord Montague		6 (or 8)	———— Bush (or Bosch)

All Massachusetts ships, except the *Defence* (Connecticut), the *Tartar* (Rhode Island), and the *Abigail* (New Hampshire).

The three groups given above are complete but there is much confusion in the following class. There are said to have been nineteen transports.

APPENDIX I

PROVINCIAL VESSELS (TRANSPORTS, SUPPLY SHIPS, CARTELS, DISPATCH BOATS, ETC.)

	Commander
Union	Capt. Elisha Mayhew
Humming Bird	Capt. ——— Honiwell
Hannah and Mary	Capt. David Cannida
Sally	Capt. Joseph Smith
Dove (or Doe)	Capt. ——— Rackwood
Charming Molly	Capt. ——— Byles
Fishhawk	Capt. ——— Newmarch
Seaflower (schooner)	Capt. ——— Wadlin
Seaflower (sloop)	Capt. Jonathan Sayward
Good Intent	Capt. ——— Bradford
Elizabeth	
Philadelphia	Capt. John Stinson
St. Peter	Capt. ——— Davis
Beaver	Capt. ——— Cahoone
Diamond	Capt. Ephraim Doane
Victory	Capt. William Adams
St. Jean	Capt. [Joseph?] Richardson (see *Resolution*)
Amplus	Capt. ——— Donnell

OTHER PROVINCIAL CAPTAINS WHOSE SHIPS ARE NOT KNOWN:

Samuel Barnes
Aaron Bull
Zebulon Elwell
Michael Hodge
William Jackson

James Jordan
John Le Croix
Joshua Loring
Samuel Miles
Edward Stow

Robert White

Also Captains Arno, Barton, Bingham, Branham, Chapman, Church, Clark, Coit, Cooper, Daggett, Dodd, Fitch, Gears, Giddings, Hammond, Jones, Lee, Lovett, Mumford, Robbins, Sanford, Sherburne, Spry, Stone, Talcott, Ward, West.

APPENDIX II

PETER WARREN LETTERS

The following important series of nine letters from Commodore Peter Warren to General William Pepperrell has apparently never been published. The originals are owned by the New York Historical Society which has courteously permitted their use in this work. The letters are signed by Warren but are in the hand of a secretary or clerk. Most of the series bear the signature and endorsements of N. L. Waldron, whose identity has not been established.

These letters should be compared with the correspondence between Warren and Pepperrell published in *The Pepperrell Papers* (*6 Mass. Hist. Soc. Coll. X*). The letters now printed supply the beginning of the correspondence and fill in several gaps. The first letter from Warren in *The Pepperrell Papers* is dated May 1, 1745, while two earlier letters are here given. The third of the following letters (May 1st) mentions another letter written that same day which is the first letter printed in *The Pepperrell Papers*.

The Letters

Superb off Cancoa [Canso] the 23 April 1745.

Sir

I arrivd off the Harbour of Cancoa, this Morning, where Captain [Philip] Durell, in his Majesty's Ship Eltham joyn'd me, and Inform'd me, of your being still at Cancoa, with the Troops, and that Captain [Edward] Tyng with some of your Cruizers, were off Lewisbourg, to Intercept any Provisions, or Succours, being carried Into that Port.

As I apprehend it will be my part with his Majesty's Ships, to use our Endeavour to Prevent an Introduction, of such, by any

APPENDIX II

Force Superior to yours, I shall make the best of my way, off Lewisbourg, where I shall be glad to hear from you as often as possible. Give me leave to assure you nothing shall be wanting, on our parts to promote the Success of this Expedition, which I think of the utmost Consequence, to our King and Country.

I wish you cou'd spare me a good Sailing Schooner, to Correspond with you.

I propose to be off, till you Receive this, and if you have any particular Commands you'l send the Sloop to me, who may hoist his Ensign at his Mast head, to Speak with me.

Excuse this Inacurate Srawl in hast, I hope to kiss your hand soon, at Lewisbourg, and am with great Regard.

       Sir
        Your
         Most humble Servant
         P Warren

PS: I shall be very glad you will send me your Plan of Operation, as soon as possible— And you'l please to have directions with the Officer, that you leave at Cancoa, that if any Vessells arrive with Provisions for the Ships under my Command, to let them know, tis my directions, they remain at Cancoa, till they receive Orders from me.

        To Lt: General Peperel

I shall be much Oblig'd to you for a draugt of Lewisbourg

    [Superbe] off Lewisbourg the 25 April 1745

I Receiv'd your letter of Yesterdays date this Morning informing me, of the arrival, at Cancoa, of the Connecticut Convoy, upon which I Congratulate you.

Agreable to your desire, I send you the Prince of Orange,[1] who with Captain [John] Rouse I think cant be better Employ'd, then in Cruizing, to the westward of Cancoa, for the French Ship, you mention, that was in Chace, of the Sloop, or any other of the Enemys Vessels, that may Interupt our Communication with Boston.

---

[1] The *Prince of Orange,* a Provincial ship, mounting fourteen guns, with eighty men, Capt. Joseph Smithers or Smithurst commanding.

I have sent his Majesty's Ship, the Mermaid to Escort you, and the Troops hither but if he shall hear, any thing of the French Ship's hovering about, or near Cancoa, and you think you shant want his Protection, he is at Liberty, to Cruize for her, Five, or Six days, and is to joyn me again here, for 'tis my opinion, that the Ships of warr, shou'd keep together, off Lewisbourg, least a Strong Convoy, shou'd come from France, which might be of the worst Consequence, to the present Expedition.

I hope this letter, will meet you in your way hither, Captain [Edward] Tyng telling me he had sent you word, there was no Ice on the Coast, to prevent your landing, Give me leave to Recommend dispatch, for delays may frustrate all our hopes.

I think there is but Two small Sloops, in at Lewisbourg, now, but no man can judge, how soon they may be Supply'd, with Provisions, and Succours from France.

I beg leave to tell you, as a Judge of the Uncertainty of Sea Affairs, tis possible Succours may be Introduc'd, let our care, and diligence, be ever so great, Especially in a Country so Subject to Fogs, and bad Weather.

If any Provision Vessells, are arrivd from Boston, for his Majesty's Ships, under my Command, I wou'd have them come to us with you.

I want much to hire a good Sailing Schooner, which may be of great Consequence to his Majesty's Service, If this you sent me cou'd be Spared, she woud a ——— [MS. torn]

Wee took a ——— [MS. torn] Shallop, Yesterday, the two former laden w ——— [MS. torn] for Lewisbourg, the Men having made their escape ashore, wee cou'd not procure any Intelligence.

When it shall please God to make you Master of Lewisbourg Harbour, which wou'd be the only certain means to Prevent the Introduction of Succours, and in that Case, I think part of the Squadron, wou'd be sufficient, to Cruize off here, while the others may go further in quest of his Majesty's Enemys.

The Road Island Briggantine being leakey, I shall send him to Cancoa, as soon as I can speak with him, the weather being now thick.

APPENDIX II 187

I am inform'd, an Officer, of Captain [John] Rouse's, has some Cloaths on board, to sell, if you Please to let them be sent down here, he shall be Paid for them, my Men being almost Naked.

If the Mermaid, shou'd go after the French Ship, I think it wou'd not be amiss, for Captain [John] Rouse, to go with her, as he Sails well, and can go into Shoaler water.

You'l Please to leave such directions, as you think proper, for the Prince of Orange, and Road Island Brigg, I having given them no other directions, but to wait upon you, at Cancoa.

As I find Cancoa is to be the Magazine, for Stores, I presume you will judge it proper, to leave a Considerable Garrison there, for their Protection. I am with great Regard

       Sir
       Your
        Most humble Servant:
         P Warren

Lieut. General Peperel

Sir

My French Pylote Informs me, that there are two Harbours, at the North:East part of this Island, One at about Fourteen Leagues distance, the other Twenty, where he says all the French Ships, will go, when they know this place is Invested and Blockaded.

I therefore think it will be proper, after you are setled ashore, to send two, or three, of the Country Vessels, with a Man of warr, to those Harbours, to demolish any Vessels, that may be there, and all the Fishing Vessels along the Coast, and shall be glad to have your opinion of this Scheme.

It will be almost Impossible, to prevent that Briggantine's escaping out of Lewisbourg, without some small Vessels, and some of those Arm'd, to watch close in, with the Harbours mouth, while the Ships lay in the Offing.

As I find by Captain [William] Fletcher, you like Gaborous Bay, for the Schooners, wou'd it not be proper, to have a good Battery there to cover them, even if you Remov'd that from Cancoa, for God sake think of sending to Boston for Provisions. I shall be glad to know when you do, or to Cancoa, for the Ships have very little Provisions, and I expect two Months there, which I wou'd order down here.

When your Troops have Invested the Town, (if you dont attack it by Storm) if any French Ships, shou'd escape us, and Run ashore, I apprehend you will be able to prevent the Men, getting into the Garrison, and wee will be Sure to take, or destroy their Ships, if possible, it will certainly be of the greatest Consequence, to the Success of the Present Expedition, to Secure the Entrance of the Harbour, as soon as possible, as the only certain means, to prevent the Enemy being Supply'd with Provisions, or Succours of any kind.

I am sorry to hear the Ship, that engag'd Captain [Edward] Tyng, is got in, tho as I am told, her Cargo is wine, and Brandy, it wont be of great service, to them, if they are Short of other Provisions.

Pray Issue out the Signals, I gave you, for the Schooners, otherwise they will give us great trouble, in Chacing them, and direct them when wee chace them, not to carry us, out of our way, but come to us directly.

I find the Eastwardmost End of this Island, is the part the French generally make, therefore it will be proper, to guard it, with some of the Squadron, tho it will weaken those here.

Pray send me, two, or three, good sailing Schooners, and the Cloaths for my Men, as soon as possible, and please to forward the Inclos'd for my Provisions, by the first Vessell you send to Cancoa.

If you can give me timely notice, when you Intend to make any attack upon the Garrison, I wou'd use my endeavours, to alarm them, by Standing in with the Squadron, as near as possible.

If you can spare Capt: [William] Fletcher, he will be a proper Person, to cover any other small Vessels, that will be necessary to lay close off the Harbours Mouth, to Intercept the Brigg.

You'l be good enough to excuse any Inacurate Scrawls, I shall send you, in a hurry, and please to make no Ceremony with me, in sending any Intelligence you may think necessary for my knowledge.

APPENDIX II

I send you with this, another letter which I wrote in a hurry, and Intended you by Captain [William] Fletcher.

My Compliments to General Walldrow [Samuel Waldo], and all the Gentlemen ashore, and believe me to be with the greatest Respect, and Regard,

Your Most humble Servant
P Warren
Sir

Superbe off Lewisbourg
the 1 May 1745.
Lieut. General Peperel

Sir

The Account you give us, of taking the Grand Battery, gives me, and all my Captains, who are now with me, great joy, as wee hope it a happy beginning, to your future Success. By the Enemys not defending it, I apprehend, their stand will be, in the Town, which I cant think, they will be able to support, and if wee cou'd once get possession, of the Island Battery, nothing from Sea, of the Enemys, cou'd gett in, and they must Starve in the town, If you intend to attack, that, and our Boats, and Men, can be usefull, and the weather will permitt, you'l please to let me know. Herewith I send you, an Invoice of the French Prize's Cargo, which wou'd have been very valuable, to them, and is in a great measure, so to us, I have order'd her into Chapeaurouse Bay, where she may make the figure of an Arm'd Vessell, If any thing in her, will be agreable to you, or the rest of our Friends, on shore, I will endeavour to procure it. The Bearer Mr: Agnue, who is the Senior Officer of the Marines, in the Squadron, waits on you, with this, as my Aid du Camp, and will Receive your Commands verbally, when you have not leisure to write, which must often happen. I am glad to find so Glorious a Spirit in our Americans, it will greatly Recommend them, to their Mother Country, and if they can make this acquisition, it will be the greatest to them in particular, and to our Country in general, that has for many years been made; you'l please to lett me know in what Shape, the Squadron can — Contribute to it. Not a word of News, in our French Prize, but that some Men of warr, may be soon expected, I hope Lewisbourg will receive them civilly, under the English flagg. I thank you, for sending the Connecticut Sloop, I shall want three, or four Schooners, very much, Captain [William] Fletcher chac'd a Sloop, and Schooner, into some Harbour, about three, or four Leagues, to the Eastward, which wee might have Intercepted, if wee had Schooners, to have follow'd them. Pray will it be right, to destroy the Houses, along shore, as wee may fall in with them, and do it by our Boats. The Schooners you send may take any Guns, that are proper for them, out of the French Prize. I wish you the greatest Success, and am with Perfect Esteem, and Regard.

       Sir
        Your
         Most Obedient humble
          Servant
           P Warren

Superbe off Lewisbourg
the 2: May 1745 —
 Lieut: General Peperel

    Comre Warren's Plan of Operation, May 4th

 A Plan, of Operation, for the Speedy Reduction of the Town, and Garrison of Lewisbourg, Propos'd by Peter Warren Esq:, Commander in Chief, of his Majesty's Ships, and Vessells etc., to Lieutenant General Peperell, Commander in Chief of all the American Troops, and to his Council of Officers, and to all the Captains of his Majesty's Ships of warr, Employ'd upon this Expedition, for their Opinions and Approbation.

 As the Enemy have abondon'd the Grand Battery 'tis proposed, to attack the Island Battery, as soon as possible, with all the Whale Boats and the Boats belonging to his Majesty's Ships, and the Private Ships of warr, man'd, and arm'd.

 If the Whale Boats, can carry five hundred Men, His Majesty's Ships, and the Private Ships of warr, can make an addition, of between Two, or Three hundred Men more, in their Boats, who shou'd be arm'd in the following manner Viz. —

APPENDIX II

Every Seaman, a Musquet, Pair of Pistols Hand Granade, Quick Match, and Cutlash.

Every Marine, his Musquet, and Bayonet

A Box of Spare Musquet, and Pistol Carteridges, in one of the Boats, of every Ship, in proportion to the whole number of men, sent by each particular Ship, One or two days Provisions, and a small Cag, of water, in each Boat, or in each Long Boat, one Cask of water, the Scaling Ladders in the Whale Boats, if in the night, Lanthorns, Candles, Tinder box, Steel, and a good knife in each mans pockett.

That his Majesty's Ship Superbe, shoud anchor in Chapareux Bay, and be the Rendezvous, where all the Boats shou'd meet, and when they are aboard as a Signal, to let the General know it, a Dutch flagg shou'd be hoisted, at the Fore top Gallant Masthead and if they proceed before dark to go upon the attack, the Instant they are ready, and put off; from the Ships side, the Dutch Flagg to be hawld down, but if it shou'd be thought proper, to put off in the Night, then the Signal shou'd be two Lights, at the Main Top Gallant Masthead, and three Minute Guns, as soon as they put off.

There shou'd be two, or three, Schooners with a Surgeon, on board of each, lie as near as possible to the Battery, and if the attack is made in the night, as soon as it begins, the Schooners, shou'd each of them show a light, and the Officers that are upon the attack shou'd be acquainted of those Schooners lying there to receive any men, that may be wounded, upon the attack, and his Majesty's Ships, and the Country Arm'd Vessells, shou'd lie as near as the weather will permitt.

The Command of the attack, shou'd be given, to any such person, as General Peperell shou'd appoint, and those who are the best Pylotes, to the proper landing place, shou'd be the headmost of all the Boats and some people, who know the way to march up to the Battery, shou'd be left, at the water side, to show the people as they land, the way to follow each other, and the word shou'd be ———— and a proper Guard, shou'd be left at the landing place, to prevent the Enemy, from the town, attacking our Forces, in the Rear, it is not to be suppos'd that the Enemy from the town or from any other of their Battery's will fire; at the Island Battery, while their own people are there, but shou'd they abandon it, it is probable, they then will, in which case if our people find themselves too hard prest, they shou'd have proper Spikes, to Spike up all the Cannon, or even to throw them over the wall, before their Retreat.

If about an hour, or two before the attack, of the Island Battery, a feint was to be made, by the Troops, on shore, (if not thought prudent effectually so to do) as if they Intended, to storm the town, in Several places, it wou'd greatly take off the attention of the Enemy, from the Island Battery, and probably be the means, of their drawing off some of their Troops from thence; shou'd the forces succeed, in their attack upon the Island Battery, and shou'd not the Troops on Shore, think proper to storm the town, or if they fail of Success; if they did, I wou'd than propose to go into the Harbour, with all his Majesty's Ships, and all the Country Vessells, except two, or three, of the small Arm'd ones, and about one third of the Schooners, and Sloops, who shou'd be left in Chapareux Bay, and who with the French Prize there, wou'd be sufficient to secure a Retreat to Cancoa, let what will happen, but I'm of opinion, that is not in the least to be apprehended, or Provided for.

If any of the Ships, shou'd be in danger of Sinking, by the Enemys Shott, they shou'd in that case Run, or Hawl ashore as near the Grand Battery as possible, (not to be in the way of the Battery's fire upon the town, nor in the Line of direction of any of its Cannon) in order to save their Guns, Arms, Ammunition and Provisions.

In going in, all the small Vessells, should have no great Guns, shou'd keep of the Starboard side of the Ships of warr, and Run into the North: East: Harbour and land every man on the side of the Royal Battery in order to go round to joyn the General, and the Troops.

The Arm'd Sloop, and a Brigg, or two, shou'd be appointed, to secure all the Boats, and Vessells in the Harbour, near the town, and to send as many Boats, as they can procure on board the Ships of [warr?] and the Country Arm'd Vessells, to lie on the off side from the Town Batterys, ready to land men, from every Ship if it shou'd be thought necessary.

APPENDIX II 193

When I propose to go in, I wou'd hoist a Red Flagg, at the Foretop Gallant Masthead, about an hour before that, all our Troops from the Royal Battery, except a proper number, to manage the Guns there, against the Enemy, shou'd march to joyn the General, and Army, who shou'd when I hoist the Red Flagg, attack the town, in such places, as not to be annoy'd by the Shott, which our Ships shou'd fire, at the Enemys Batterys in the town.

The Officer at the Grand Battery, shou'd be directed, to be very carefull, in firing at the Enemy, that he does not Hull any of our own Ships, that may lie between that Battery, and the town, and if wee shou'd land Men, from the Ships, to joyn the Troops, on the attack ashore, the word shou'd be ———.

I wou'd further propose, in order to the Generals knowing, when I think wee can get in, to hoist a Dutch Flagg, at the Foretop Gallant Masthead, at about ——— hours before wee Expected to get into the Harbour.

The Season of the year advancing a pace, that the Enemy, may expect Provisions, and Succours, from France, makes it highly necessary, that wee shou'd take some Vigorous measures, for the Sudden Reduction of Lewisbourg, these are the most so that occurs to me.

As I wou'd be farr from being Obstinate in my opinion, I shall always be very ready, to joyn in any other plan, that may be thought more Conducive to the attaining the end, for which wee are all come here, which will be the greatest acquisition, to our Country, in general, to the Northern Collonys in particular, and an Everlasting honour, to every person contributing thereto.

I shall be greatly pleas'd with your Candid Opinions, upon this plan.

I shou'd be glad to be inform'd of the following Quere's, if possible.

Whether you have any Deserters, from the Enemy, that may be rely'd on, or whether you have had any from you to them.

What number of men, and Guns, in the Town, and Island Battery, what Regular, and what not.

What number of Cannon, they can, bring to play upon the Ship's from the town, if the Island Battery shou'd be taken.

What Quantity of Powder or Ammunition, they have ———, what number of Mortars or how many Shells.

How many Women, Children, and Old Men, unfitt to Bear Arms.

What Quantity of Provisions, they have,

Is the Enemys Communication by Land, Entirely cutt off, by our Troops.

How high is the Wall, that goes along the water side, in the Harbour, or is there any ditch.

How near can the Ships come to the Town Batterys.

P Warren

Sir

Superbe off Lewisbourg the 4th: May 1745.

I have this day, laid the above Plan, before the Captains of the Squadron, under my Command, who are of opinion with me, that the assistance propos'd shou'd be given, for the attack of the Island Battery when the general thinks proper, to undertake it, and the Weather will permitt; But they think with me, that they can't advise, going into the Harbour, with the Ships, 'till the Island Battery is taken, and the Quere's contain'd in the said Plan of Operation, can be in some measure resolv'd, or made known to us, which wee hope you'l use your endeavour to do, as soon, and as authentick as possible, and that you will let us know, in what Shape besides that of Cruizing (to prevent the Introduction of Succours, or Provisions into the Garrison), wee can be usefull, with the Ship's, towards the Reduction of Lewisbourg, and they with me, do assure you, wee will give you all the assistance, in our power, upon all occasions, and that wee are

Sir

Your Most humble Servants:
P Warren
Phi Durell

J Calmady
James Douglas
Rich Tiddeman
Edw Tyng
    Lieut: General Peperel

APPENDIX II 195

Superbe off Lewisbourg the 18 May 1745

Sir

Herewith I send you, a Copy, of Orders, which I intend to Issue out, to all my Squadron, and hope it will meet your approbation, and that you will appoint a Committee of your Council, to come to the propos'd Consultation, of Land, and Sea Officers, in order to consider, and determine, upon the properest plan of operation, against the Enemy, when the Two Ships of warr joyns us from Boston.

If you think it adviseable, to attack the Island Battery, before their arrival, or the first fair opportunity of wind, and weather, upon giving me notice thereof, I can assist you with upwards of two hundred Men, with the Boats of the Squadron who may either be sent in the night that the attack shall be propos'd or a night before if you think proper; your Whale Boats and the others in Lewisbourg can I presume carry Two hundred Men

I stood this day within Gun shott of the Island Battery and I really believe there are very few Men in it but there is a great Surff on the Seaside of it, so that if you think of attacking it you must wait a Smooth time when the wind is Northerly or Westerly and I can by the Signal of a Dutch Flagg at my Fore top Gallant Masthead let them know at the Grand Battery when the Men and Boats are ready to go in from the Ships as soon as the Night comes on dark enough to prevent their being discover'd, and it will lye with the Officer that Commands the Boats from the Grand Battery, whether he will joyn our Boats under the Lighthouse point, and go altogether upon the attack or whether they shou'd joyn him at the Grand Battery, or any where else, I am of opinion, as the Oars of our Boats, will make some noise, the Whale Boats had better joyn ours, unless it shall be thought better to Send our Boats into the Harbour the Night before they make the attack.

As I propose to be close in with the Harbour, every morning, while the weather is fair, and especially with the wind Easterly, a Whale Boat may be sent out to me, at any time before day, with your opinion, upon the propos'd attack, and I will order a Schooner, close in shore to take the Boat up.

I think the Inclos'd Signals will not be Improper.

If you approve of this, you'l please to send One, two, or three Pylotes, off, to go in our Boats.

If wee fail in all these attempts give me leave to assure you if at a General Council it shall be thought practicable and adviseable to go in against the Town and Batterys with all our Naval Force of every kind I shall be very ready and willing to do it, and will make the best Disposition I can to obtain the wish'd for Success.

I hope you'l pardon my Anxiety to bring matters to a Speedy and happy Conclusion being prompt'd thereto by the consideration of the danger of delays, the uncertainty of winds and weather, especially in this uncouth Clymate, and the Unguarded Situation of all the Collonys and Ships Trade to the Northward of Carolina, for whose protection I am appointed Commander in Chief of all his Majesty's Ships and Vessells Employ'd and to be Employ'd upon the Continent to the Northward of Carolina, who must while I have all the Ships, intended for their protection, and even others that are appointed upon services of very great Consequence, here with me, be extreamly expos'd to the Insults of his Majesty's Enemys.

I am well assur'd you will Consider this and push on every particular under your Direction to use their utmost endeavours to bring to a happy period, the great End for which wee are all come here, in doing which I sincerely wish you Success and am with Great Esteem and regard

    Sir

      Your Most Obedient humble Servant

              P Warren

PS That was not [Capt. Clark] Gayton as I took it to be Yesterday [Capt. Joseph] Smythers and he are still missing, shall I send [Capt. John] Rouse and One of the Sloops to the North East of this Island to look into the Harbour and Intercept anything from Canada

L General Peperell

Sir

      Superbe off Lewisbourg the 20: May 1745

Last Night wee took the Vigilant, French Man of warr, of 64 Guns and about 500 Men, from Brest, bound to Lewisbourg, for which place, she has on board some Warlike Stores. She being a fine Ship, and this her first Voyage, I intend to Commission her for

APPENDIX II 197

his Majesty, and hope you will think it, of the utmost Consequence, to assist us, with Men, to Mann her, as soon as possible, in order to make us Strong enough, for any Squadron of the Enemys, that may come here, I assure all such Men, as you shall let us have, for her, that they shall be discharg'd, upon our arrival at Boston, if they desire it, she is much Shatterd in the Engagement, and I shall send her in to Chapeaux Rouge bay to sett, and beg that you will direct Vessells, to come to take the Prisoners, from us, upon our appearance off, otherwise all the Cruizers will be useless, with such Numbers on board, I hope this will be a very happy event, for our future success, which I sincerely wish, and am —
     Sir Your Most Obedient humble Servant
             P Warren
L Gen Pepperell
    To On his Maj : Service
Lieut. General Pepperell
            Peter Warren

        Superb off Lewisburg the
         23d May 1745
Sir
 Brigdier Donil [Col. Nathaniel Donnell?] and Collonel [Samuel] Moor, Inform'd me Last Night of your Jntention to Attack the Jsland Battery to Night with your Whale Boats and that you woud be glad of the assistance of the Boats of the Squadron Mann'd and Arm'd, upon so short a Notice twill bee Impossible for me to gett so many of them together, as I woud wish, but as the Weather is now very favourable for such An Attampt, I woud not defer going upon it, with such as wee can Muster, which I perswade my Self will be Enough to Carry two Hundred Men at least which is as Many as the Ships Can with any prudence spare, Considering how the French Prize has weaken'd us, and those shall be ready to Meet the whale Boats (who I presume will have all the Ladders) at the time and place that you shall appoint this Night of which you will please to send me the earlyest Notice. as I have Orderd them to Rendezvous on board of Me, by four a Clock this afftternoon. I receiv'd Letters from Governor Shirley by the Princess Mary

(on whose arrival I Congratulate you) I answer'd them by the Schooner you sent Me and dispatch'd her by Ten a Clock last Night, Mr Shirley informd Me of his haveing appointed Captain [James] Mackdonald a Collonel to Command such Marrines as I shall think fitt to Land, which shall be every one in the Squadron if they can bee of any Service to the present Expedition, and I believe you will find Collonel Mackdonald with them will bee of the greatest Consequence to it, as he has the Character of being a good and Experienced Officer.[2] In Leu of our Marrines wee Must have some of your Men to Man our Ships till the Marrines return, for what with Sickness, and Spareing Some Men to the French Man of Warr, lately taken, wee are in No Condition to Attack the Enemys Ships that are hourly Expected here both from France and the West Jndies, therefore when you send for the Marrines youl please to send an Equal Number of Men to us, Capt Mackdonald knows how many Marrines there are in the Squadron. As the French Prize is Now in Chapperouge Bay, give mee leave to tell you as I Shall Commission her for his Majesty it May be of the utmost Consequence to this Expedition to Man her and fitt her as soon as Possible she being of greater force then any Ship here. you will please to Consider this, that tho it May weaken us Somewhere it Will be putting Strenth where it can be well Applyd. I wish my situation woud Allow Me More frequent Oppertunitys of Concerting Meazures with you, but this I beg you will bee assured off that all thee Ships Sea Men and Marrines under My Command as well as My Self in Person Shall bee ready and I am sure are willing to hit upon any Scheme that Shall be Agreed upon for the reduction of Lewisburg to his Majestys Obedience, I am with regard and Esteem

Sir

Your Most Obedient humble Servant

I am in pain for [Joseph] Smithers,
for god Sake Send some of the Transports
and so forth
Gen. Pepper

---

[2] McDonald irritated Pepperrell with his reflections on the military conduct of the Provincial soldiers. Pepperrell wrote Shirley "we were glad to get rid of him, for the most he did was to find fault that our encampment was not regular, or that the soldiers did not march as hansome as old regular troops, their toes were not turned enough out, etc."

APPENDIX II 199

the Prisoners, they may take two a ——— [MS. defaced]
who to send with them to Boston I presume youl Make a feint
upon the Town when the Boats Attack the Battery

Your
P W

To send the plan for the Island Battery
To send out Schooners to take the prisoner
To help man the prize
[MS. defaced]

———•———

Superbe off Louisbourg the 12th June 1745
Sir

I see the Sunderland, and Canterbury, with three Ships, that I suppose to be prizes, I expect to speak with them this evening, and as I would not loose a moments time, I must desire you will please to order off the men which you agreed to assist us with, among them, I beg for Collonel [Samuel] Moor, and his Regiment, many of them being used to the sea, and I shall be glad to have himself, and 100 of his men with me, in my own Ship; I find wee cant hope for many men, out of the Transports, wee possibly may get 100, You'l also please to send the Cohorns, and Shells, and to order Captain [Thomas] Saunders, and every sloops boat, and Vessel, out of the Bay, except such as you shall want for your own Commands; to take the Ships Spare Topmasts, and Yards, to prevent their being Render'd useless, by the Enemys Shott: A moments time ought not to be lost, that wee may go in with the Ships, the very first opportunity, of wind, and weather, I hope you'l please to observe my Signals, that I gave you, to let you know when I am ready to go in, and I perswade myself, I need not recommend your making a vigorous attack, to assist on the land Side of the Town, at the same Instant, that I do with the Ships, and that you will give proper directions to have all the ladders ready in the Whale Boats Shalloways, and others, that are already, or that I may send into Lewisbourg Harbour, and that they lye ready, when they see us coming in, to come off upon the Signal that I have appointed for that purpose, and our people shall be ready to assist in Manning them, if necessary to land with our Boats, I send you a copy of the disposition, I have made for the Ships going upon the attack, that you may know our order of Battle, and Signals, and give them to the proper Officers, to whom they relate, particularly the Signal for boats to the Officers that Commands at the Grand, and Lighthouse Batterys.

I am with great regard and Esteem,

Your Most Obedient humble Servant

P. Warren,

L General Pepperell Esq

APPENDIX III

THE EXPEDITION AS SEEN IN CONTEMPORARY NEW YORK

The following extracts are taken from *The New-York Weekly Post-Boy,* the issues of June 10th, July 15th, July 22nd, and August 5th, all in 1745. There is a file of this newspaper including the issues of the above dates in the New York Historical Society and that Society has kindly permitted the use of their copies.

THE NEW-YORK WEEKLY POST-BOY

The Issue of June 10, 1745.

Cape Breton Island, on which Louisburgh is built, lies on the South of the Gulph of St. Lawrance, and commands the Enterance into the River, and the Country of Canada. It is reckon'd 140 Leagues in Circuit, full of fine Bays and Harbours, extremly convenient for Fishing Stages. It was always reckon'd a Part of Nova Scotia. For the Importance of this Place see our Post-Boy, No. 122. As soon as the French King had begun the present unjust War against the English, the People of Louisburgh attack'd the New-England Town of Canso, consisting of about 150 Houses and a Fort, took it, burnt it to the Ground, and carried away the People, Men, Women and Children, Prisoners. They then laid Siege to Annapolis Royal, and would have taken, it, if seasonable Assistance had not been sent from Boston. Mr. Duvivier went home to France last Fall for more Soldiers, etc. to renew that Attempt, and for Stores for Privateers, of which they proposed to fit out a great Number this Summer, being the last Year unprovided: Yet one of their Cruisers only, took 4 Sail in a few Days, off our Coasts, to a very considerable Value. What might we have expected from a dozen Sail, making each 3 or 4 Cruises a

Year? They boasted that during the War they should have no Occasion to cut Fire Wood, for that the Jackstaves of English Vessels would be a Supply Sufficient. It is therefore in their own Necessary Defence, as well as that of all the other British Colonies, that the People of New England have undertaken the present Expedition against that Place, to which may the God of Hosts grant Success. Amen.

[A dispatch published in the same issue:]

Boston, May 6. By the Shirley Gally, Capt. [John] Rouse Commander, who arrived in Nantasket last Thursday from Canso, to which Place he had carry'd the General, [Pepperrell] and convoy'd the main Body of our Fleet, we learn, That Commodore [Peter] Warren, after having receiv'd the General's Dispatches by Col. [John] Bradstreet, whom the General had sent to wait upon him on board the Superbe, in order to communicate to him the Plan of Operations propos'd to be carry'd on by our Forces against the French Settlements at Cape Breton, proceeded from Canso with the Superbe, Eltham, Launceston and Mermaid, to his Station off Louisbourg Harbour, where he is now cruizing, together with the Vessels of War employ'd by this Government in the same Service, in order to cut off the Enemy from all Supplies of Recruits or Stores, before the Arrival of our Land Forces at Cape Breton, where it is expected they are before this time landed. Capt. [John] Rouse also informs us, that before he left Canso Harbour all the Massachusetts, New Hampshire and Connecticut Transports were arrived there, and 4,000 Men, exclusive of Commission Officers, were in good Health and Spirits. That the General had review'd them on Canso Hill, and form'd the several Detachments which are to go upon Action immediately after their Landing at Cape-Breton; for which Purpose they have been compleatly equipp'd there upon the Spot; and Orders are given for them to proceed from Canso to Chappearouge-Bay in distinct Divisions of Transports, and to be landed in separate Corps under their respective Officers, who are to command in the different Parts of the propos'd Action; but that they had been detain'd at Canso till his sailing from thence by the great Quantity of Ice in Chappeaurouge-Bay, which had made it impracticable for our Transports to get in near enough to the

As the Cape Breton Expedition is at present the Subject of most Conversation, we hope the following Draught (rough as it is, for want of good Engravers here) will be acceptable to our Readers; as it will serve to give them an Idea of the Strength and Situation of the Town now besieged by our Forces, and render the News we receive from thence more intelligible.

PLAN of the Town and Harbour of LOUISBURG.

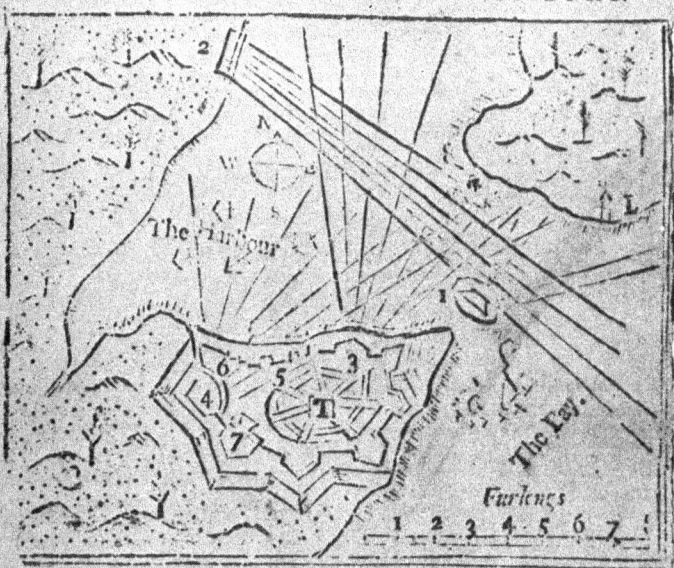

EXPLANATION.

1. The Island Battery, at the Mouth of the Harbour, mounting 34 Guns, --- Pounders. This Battery can rake Ships fore and aft before they come to the Harbour's Mouth, and take them in the Side as they are passing in.
2. The Grand Battery, of 36 Forty two Pounders, planted right against the Mouth of the Harbour, and can rake Ships fore and aft as they enter.
3. The Town N. East Battery, which mounts 18 Twenty four Pounders on two Faces, which can play on the Ships as soon as they have entered the Harbour.
4. The Demi-Lune or Circular Battery, which mounts 16 Twenty four Pounders, stands on high Ground, and overlooks all the Works. This Battery can also gaul Ships, as soon as they enter the Harbour.
5. Three Flanks, mounting 2 Eighteen Pounders each.
6. A small Battery, which mounts 8 Nine Pounders. All these Guns command any Ship in the Harbour.
7. The Fort or Citadel, fortified distinctly from the Town, in which the Governor lives.
8. A Rock, called the Barrel.
T The Center of the Town. L The Light House.
Every Bastion of the Town Wall has Embrasures or Ports for the Number of Guns to defend the Land Side. The black Strokes drawn from the several Batteries, shew the Lines in which the Shot may be directed.

From The New-York Weekly Post-Boy.

APPENDIX III

Shore for the Men to Land. — That in the mean Time the General had taken Possession of the Island for his Majesty by causing a Block House to be erected upon it, near the Place where the Old one stood, and hoisted the British Flag in it; and that he had inclos'd it with a Ditch, Ramparts and Pickets, and fortify'd it with a Battery of eight Cannon, nine Pounders, and posted a Detachment of 80 Men in it, under a Commandant, which was to remain there during the Expedition; that Island being most commodiously situated, not only for a Place of general Rendezvous for our Forces, but also for maintaining the necessary Intilligence between the Camp and Fleet and this Place, and for divers other Services of the Expedition; particularly as that Part, which is called the Pond, affords a secure Station for our Transports against any Surprize from the Enemy, not only by their lying under Cover of the Battery, but as no Vessel of Force can either enter or annoy them there, and is a good Place for lodging any Artillery or heavy Stores, not immediately wanted in the Camp, and for a Place of Resort or Retreat upon all Emergercies — But we hope, besides the Usefulness of this Island to the Expedition, that more beneficial Consequences may attend our taking Repossession of it, viz. the recovering from the Enemy that most valuable Fishery, which was before carry'd on by his Majesty's Subjects there; and where, notwithstanding the late Incroachments of the French upon it, from 200 to 250 fishing Scooners and Shallops, were annually employ'd in it, and about forty topsail Vessels for the European Markets; which Fishery is capable of being greatly encreas'd, as Canso is incomparably the best situated of any Harbour in these Seas for carrying on a Fishery with small Vessels, and has many Advantages beyond either Cape-Breton or Newfoundland for that Purpose; not to mention, that our regaining the Possession of this Island (if it is held) will deprive the Enemy of many other Advantages they have reap'd by their breaking up the Garrison and English Settlements there, and particularly as it has given 'em a free Communication with the French of Nova-Scotia (thro' the Gut of Canso) from whence they have drawn the chief Part of their Provisions and Live Stock at Louisbourg this last Summer, and will very much contribute to keep the neutral French (as the Nova-Scotians are called) in those Parts, in a proper Awe and Respect of the English, and deter them from any Thoughts of joining the French Enemy and Indians, in any Attempt against his Majesty's Garrison at Annapolis Royal.

Also since our last, besides the Intilligence gain'd by the General from the three Cape-Sables Indians of general Orders being sent from Cape-Breton for assembling all the Indians at Menis this Month, to join some French Troops in order to make a fresh Attack upon his Majesty's Garrison at Annapolis Royal, and that two Ships of War were expected about that Time in the Bason of Annapolis from France, to assist in the Attack; we have receiv'd Advices from Annapolis Royal, that the French Priest of St. John's River, and others there, had given the Garrison an Account, that near 200 Canadeans, with some Indians, were assembled in Schiegnecto, and advancing towards Menis; and that M. Duvivier was expected soon with the new French Governor of Cape-Breton, and three Ships of War, which were, immediately after landing the Governor and Stores at Louisburg, to proceed to Annapolis Royal: Also that a Party of Twenty or Thirty Indians had seiz'd a Sloop at Menis, belonging to Mr. Gautier, a French Trader, which he had left there in the Winter to load with Wheat, and went to fetch in the Spring for the Inhabitants of St. John's River, who were in great Want of Wheat; and that a small Shallop likewise sent to Menis upon the same Account, was detain'd there.

And we have Accounts from Albany, that they have receiv'd Intelligence from Canada of a Body of French and Indians fitting out from thence, under one Monsieur Bilâtre, as Commander in chief, and a Son of Monsieur Lanoo's, and one Monsieur Artel who are to have the next Command under him. — That the Party is to consist of 5 or 600 Men, and is design'd, as some of the Albany Indians say, against Annapolis Royal, and others of 'em report, against the Checasia Indians; which last seems only a Blind. Likewise that they had other Intelligence about the middle of April, that within a few Days there was to be a great Meeting of Indians in Lake Champlea, where they were call'd by the French from their Hunting; from all which Accounts, it can't be reasonably doubted but that the French were meditating another Attack against Annapolis Royal, in which they expect to be join'd by a Naval Force

APPENDIX III

from France sometime this Month. But there is the utmost probability, that our present Enterprize against Cape Breton will either cause the Enemy to desist from making their Attempt against Annapolis-Royal, or frustrate it; so that what ever may be the Success of the present Expedition in other Respects, there seems the utmost Probability of its producing these two good Consequences, viz. the Recovery of Canso with our Fishery there, and Preservation of Annapolis Royal, at least for the present.

[Published in the same issue:]

Boston, May 13. On Friday last the Schooner Montague, one of the Ordnance Tenders, arriv'd here Express from Annapolis Royal, and brought Advice, that Governor [Jean Paul] Mascarene had receiv'd undoubted Information, that 600 French and Indians came in the Winter from Canada to Chignicto, being the same which were seen passing on the Skirts of New-England, and arriv'd at Menis on the 19th April last, part by Land, and part by Sea in the Vessels they found up the Bay; that they had with them 12 Officers, an Engineer and a Surgeon, and were come in Expectation to join the Forces which the French intended should come with Mons. Duvivier from France and Louisburg; and that 2 Men of War were expected to be early on our Coasts to prevent any Succours from being sent to the Garrison: That upon the Report of Part of the New-England Fleet's being seen off the Eastern Coast of Nova Scotia, their Thoughts at Menis were various, some thinking 'em to be the Fishery, others a Force going to take Possession of Canso: That since the News of the Canadeans being arrived at Chignicto, which the Garrison had receiv'd 5 Weeks ago, there had been a grand Expectation among all the Settlements in Nova Scotia, of a very vigorous Attempt's being made upon his Majesty's Garrison at Annapolis Royal; and that a secret Correspondence was discover'd to have been carried on between the Inhabitants of Annapolis-River about the Fort and those of the Bay, for which several of the former had been seiz'd and were now confin'd in Prison: But that as that Fort was now in good repair as to its Out-works, there was no fear of the Enemy's doing much harm to the Body of the Place with their Firelocks. And upon the Whole, those

Letters add, "That if the Enemy's Projects had not been defeated by those of this Government, the Garrison might have had a great deal of Work this Spring."

We hear from Newport, that on the 4th Instant was launched there, before a vast Multitude of Spectatores, a fine Ship of 400 Tons, design'd for a Privateer, and to carry 20 Guns on her Main Deck.

Yesterday his Majesty's Ship Princess Mary sail'd from Nantasket Road, in order to join Commodore [Peter] Warren off Louisburg, to the great Satisfaction of all Wellwishers to the important Expedition, who had been under much Concern that that gallant Ship has been so long from her Station, at this critical juncture.

[Published in the same issue:]

AS CAPE BRETON AT PRESENT ENGAGES THE ATTENTENTION OF OUR READERS, PERHAPS THE FOLLOWING ACCOUNT OF THE IMPORTANCE OF THAT PLACE, WILL NOT BE DISAGREEABLE TO MANY OF THEM.

The Island of Breton, or as the French call it, the Isle Royal, lies between Newfoundland and Nova Scotia, and is about 30 Leagues long, and near 10 broad. The Soil is but indifferent, but the Coast is full of Good Harbours, in most of which the French have small Settlements and Stages for the Fishery; but there are no Fortifications of any Consequence except at Louisburg. This Town is about three quarters of a Mile long, and nearly oval. It is regularly fortified on the Land side, and the Harbour is defended by several Batteries.

This Island was given to the French by the (wise) Treaty of Utrecht, and by the Advantage of it they have carried on a prodigious Fishery, annually employing 1000 Sail of Vessels, from 200 to 400 Tons, and 20,000 Men. It is computed that they cure five Millions of Quintals of Fish, Communibus Annis: And in 1730. they carried to Marseilles only, twenty two hundred thousand Quintals.

From hence it plainly appears to have been a vast Nursery of Seamen, and a prodigious Addition to the Riches and Strength of

APPENDIX III

France, and that the Reduction of it must be a proportionable Increase of the Number of British Seamen, and of the Wealth of Britain, and the British Dominions in America: For the French, if removed from thence, have no other Shelter for their Fishery nearer than Old France, and must therefore of Necessity drop it in a great Measure.

From the Situation of the Island, it commands Navigation up the great River St. Lawrence, and so cuts off all Communication with Quebeck, by which Means the whole Country of Canada must in a little Time fall into the Hands of the English, if they are once master of Cape Breton. — Some of the many Consequences of which are as follow:

The French Sugar Islands would lose the chief Vent for their Rum and Molasses, and the Supply of Lumber and Provisions they now have from Canada; and the English Islands would gain both. Great Britain must have a boundless Vent for all Kinds of coarse Woollens, and many other Kinds of their Manufactures, and command the valuable Trade in Fur, with all the Indian Nations. — And those of them who live near the English Settlements, will have no French Missionaries to stir them up to a mischievous and expensive War.

While on the other Hand, so long as the French keep Possession of that Place, all the British Plantations in North America, will be liable to perpetual Annoyance from their Parties and Indians by Land, and all the British Navigation to and in America, from their Privateers and Men of War, as we have sufficiently experienced the last Summer.

The only Reflection I shall make on these Facts, is, that every Man who loves his Country, ought to pray for the Success of the present Expedition.

THE NEW-YORK WEEKLY POST-BOY

The Issue of July 15, 1745

Boston, June 3. On Thursday last arrived here Capt. Smith in a Transport with Expresses in 8 Days from Lieut. General Pepperel and Commodore Warren; by whom also came Letters from most of the Officers in the present Expedition against Cape Breton, from which we learn, That since the last Account, our Forces had made their Approaches so near the Town of Louisburg, as to have compleated a Fascine Battery of 42 and 18 Pounders within 200 Yards of the West Gate; with which they had annoyed the Enemy's Work, so that they had beat down the Draw-Bridge before the Gate, and almost the whole Gate, as also the Parapet of the Demi-Lune Battery fronting that Way, and had got a considerable Breach there, so that they had a fair View into the Town; where though they could observe the Enemy at work in raising a Fascine Battery within the Gate against them, they kept such an incessant firing, and so successfully, they doubted not of soon having such a Breach, as would render the Place easy of Assault. — We also learn, That they had on the North-Side of the Harbour fronting the Magazine and Demi-Lune on that Side, raised another Fascine Battery, and had got some 42 Pounders already there, and began to play them on the Town and Battery the Day that Capt. Smith came away, which being within a point blank Shot, must not only damage the said Battery and Town on that Side, but much annoy the Enemy in the Works they are carrying on within to hinder our Approaches at the West Gate; so that the Town was now exposed to five continual Fires, which had beat down many Houses, with the Roofs, etc. of the principal Ones, and in that Way done as much Damage as could be expected. — We farther have sure Intelligence, That our People, in reconnoitering the Harbour, Shores, etc. had discovered a Number of Cannon on the Lighthouse Side of the Harbour, in the Water just below Low-water Mark; which it is supposed were designed for a Battery to be built at the Lighthouse this Year; but upon Discovery of our Fleet, tumbled down the Precipice into the sea, to prevent their falling into our Hands; but that notwithstanding they were exposed to the Island-Battery, our People had weighed and got up most of them; for the Security of which and the building a Fascine Battery there, there was a proper Detachment posted: but to prevent the Recovery of those Cannon the Enemy had sallied from the Town, and about 100 of them in Boats landed on the Light-house Point, who were no sooner on Shore, but a Party of ours got betwixt them and their Boats, so that they flew immediately to the Woods for Shelter, their Return to the Town being impossible; one of those was taken Prisoner,

APPENDIX III

who proved to be a Seaman belonging to a Snow from France, that got into the Harbour in a Fog, undiscovered by our Cruizers, from whom they got Intelligence, that an Armament was coming from Brest to reinforce that Place, and proceed to Annapolis, consisting of 3 Men of War, a 70 Gun Ship, two of 56 Guns, and two Company Ships of 36 Guns each. — And we have further certain Accounts, That on the 18th ult. the Mermaid, Capt. [James] Douglass, a 40 Gun Ship, and the Shirley-Galley, Capt. [John] Rouse, one of our Cruizers, fell in with a French Man of War, and engag'd her, the former Broadside and Broadside; and the latter being too small to lay along-side, and going well, annoyed her astern, or ahead, or on the Quarter, as he could best; and as she prov'd a Ship of Force, they knowing how the Commodore bore of them, fought and sailed till they fell in with him and the Fleet; but Night coming on, it was 9 o'Clock before the Commodore got along side near enough to engage, when after 2 or 3 Broadsides, she struck and ask'd for Quarters, and was the next Day secured; she is call'd the Vigilant, a new Ship never at Sea before, of 64 Guns, and 560 Men, and was commanded by the Marquis du Maisonfort; but the Command of her is now given by the Commodore to Capt. [James] Douglas, who so gallantly engag'd her in the Mermaid, and the Command of the Mermaid to Mr. [Capt W.] Montague. It is unknown of what Consequence the Caption of this Ship is, as she proves to be laden with warlike Stores of all sorts for the supporting a Siege, reinforcing their Fortifications, and the supplying of the Indians, amongst which are a great Number of heavy Cannon, with their Materials, besides Small-Arms, Bomb Shells, Cohorns, etc. even down to an Indian Hatchet; and exclusive of the Ship's Provision, 1000 Half Barrels of Gunpowder; 'tis also said, she has on board three Year's Pay, and all the Cloathing for the Garrisons at Cape Breton and Canada; and as there is a good Look out for the Remainder of those Ships, it is not doubted but they will meet the same Fate. The Vigilant in her Passage from France had taken two large Ships from S. Carolina, laden with Rice for London, which were also expected soon after them they having parted with them but a few Days before. After this Ship was taken, she was with a great Number of Flags of all Sorts, in Procession towed across the Entrance of the Harbour by the Mermaid, in View of the Town, into Chappeaurouge-Bay; and as the Enemy's Dependance must have been on the Arrival of these Ships. seeing of their Commodore taken must intimidate them much: There is a Person of Distinction on board, but whether it be a new Governor, or M. Duvivier in Disguise, was not discovered when Capt Smith came away — . We farther have certain Intelligence, that the Princess Mary, Capt. [Richard] Edwards, had joined the Fleet the Day of Capt. Smith's Departure; and that he also met the Hector, Capt. [Frederick] Cornwall, off Forchette, about 4 Leagues from Chappeaurouge, the next Day, bound down along with a fair Wind; so that the Fleet consists now of the Superbe and Princess Mary, of 60 Guns each, the Mermaid, Launceston, Eltham, and Hector, of 40 Guns each, the Bien Amie, 24 Guns, and three 20 Gun Ships, three Snows of 20 Guns, one Brig. and the Rhode Island and Connecticut Colony Sloops, all well mann'd and fitted; which it is not to be supposed any Force will come from France equal to this Year; besides we hear the Commodore expects also three other Ships of War to join him from Newfoundland; which with the Ships expected to Annapolis, Piscataqua, etc. with Stores, it is not doubted will protect our Northern Colonies from any Invasion this Year. — We learn further, That the Fluxes that had got amongst our People were over. — That the Army was in a general good Health, and high Spirits. — That since the last Account, we had lost but two Men killed at one of our Batteries, and one wounded with the Loss of a Leg. — That the Lieut. General [Pepperrell] and Commodore [Warren] had determined upon Measures of prosecuting (as soon as Affairs were in a proper Disposition for that Purpose) some more vigorous Attack, of which we hope shortly to have a good Account. — That two of the Men of War and Capt. [Jonathan] Snelling has taken in one of the Eastern Harbours a Ship from France laden with Stores and Provisions, with 27 Men; and the Rhode Island Sloop has taken a Brig from France, laden with Provisions, etc. both which Vessels confirm the Account of an Armament coming from Brest.

By the Way of Piscataqua we hear, That three Sail of Men of War arrived at Newfoundland from England, bound to join Commodore Warren, at Cape Breton; when they arrive, 'tis thought

APPENDIX III

he will be an Over-match for any French Ships that can come to the Relief of Louisburg.

A few Days since, a Billander well mann'd and arm'd was sent by this Government to the Relief of Annapolis Royal, besieg'd by the French and Indians; but Yesterday we had the agreeable News, by a Schooner from that Place, that about ten Days ago the Enemy had raised the Siege and were drawn off. We are likewise informed, that Capt. [John Henry] Bastide, his Majesty's chief Engineer in Nova Scotia, with some Gunners, were gone from Annapolis Royal, to the Army before Lewisbourg.

Yesterday Capt. Ingersol, in a Privateer belonging to this Town arrived at Salem, with a large French Sugar Ship, taken in Company with Capt. Morris of Rhode Island.

THE NEW-YORK WEEKLY POST-BOY
The Issue of July 22, 1745

Boston, July 8. Last Tuesday Night arrived here Capt. [Moses] Bennet with Dispatches from Lieutenant General Pepperel and Commodore Warren, by which we have the good News of the Surrender of the important City and Fortresses of Louisburg, at Cape Breton, to our Forces on the 17th of June last, after a Siege of near 7 Weeks; Our Fascine Batteries opposite to the West Gate having almost beat down their circular Battery; and the new Battery at the Light-House side has with our Cannon and a large Mortar plaid so incessantly and warmly on the Island Battery, that Numbers of the French abandon'd it and ran down into the Sea to avoid the Fire; For further Particulars of this important Event, we refer to the following Letters, written by Gentlemen in the Army, well acquainted with the whole Affair.

LETTER FROM AN OFFICER OF NOTE IN THE TRAIN, DATED LOUISBURG, JUNE 20, 1745.

"Glory to God, and Joy and Happiness to my Country, in the Reduction of this Place, which we are now possessed of. It's a City vastly beyond all Expectation, for Strength and Beautiful Fortification, but we have made terrible Havock with our Guns and Bombs, and according to the French Account we have fired Nine Thousand Shot, and Six Hundred Bombs into it. — It was impossible for us to keep a true Account of the Shot and Bombs, but I verily believe the French Account is true, and there is but one House in the Place but has received Damage. The City was delivered up by Capitulation, wherein the Inhabitants were to have their personal Effects, and the Honours of War, and to be transported to France at our Cost, and well off too, for such a fine City, which will be an everlasting Honour to my Countrymen — We find here 148 Embrazures, in the Walls, 83 Cannon, whereof 6 are English six Pounders; also 5 fine Brass Mortars and Iron ditto. I have not been to the Island Battery; shall let you know more by the next. —

EXTRACT OF A LETTER FROM AN OFFICER OF NOTE, DATED LOUISBOURG, JUNE 18, 1745.

"Yesterday, after a tedious Siege of 7 Weeks, on a Capitulation agreed on, a large Detachment of our Troops entered this City, and all the Army are preparing to take their Posts accordingly. The whole Loss we have sustained by the Enemy and Sickness, will not exceed 120 Men: a Number inconsiderable in proportion to the Hazard, and the Consequence of the Acquisition. The Enemy acknowledge we killed of them within the Walls during the Siege, 87 Men, and out of two Parties, one that sallied out to oppose our landing, the other to cut off a Guard posted near the Light House, a yet larger Number. The whole Town is so wreck'd by our Cannon and Bombs, that scarce 3 Houses in it are at this Hour tenantable. The great Fire we made on the 16th Instant, effected our Wishes. The Strength of this City vastly exceeds my Expectation. Had the Enemy's Ammunition held out, or any Naval Force under Cover of the Fogs, been able to have entered, and afforded Succour to the Besieged, we should have had very little Room to have expected so happy an Issue. The Capitulation was absolutely necessary, and well timed; for had the Resolutions which were taken a very few Hours before to make a general Attack by Land and Sea, and which we were with all Diligence preparing for, by making Ladders, Fascines, etc. and fixing up Shallops and Whale Boats, we should have greatly suffered; but happy was it for my poor Countrymen, the Enemy beat a Parley, sent out a Flag, and a speedy Agreement followed, or I really think we must have lost more than half our Army. At all Events the Conquest is secure by an Entry of about 2000 English Troops, 11 Men of War, and all our Transports into this Harbour, and the Embarkation of this and the Island Battery Garrisons, consisting of about 550 Men, French and Swiss, aboard the several King's Ships. There yet remains in the City about 1500 Men, Youths called Soldiers, which must needs be sent to Boston, where or in its Neighbourhood, hope they'll become good Settlers, It is determined that they embark on Monday next at farthest.

A LETTER FROM ONE OF THE CHAPLAINS IN THE ARMY
DATED LOUISBURG, JUNE 19.

"God in his infinite kind Providence now gives me the Pleasure to date a Letter to you at and in the City of Louisburg. Last Saturday the Commodore was on Shore, and he with the Land Council of War had determined, as soon as the Wind would permit, to make a general Attack; but God, who does all Things well, in his great Goodness prevented us; for the Council had but just broken up, and before the Gentlemen were dispersed, there came a Flag of Truce from the City, desiring that there might be a Cessation of Arms till they in the City could get together and conclude upon Articles of Capitulation. It was allowed them till the next Morning at 8 o'Clock, at which time they sent us Articles which we thought not proper in any wise to agree to, and too tedious now to relate. Then we proposed to them Terms which follow: That they should resign to us the City, with the warlike or King's Stores, and that they might have all their personal Estate, and that they should be transported to France in the Ships and Vessels of theirs that were in the Harbour, and that we would furnish them with what more necessary. These Terms were sent into the City, and their Compliance with them returned about 6 o'Clock. Hostages were given by each Party capitulating: The next Day the Commodore sent 2 or 3 Companies of Marines to take Possession of the Island Battery, and then came into the Harbour with his Ships, the Wind favouring, and about 6 o'Clock the General and Gentlemen on shore entred the City, two Regiments of Foot marching before him; at which Time I also came in; and we are now in Possession rejoicing. — O that we may rejoice with true Thankfulness! The City is, I had like to have said, infinitely, stronger than it was ever represented. — If we had endeavoured to have stormed it, it is very uncertain whether we should have succeeded, in my Opinion; but sure I am, Success would have been attended with the Loss of great Numbers. People are generally pleas'd with the Terms on which the City was given up; and I think every one has the greatest Reason to rejoice, and thank God that he in his Providence prevented our attempting it by Storm. — All that have been killed by the Savages and French on Scouts, those that were killed by and drowned in the unfortunate Attempt on the Island Battery, and those that have been killed by the Enemy's small and great Shot from the Town; and lastly, those that have lost their Lives by the unhappy splitting of some of our Cannon, and our large 13 Inch Mortar, does not amount to but about 150. We found, when we came into the City, about 150 of our People taken at the Island Battery. The Time of our Siege, from the Time we landed till the City was delivered up to us, was 6 Weeks and 5 Days. We have lost few, very few by Sickness."

As Capt. [Moses] Bennet arrived in the Night, he first carried the General and Commodore's Dispatches to his Excellency, then at Dorchester, and on his Return, communicated the joyful Tidings to the Hon. Col. Wendell's Company of Militia, then on Duty as a military Watch, who, (not able longer to conceal their Joy) about 4 o'Clock, alarm'd the Town, by firing their Guns and beating their Drums, and before five, all the Bells in the Town began to ring, and continued ringing most part of the Day. The Inhabitants thus agreeably surprized, laid aside all Thoughts of Business, and each one seem'd to strive to out-do his Neighbour in Expressions of Joy. Many Persons who were gone to Cambridge to be present at the Commencement, came to Town to rejoice with us, as did many others from the Country, and the Day was spent in firing of Cannon, feasting and drinking of Healths, and in preparing Fire-Works, etc. against the Evening. And to add to the Pleasures of the Day, Col. Pollard and his Company of Cadets were under Arms, and made a very fine Appearance. Now the Churl and the Niggard became generous, and even the Poor forgot their Poverty; and in the Evening the whole Town appeared as it were in a Blaze, almost

APPENDIX III

every House being finely illuminated. In some of the principal Streets were a great variety of Fire-Works, and curious Devices for the Entertainment of the almost numberless Spectators, and in the Fields were several Bonfires for the Diversion of the less polite, besides a large one in the Common, where was a Tent erected, and plenty of good Liquor for all that would drink. In a Word, never before, upon any Occasion, was observed so universal and unaffected a Joy; nor was there ever seen so many Persons of both Sexes at one Time walking about, as appeared that Evening, the Streets being as light as Day, and the Weather extreamly pleasant. And what is very remarkable, no ill Accident happen'd to any Person, nor was there any of those Disorders committed, which are too common on such Occasions.

There has likewise been great Rejoicings at many other Towns, on the glorious Success of his Majesty's Arms.

It is said, that just as the Express came away, a large Store-Ship bound to Canada appeared off the Harbour of Louisburg for a Pilot, which was taken and carried in, and by her they had Advice, that she came out of France with several other Vessels bound to the same Place.

We hear, that upon the Surrender of the Place, Capt. [W.] Montague, Commander of the Mermaid Man of War, was dispatch'd to England in a Sloop, with the news of the Success.

Several Transports with Troops, and others with Provisions and Stores, lie ready to sail for Cape Breton.

[Published in the same issue]:

New York, July 15. Last Tuesday late at Night arrived an Express from his Excellency Governor Shirley to his Excellency our Governor, with an Account of the Surrender of Louisburg, with all the Fortresses thereto belonging, to the Obedience of his Majesty; Upon which Occasion his Excellency, with the Gentlemen of his Majesty's Council, and several other Gentlemen and principal Merchants, were entertained at Dinner the next Day by the Mayor and Corporation of this City, when all the loyal Healths were drank, with those concerned in this considerable Conquest, and to the Continuance of Louisburg under British Colours for ever, while the Cannon of Copley Battery and several Vessels in the Harbour were firing. In the Evening there was a magnificent Bonfire erected, at which the same Healths were repeated: At Night the whole City was splendidly illuminated, and the greatest Demonstration of Joy appeared in every Man's Countenance upon hearing the good News. The Gentlemen at Dinner made a handsome Collection for the Person who brought the Express, which he voluntarily engaged to convey hither; And there being present at this Entertainment many of the Persons who, at the Instance of his Excellency our Governor, had engaged with him in a Subscription, immediately after the Dissolution of the late Assembly, for the purchasing a Quantity of Provisions to be forthwith transported and consigned to Governor Shirly, for the Service of the Expedition; The Vote of the General Court of the Massachusetts Bay was read, returning their Thanks to his Excellency Governor Clinton, for that Instance of his Zeal in promoting this important Expedition; and to desire he would acquaint the Gentlemen concerned in the said Subscription, how acceptable this Mark of their publick Spirit was to that Court.

THE NEW-YORK WEEKLY POST-BOY

The Issue of August 5, 1745

THE FOLLOWING BEING A MORE PARTICULAR AND METHODICAL ACCOUNT OF THE SIEGE AND SURRENDER OF LOUISBURG, THAN ANY OTHER YET PUBLISHED, WE NOW GIVE IT TO OUR READERS.

By Dispatches brought from General Pepperell and Commodore Warren, by Capt. [Moses] Bennet, as formerly mention'd, we were advis'd, that on the 17th of last Month, the Enemy surrender'd to His Majesty the City of Louisburg, and the whole Island of Cape-Breton, upon the following Terms, viz. "That they should march out of the City with their Arms and the other Honours of War, and carry off all their personal Effects, and to be transported to France at His Majesty's Expense." — The Number of the Enemy found in the City after the Surrender, were about 600 regular Troops, French and Swiss; and according to the best Accounts that could be got before the Express came away, about 1400 other effective Men under Arms, Inhabitants of the City and of other

APPENDIX III 217

Settlements on the Island, from whence the Enemy had drawn in about 900 to strengthen the Garrison, upon the Discovery of our Cruizers sent before the Embarkation of our Troops, to cruize constantly off the Harbour, to prevent any early Vessels from getting into it with Provisions or Intelligence, and which were discovered, notwithstanding their Orders to cruize out of Sight of the City: This Discovery was probably occasion'd by the long stay of our Troops at Canso, which lies about 20 Leagues from Louisburg, where they were detain'd about three Weeks, and hindred from landing in Chappeauroge-Bay, by the great Quantities of Ice which are always found on that Coast in the Spring, and which happen'd to continue very late this Year. What greatly facilitated this Conquest, was probably the Conduct and Bravery of our Troops at their first landing, when a Party of the Enemy of about 100, came out of the City to oppose 'em, with Capt. Morepang [Morpain] accounted their Hero, at their Head; but a Party of our Men landing under the Fire of some of our smaller Cruizers, row'd on Shore very briskly in their Whale Boats, and so resolutely march'd up and attack'd the Enemy, that they kill'd 8 on the Spot, wounded several others, and took ten Prisoners, among whom was Mr. Boullarderie, who was formerly a Capt of Foot in France, an Officer of great Bravery, and so.c'd Mr. Morepang to make a very precipitate Retreat with the rest into the City. This was done without the Loss of one Man on our side; and in this their first Action our Men took so good Aim, that one of the Slain was found with five Balls lodg'd in his Breast. The good Behaviour of our Troops on this Occasion, and their March towards the City, struck such a Terror into the Enemy, that they quitted their Grand Battery, lying at the Bottom of the Harbour, and right against the Mouth of it, having in it 28 Cannon of 42 Pound Shot each, spik'd up, (the other Cannon belonging to that Battery having been carry'd into the City some Time before.) This Battery, of which our Troops had thus possess'd themselves (the Guns found in it being soon unspik'd) was of great Importance to them; for thereby they had obtain'd in a great Measure the Command of the Harbour, and were capable of annoying the City with some of their own Cannon. Our Troops then rais'd a Battery against the West Gate of the City, according to the Plan of Operations projected here before their Departure, and from Time to Time made such Advances, notwithstanding the furious Fire they frequently sustain'd from the Enemy's Works, under the direction of an Engineer of great Repute, that for a very considerable Time before the Surrender, they were within Musket Shot of 'em, and being generally good Mark's Men, pick'd off the Enemy with their Small Arms from their Walls and in the City, in such a Manner, that at last they could not shew their Heads without running a very great Risque of their Lives: Our Troops also erected a Battery between the West Gate and the Grand Battery, which was of Service, not only to annoy the City in general, but also to drive the Enemy from a Work which they had rais'd within the Walls over against the Breach made at the West Gate, and by the Fire from these Batteries the West Gate was demolished, and a practicable Breach made there as our Troops and the Enemy judg'd, the circular Battery ruin'd, and all the Guns in it, except three, dismounted; and the whole City was so exceedingly batter'd that all the Buildings in general were render'd scarce habitable, there having been thrown into it from these Batteries, according to the French Account (it being impossible for our People, as one of the principal Officers in the Train of Artillery writes, to keep an exact Account) 9000 Shot, and 600 Bombs; and as the Island Battery, which stands on a Rock in the Sea at the Harbour's Mouth, and guards the Entrance of it, (and which a Party of our Men had in vain attempted to take by Storm, in their Whale Boats) was a Place of great Consequence, our Troops rais'd a Battery on the opposite Shore near the Enemy's Light House, which, considering the steepness and difficulty of the Ground, over which the Artillery was carry'd and the short Time wherein it was made, was a very extraordinary One, and from which the Execution done by our Cannon and Mortars was so great, that the first Day's Fire made the Enemy forsake their Guns, and drove several of them into the Sea for Shelter. —

While the General with the Land Forces was thus employ'd on Shore, the Commodore with his Squadron was as vigilant and successful at Sea, for nothing escap'd 'em, except two Brigs, which by thick foggy Weather, frequent on these Coasts, got into the Harbour with some small Supplies, and they had the good Fortune to take a 64 Gun Ship, bound from France to Louisburg, with Stores for the Garrison. This Ship fell in first with the Mermaid, Capt. [James] Douglass, who attacked her, but finding her too heavy for him, very directly led her down to the Commodore, who immediately came up and engag'd her Yard Arm and Yard Arm, and being surrounded with the rest of the Squadron, she was taken with very little loss on our Side, the Commodore who was in the hottest of the Action not having lost a Man, and without any great Loss of Men on the Side of the French. — Two Days before the Parley, the Commodore, after a Consultation had with his Officers, determin'd to enter the Harbour with his Ships, having some time before settled the Line of Battle. — But the Land Forces, to return to them, having repuls'd every Party that sally'd out against 'em, and having gain'd Advantages in diverse Skirmishes on the Island, and a Party of our Scouts having had an Obstinate Fight for four Hours with a larger Party of the Enemy, French and Indians, wherein our Men prevail'd, and finally routed 'em, killing about 40 on the Spot and taking divers Prisoners; and on the 16th our Battery rais'd against the Island Battery having made the severe Fire before mention'd, and at the same time a most fierce Fire having been made from our other Batteries upon the City, the Enemy were distressed to that Degree that they could not show their Heads, nor stir from their cover'd Ways, and having but Forty four Barrels of Powder left in their Magazine within the City, they beat a Parley, and thereupon sent out a Flag of Truce, which came to the Camp just after the General and Commodore had come to a Resolution to make a general Assault by Land and Sea the Day following, and an Agreement to surrender the City on the Terms aforemention'd was soon made, and happily for both Parties; for although considering our Strength by Sea and Land, and the Gallantry of our Countrymen, of which the Enemy had large Experience, the Issue of the General Assault must in all probability have been in our Favour, yet many Lives must have been lost on both Sides. — Thus ended this Expedition, to the perpetual Honour of his Majesty's American Arms, with the Loss in the whole at Land of about 100 Men on our Side, and of the Enemy, by their own Confession, 87 Men within the Walls, and with the Loss at Sea of one Ship only, the Prince of Orange Snow, belonging to this Province, lost, as it is suppos'd, in a Storm as she was cruizing off the Harbour's Mouth, whereby there are unfortunately made about 50 disconsolate Widows in one of our Fishing Towns, and without Damage to any of His Majesty's Ships of War, which after the Capitulation enter'd the Harbour without having ever fir'd or had Occasion to fire a Shot at any of the Enemy's Works. —

By this happy Success of His Majesty's Arms, a very great Addition is made to the Strength and Security of all his Majesty's Dominions on this Continent, and the Dangers attending the Navigation of his Subjects in these Seas, are very much lessen'd, and that great Source of Wealth and Naval Power the Cod Fishery may with much Ease be preserv'd to the English, from whom the Enemy, immediately after their Declaration of the present War, began to take it with the utmost Violence, a Party of about 900 French and Indians being for that End sent out by Mr. Duquesnel, late Governor of Louisburg, to destroy the Settlements at Canso, one of the principal Seats of the English Fishery; who accordingly took and burnt 'em, not leaving a House standing. and made the Garrison (which surrender'd upon Terms) and all the Inhabitants Prisoners of War: And as the Reduction of this strong and important Fortress is the Consequence of an Expedition form'd, set on Foot and conducted by our Governor, with the most remarkable Application, Secrecy, Prudence and Dispatch (the first Inlistment being made on the 3d of February, and the Troops having embarqu'd and sail'd for Canso by the 24th of March) and entred into and carried on at first wholly by this Province, and afterwards with the Aid of some of the Neighbouring Colonies (under the general Command given by his Excellency) with the most surprizing Spirit, Alacrity and Zeal for the Common Cause, and supported by the Ships of War sent (most of 'em) upon his Excellency's Application to his Majesty for that Purpose) the Joy in this Province occasioned by it was very great and universal, and with the greatest Reason still continues to be so, and we hope; accompany'd with a due Sense of the Favour of Heaven most plainly and wonderfully vouchsaf'd unto us during the whole Prosecution of this Enterprize; for unto Almighty God, who loves to shew himself, and in an eminent Manner take Part with Right and Justice against those mighty Oppressors of the Earth, who like an overflowing Flood would bear down all before 'em, be ascrib'd this great and happy Conquest.

APPENDIX IV

LABOR ACCOUNT

Within a few days of the fall of Louisbourg the victorious army considered the necessity of repairing the damage done by their artillery. The Council of War, at a meeting held in the citadel on June 24, 1745, adopted the following resolution:

"Advized, that whereas many breaches are made in the walls and buildings of the town and batteries of Louisbourg by our artillery, and the Circular Battery, which did very much command the harbour, is render'd intirely useless without repair, and as the summer is the only season that such works can be effected here, the walls, citadell, hospital, magazines, kings's storehouses, and all other the king's buildings, also the batteries of the town, and the Grand and Island Batteries be repaired.

"That the said works and repairs be forthwith begun by the army.

"That the artificers employed for this purpose be allowed and paid seven shillings and six pence pr day N. E. currency, old tenor, for their labour.

"That common labourers be allowed and paid five shillings pr diem, said currency, for their labour.

"That the governments of the Massachusetts Bay, Connecticut, and New Hampshire be inform'd as soon as may be of this resolution, and application be made to them at the same time to pay the aforesaid labourers their quota in proportion to their number of troops in the army, also to signifie their pleasure relating to their going on with said repairs."

Pepperrell also wrote Warren about these arrangements on June 28th. (*6 Mass. Hist. Soc. Coll., X: 297.*)

There have been preserved several of the accounts relating to labor performed as a consequence of the above resolutions. The laborers were soldiers and their names are important in the absence of most of the official military rolls.

APPENDIX IV

The original of the hitherto unpublished document which follows is owned by Colonel and Mrs. Francis Russell Stoddard of New York, N. Y., and it is to them the Society of Colonial Wars is indebted for permission to publish it here.

The Account

City of Louisbourg to Sundrie Labourers in geting Handspikes for the Use of this Garrison Sept. 16. 1745 Dr

To Daniel Sheparson
Jonathn. Woodcock
Josiah Stereter
Wm. Freeman
Samuel Oliver
Elkanah Ring
George Usells
Benjamin Barrow
Wm. Jackson
Wm. Sawyer
Joseph Ramsden
Joseph Barden
} Each 2 Day at 6/ £3. 12 —

Louisbourg Octr. 10. 1745

Daniel Shepardson Made Oath that the men above mentioned were Duly Employd in the aforesd. Service Each One Day—

Jurat Coram Wm. Williams

———•———

Louisbourg Octr. 10. 1745

Sir

Pay Daniel Shepherdson Three pounds Twelve Shillings New England Currency old Tenr. to be by Him Jmmediate repaid to the Respective men Born on the List

We are Sir Your H. Servt.

Sir Wm Pepperrell Bart.
    Treasurer

John Storer
Comtee.
Wm. Williams

I approve of the above acct and Draft
Octobr 11th, 1745 Received of Wm Pepperell three pounds and twelve Shillings in full of this Acct.
Joel Whittemore   Daniel Shepardson
Wm Sewall

APPENDIX V

LIST OF EQUIPMENT

There is little evidence to show the character of the equipment carried by members of the expeditionary force to Louisbourg and this document taken from the Society of Colonial Wars' photostat of the original journal of the Reverend Adonijah Bidwell, chaplain of the Connecticut fleet, is therefore given here.

AN ACCOUNT OF THE CLOATHS AND OTHER THINGS WHICH I OWN IN CAPE BRETON EXPEDITION 1745
ADONIJAH BIDWELL.

- 1 Hat
- 2 Coats
- 2 Waistcoats
- 1 Watch Coat
- 2 pair of Breeches
- 4 pair of Stockings
- 2 Pair of Shoes
- 9 Shirts
- 11 Neck Bands
- 2 Caps
- 4 Handkerchiefs
- 3 Pair of Gloves

- 1 Pillow cass
- 4 Napkins
- 1 Pair of Scissars
- 1 Pen Knife
- 1 Pocket looking glass
- 1 Brass Ink Cass
- 1 Small Bottle
- 1 Port Mantle
- 1 a little box

APPENDIX VI

THE PRESENT LOUISBOURG

The following abstracts are given from a letter to the editor written by J. Clarence Webster, M.D., D.Sc., LL.D., F.R.S.C., a member of the Historic Sites and Monuments Board of Canada, whose interest in the restoration of Louisbourg has extended over many years. The letter is dated November 11, 1931.

"Since I last saw you much has transpired in connection with our proposals for developments at the old place. The Government of Canada acquired the entire area within the fortifications as well as considerable land outside, abut three years ago. There were about ten small houses on the property. These have been removed, with the exception of one, which has been kept as temporary quarters for the caretaker. In due course the site of the Grand Battery will be acquired as well as more land on which are siege positions of both campaigns. These areas form the Louisbourg National Historic Park. Plans for the development of the Park have been under consideration and are now in progress, work having been carried out during the last two years.

"Our plans include the following:—
  "1. Marking the cemeteries and surrounding them with suitable low fences.
  "2. Completion of the work of preserving the casemates.
  "3. Marking all the streets, with both the French and English names.
  "4. Removing rubbish heaps and outlining foundations of the Citadel, Governor's Garden, Hospital, Churches and other important buildings.
  "5. Opening certain of the streets so that they will be in a condition to be used. In this way it will be possible to drive from the Dauphin Gate to Rochefort Point.

APPENDIX VI

"6. Marking all important buildings.

"7. Building a Museum, fireproof in character. We shall reproduce one of the old buildings for this purpose, possibly the quarters of de Mézy.

"8. Marking various siege positions used by the attacking forces in both campagins.

"9. Already we have preserved the base of the original stone Lighthouse, near the modern Lighthouse.

"10. We have under consideration the restoration of one of the gateways, preferably the Dauphin Gate, of which we have the plans.

"These are the main items in our program at present.

"The Historic Sites and Monuments Board, assisted by a Local Advisory Committee advise the Government and direct the operations of the engineer appointed to carry on the work.

"This summer we erected and dedicated a monument at the site of Wolfe's Landing on Gabarus Bay.

"In due course we intend to have an official dedication of the Park, which we shall make an international affair, which we hope will be attended by British, American, French, and Canadian Representatives.

"We intend to lift some of the cannon belonging to the French ships sunk in the harbor, and to mount them somewhere within the fortifications.

"A large relief model of Louisbourg in the late period of its development under the French is now being designed."

APPENDIX VII

THE SOCIETY OF COLONIAL WARS AND LOUISBOURG

The Society of Colonial Wars has, from its earliest days, endeavored to create an interest in Louisbourg and particularly in the eventful campaign of 1745. It seems proper to here introduce a brief record of the more active evidences of that interest.

The First Church Service of the New York Society was held March 24, 1895, in commemoration of the one hundred and fifteenth anniversary of the departure of the New England troops for Louisbourg.

On June 17, 1895, the General Society of Colonial Wars unveiled a monument on the site of the Louisbourg walls. It was erected by the subscriptions of members. The architect was William Gedney Beatty.

The General Society in 1895 caused to be struck a Louisbourg medal, made by Tiffany & Company of New York City, from the metal of a bronze cannon found on the wreck of a French frigate sunk in Louisbourg harbor. The obverse bore the heads in profile of Sir William Pepperrell and Sir Peter Warren with the motto of the expedition: *Nil Desperandum Christo Duce* (Despair of nothing while Christ leads). The reverse was a reproduction of the medal struck by order of Louis XV in 1720 to commemorate the erection of Louisbourg fortress.

The Society of Colonial Wars in the State of New York owns a replica of the Louisbourg camp color or expeditionary flag, a valuable collection of engravings and maps of Louisbourg, and printed or photostatic copies of many books, journals and documents relating to the siege.

The official gravemarker of the General Society, intended solely to mark the graves of Colonial soldiers, is a facsimile of the Louisbourg Cross, and the War Service Insignia of the Society, awarded

THE SOCIETY'S GRAVE-MARKER
(*The Louisbourg Cross*)

APPENDIX VII

to members who saw active service in the World War, is also a copy of this cross. The original of the cross is of iron, hand-forged and gilded, and, prior to the fall of Louisbourg in 1745, stood in the market-place in that town. The original is now owned by Harvard University.[1]

The Society of Colonial Wars has issued several publications relating to Louisbourg, as follows:

(1) *The Second Capture of Louisbourg.* An address by Frederic H. Betts (1899). Published by the Society in the State of New York.

(2) The second Register of the General Society (1895) included a report of the Committee on the Louisbourg Memorial, and a roster of the officers on the expedition of 1745.

(3) The third Register of the General Society (1896) included the final report of the Committee on the Louisbourg Memorial with illustrations.

(4) The Society in the State of New York published *The Journals and Papers of Seth Pomeroy,* edited by L. Effingham de Forest (1926), including Pomeroy's Louisbourg journal.

---

[1] "Some twenty-five years ago, when we were rebuilding the eastern transept of Harvard College Library, I discovered in a gloomy corner an iron cross about thirty inches in height, which had stood in the market-place at Louisburg and was brought to Cambridge as a trophy. I thought it a pity to hide such a thing, so I had it gilded and set up over the southern entrance to the library." Fiske, *New France and New England* (*1902*), *256.*

BIBLIOGRAPHY

GENERAL WORKS

* Baker, H. M., The First Siege of Louisburg (1909).
* Belknap, J., History of New Hampshire (1831).
* Bourinot, J. G., Cape Breton (1892).
* Burrage, H. S., Maine at Louisburg (1910).
  Douglas, W., A Summary, Historical and Political of the First Planting, etc. (1749).
* Drake, S. A., The Taking of Louisburg, 1745 (1890).
* Drake, S. G., A Particular History of the Five Years French and Indian War (1870).
  Fiske, J., New France and New England (1902), 249–257.
  Hoyt, A. H., Pepperrell Papers (1874).
* Lincoln, C. H., Correspondence of William Shirley (1912).
* Macpherson, K. L., Scenic Sieges and Battlefields of French Canada (und.) (Montreal).
* Massachusetts Historical Society Collections, 6th series, volume X (Pepperrell Papers) (1899).
* McLennan, J. S., Louisbourg From Its Foundation to its Fall, 1713–1758 (1918).
  Parkman, F., Half Century of Conflict (1892), 2: 83–170.
* Parsons, U., The Life of Sir William Pepperrell, Bart. (1855).
* Wheeler, E. P., Lieut. Gen. Sir William Pepperrell, Bart. (1887).
  Winsor, J., Narrative and Critical History of America (1887), 5: 434–448.
  Wood, W., The Great Fortress (1915).
  Wrong, G. M., The Conquest of New France (1918).

ROLLS OF SOLDIERS AND SAILORS

* Burrage, H. S., Maine at Louisburg (1910).
* Chapin, H. M., A List of Rhode Island Soldiers and Sailors in King George's War (1920).

* Copy in the library of the Society of Colonial Wars in the State of New York.

Chapin, H. M., New England Vessels in the Expedition against Louisbourg, 1745. (1923).
* de Forest, L. E., Journals and Papers of Seth Pomeroy (1926), 52–54.
* Drake, S. G., A Particular History of the Five Years French and Indian War (1870), 227–248.
* Massachusetts Historical Society Collections, 6th series, volume X (Pepperrell Papers) (1899).
* New England Historical and Genealogical Register, 24: 367–380; 25: 249–269; 55: 65–70; 66: 113; 77: 59–71, 95–110.

JOURNALS

ANONYMOUS

An unknown sailor, a member of the crew of the sloop *Union*. Journal: March 24, 1745 — August 23, 1745 (many days without entries). Published as *A Journal of the Voige in the Sloop* UNION, *Elisha Mahew, Master, in an Expedition against Cape Briton* (*Providence, 1929*), with an introduction by Howard M. Chapin.

* BIDWELL, ADONIJAH

Born, October 18, 1716; died, June 2, 1784. A resident of Hartford, Connecticut. He was Chaplain of the Connecticut fleet. Journal: April 14, 1745 — October 8, 1745. Published in *New England Historical and Genealogical Register* (*Boston, 1873*), *vol. 27*. A photostatic copy of the original manuscript is owned by the Society of Colonial Wars in the State of New York.

* BRADSTREET, DUDLEY

Born March 12, 1707/8. He was a resident of Groton, Mass., and in October, 1745, he was commissioned a second lieutenant to fill a vacancy in Capt. John Warner's company, the Fourth Massachusetts Regiment (Willard's). Journal: April 22, 1745 — January 17, 1746. Manuscript owned by the Massachusetts Historical Society and published in its *Proceedings, second series, XI: 417–446*. Reprinted in *Three Military Diaries kept by Groton Soldiers in Different Wars* (*1901*), with notes by Samuel A. Green.

CLEAVES, BENJAMIN

Born, January 4, 1721/2; buried, August 16, 1808. Journal: March 6, 1744/5 — July 24, 1745. Cleaves was clerk of the company commanded by Capt. Benjamin Ives, Jr., in Col. Robert Hale's Fifth Massachusetts Regiment. The journal gives a roll of Capt. Ives' company. Manuscript owned by the New England Historic Genealogical Society and published in *New England Historical and Genealogical Register* (*Boston, 1912*), *66: 113–124*.

COBB, SYLVANUS

Journal: October 11, 1746 —. This is mentioned by Samuel G. Drake in his *A Particular History of the Five Years French and Indian War* (*1870*), *230*, but the location of the manuscript is unknown.

*CRAFT, BENJAMIN

Journal: April 24, 1745 — September 5, 1745. Manuscript owned by Essex Institute, Salem, Mass. Published in *Essex Institute Historical Collections* (*Salem, 1864*), *6: 180–194*. Also in *The Crafts Family* (*1893*), *659–670*, by J. M. and W. F. Crafts.

CURWEN, SAMUEL

A Captain Lieutenant in the 8th Massachusetts Regiment, Col. John Choate's. Journal: March 23, 1745 — July 25, 1745. Extracts published in *Journals and Letters of the late Samuel Curwen* (*1842*).

DURELL, PHILIP

Captain of the British man-of-war *Eltham* and later of Admiral Warren's flagship, the *Superbe*. Durell wrote a letter to London bearing the date June 20, 1745, which was published soon after its receipt in England. With it were published letters from an officer of marines, and from two others, apparently sailors, all three of these supplementary letters being anonymous. The original publication (folio, pp. 8) is exceedingly rare. There are copies in the New York Public Library, Boston Public Library, and Boston Athenæum. The full title is given: *A Particular Account Of the Taking Cape Breton from the French, by Admiral Warren and Sir William Pepperell, The 17th of June, 1745. With a Description of the Place and Fortifications; the Loss it will be to the French Trade, and the Advantage it will be to Great Britain and Ireland; With the Articles of the Capitulation of Fort Louisbourg. By Philip Durell, Esq; Capt. of His Majesty's Ship Superbe. To which is added, A Letter from an Officer of Marines to his Friend in London, giving an Account of the Siege of Louisbourg, and a Description of the Town, Harbour, Batteries, Number of Guns, etc. Also The Happy Situation of that Country; and an Account of M. Chambon, Governor of Louisbourg, being laid in Irons for surrendering it; In a Letter from a Gentleman in London, to a Merchant in the West of England (London, 1745).*

DWIGHT, JOSEPH

Joseph Dwight held three commissions during the Louisbourg expedition: Colonel of the Massachusetts Train of Artillery (February 20, 1744/5); Brigadier General (February 20, 1744/5); and Colonel of the Ninth Massachusetts Regiment and Captain of its First Company (June 18, 1745). There is supposed to be in existence a journal kept in 1745 and it was understood to be owned by Winslow Dwight, Esq., of Boston, and to be in the custody of the Massachusetts Historical Society. Mr. Dwight kindly gave his permission for the journal to be used in this work but it could not be located.

*EMERSON, REVEREND JOSEPH

Born, August 25, 1724; died, October 29, 1775. Graduate of Harvard, Class of 1743. Minister of the West Parish of Groton, Mass., now the Town of Pepperell [sic]. He was a chaplain on the frigate *Molineux*. His journal runs from March 15, 1745, to August 14, 1745. Manuscript owned by the Massachusetts Historical Society. Published in *Massachusetts Historical Society Proceedings* (*Boston, 1910*), with biographical notes.

GIBSON, JAMES

He was a gentleman volunteer at Louisbourg, and was without military rank. As a leading merchant of Boston his support of the expedition was highly important. He is supposed to have paid several hundred soldiers out of his own pocket. Journal: April 30, 1745 — July 4, 1745. Originally published in London, 1745. Reprinted in Boston, 1847, under the title *A Boston Merchant of 1745: or, Incidents in the Life of James Gibson*. Another edition issued at Boston in 1894 under the title *A Journal of the Siege of Louisbourg and Cape Breton in 1745. By Capt. James Gibson, with a Sketch of the Author*.

*GIDDINGS, DANIEL

Born, about 1704; died, October 25, 1771. A resident of Ipswich, Mass. A lieutenant in the 6th company, commanded by Capt. Jeremiah Foster in the Fifth Massachusetts Regiment (Hale's). Journal: March 11, 1745 — November 10, 1745, with omission of July 11, 1745 — November 6, 1745. The manuscript was owned in 1912 by J. J. Currier of Newburyport, Mass. Published in *Essex Institute Historical Collections (Salem, 1912), 48: 293–304*.

GORHAM, JOHN

The *Wast book* of Lieut. Col. John Gorham of the 7th Massachusetts Regiment contains a few references to the Louisbourg expedition. Manuscript owned in 1903 by John M. Gorham of Cleveland, Ohio. Published in *The Mayflower Descendant (Boston, 1903), vol. V*.

* GREEN, BENJAMIN

He was commissioned on March 1, 1745, as "secretary of the expedition." Journal from March 24, 1745, to August 22, 1745. Original owned by the American Antiquarian Society. Published in *American Antiquarian Society Proceedings (Worcester, 1910), vol. 20*. The journal was then edited by Charles H. Lincoln and was given the title *The Journal of Sir William Pepperrell*, although Pepperrell did not write it.

JUDD, PHILIP

A sergeant. Company and regiment unknown. Journal from June 1st to November 27, 1745. Manuscript (two large pages) owned by the Connecticut Historical Society. It has never been published but the Connecticut Historical Society has stated its intention to publish it in the near future.

* LETTRE D'UN HABITANT DE LOUISBOURG

The anonymous account of an eyewitness of the 1745 siege. The only account from the French viewpoint except the official reports. Of the original edition published in 1745 copies are extremely rare. None are known in the United States or England. It was reprinted in the *University of Toronto Studies (Toronto, 1897), History, second series, 1: 1–74,* edited by George M. Wrong.

PEPPERRELL, SIR WILLIAM

After the fall of Louisbourg, General Pepperrell sent to his friend, Captain Henry Stafford, in England, a journal of the siege. This was published in London in 1746 under the title, *An accurate Journal and Account of the Proceedings of the New England Land-Forces during the Late Expedition against the French Settlements on Cape Breton to the time of the Surrender of Louisbourg.* It was attested by Pepperrell and by General Samuel Waldo, Colonel Samuel Moore, and Lieut. Cols. Simon Lothrop, and Richard Gridley. This Journal was the same except for a few verbal differences as the one published as an appendix to Governor William Shirley's *A Letter from William Shirley, Esq., Governor of Massachusett's Bay, To his Grace the Duke of Newcastle.* Compare under William Shirley below and also *Eighth Journal* herein.

* POMEROY, SETH

Born, May 20, 1706; died, February 17, 1777. A resident of Northampton, Mass. He had a long and active military career, rising to be Colonel in the Provincial forces and Major General in the Revolution. At Louisbourg in 1745 he was Major of the 4th Massachusetts Regiment, commanded by Col. Samuel Willard. Pomeroy's Louisbourg journal covers March 14, 1744/5 — August 8, 1745. Published by the Society of Colonial Wars in the State of New York in *The Journals and Papers of Seth Pomeroy (1926),* edited by L. Effingham de Forest. Also published without annotation by Trumbull, *History of Northampton (1902), 2: 121–146.*

BIBLIOGRAPHY

* SHIRLEY, WILLIAM

Governor of Massachusetts Bay. Journal: March 24, 1744/5 — June 17, 1745. *A Journal of the Siege of Louisbourg and other Operations of the Forces, during the Expedition against the French Settlements on Cape Breton; drawn up at the Desire of the Council and House of Representatives of the Province of Massachusetts Bay; approved and attested by Sir William Pepperrell and the other Principal Officers who commanded in the said Expedition.* The text of this Journal agrees substantially with that of Sir William Pepperrell's *Accurate Journal*. See also the *Eighth Journal* herein. Shirley probably did not write this journal but he did enclose it with his report to the Home Office (*A Letter From William Shirley, Esq., Governor of Massachusett's Bay, To his Grace the Duke of Newcastle*) and both were published together. Published in London, 1746; in Boston, Mass., by J. Draper, 1746, and also by Rogers & Fowle, 1746. Reprinted in London, 1748. The Society of Colonial Wars in the State of New York has the London editions of 1746 and 1748.

STEARNS, BENJAMIN

This journal is usually attributed to Benjamin Stearns, an enlisted man in Capt. John Warner's company in the Fourth Massachusetts Regiment (Willard's), but the attribution may be incorrect. Journal: March 11, 1745—August 2, 1745. It is in part a copy of Dudley Bradstreet's journal (*q.v.*). Manuscript owned by the Massachusetts Historical Society and published in *Massachusetts Historical Society Proceedings* (*Boston, 1909*), third series, *2: 135–144*. Also published in *Acadiensis* (*St. John, N. B., 1908*), *8: 317–329*.

STORER, JOHN

Second Lieutenant Colonel of the First Massachusetts Regiment (Pepperrell's) and a member of the Council of War. He was from Maine. Journal: March 8, 1745—April 30, 1745. Published in the *Lewiston* (*Maine*) *Journal* in 1854. Extracts published in *History of the Cutter Family of New England* (*1871*), *310*.

WOLCOTT, ROGER

Born, 1679; died, 1767. A resident of Windsor and long prominent in Connecticut affairs. Major General and second in command of the Army at Louisbourg in 1745. Journal: May 30, 1745, — July 30, 1745. The journal includes some letters and a "retrospect" of the whole situation. Manuscript published in *Connecticut Historical Society Collections (Hartford, 1860), I: 131–161*. Also published in part in *Memorial of Henry Wolcott (1881)*, by Samuel Wolcott.

INDEX OF PERSONS

INDEX OF PERSONS

Aaron 34
Abbee, Daniel 106
Abbot, ——— 160
Adams, William 183
Agnue, ——— 189
Alexader ⎫
Alexadr   ⎬, Ebenezer, 1, 32, 36, 42,
Alexander ⎭   54, 128, 131-133
Allen ⎫, Charles 160
Allens ⎭
    Jacob 167
    William 130, 132
Allin, Samuel 101
Almor   ⎫, Valentine 56, 59
Almore ⎭
Ames, Simon 26
Anable, Robert 167
Arno, Capt. 183
Artel, ——— 204
Ash, Thomas 56
Ashley, John 157, 158, 160
Atchinson, Sergt. 48
Auchmuty, Robert xvi
Austin ⎫,Benajah 157
Austine ⎭
    Samuel 106

B., ——— ..7, 73, 92, 103, 123, 169
B., I. 92
Bacchus, John 168
Bagley ⎫
Baglies ⎬, Jonathan, 135, 143, 145, 148,
Bagly   ⎭   153, 154, 156, 166
Baker, ——— 155
    Ephraim, 20, 53, 155, 157, 161, 167
    H. M. .... :231
    John, 124, 125, 127-129, 131, 137,
        140, 146-151, 153-157, 159, 161-163

Balch, ——— 21, 23, 31
Ball, ——— 157
    Benjamin 157, 161
    Joseph ..101, 105, 106, 145, 147
Barden, Joseph, ... 223
Barker, Ephraim 143
    H. 131, 132
Barlow, ——— 154
Barnard, Sergt. 143, 144
Barnes, Lieut. 151
    Samuel 183
Barns, ——— 87
Barran, Isaac 151
Barrow, Benjamin 223
Barry, John 159
    Thomas 160
Barton, Capt. 183
Bastide ⎫, John Henry, 78, 89, 168,
Bastied ⎭   211
Beatty, William Gedney 228
Becket   ⎫, Robert 61, 74, 182
Beckwith ⎭
Belknap, Jeremy, xvi, 67, 73, 80, 109, 231
Belustor (see Blaster).
Bennet ⎫, Moses ..182, 211, 214, 216
Bennett ⎭
Bently, Michael 166
Benton, Jonathan 26
Bernard, ——— 123, 144
    Capt. 169
Betts, Frederic H. 229
Bickford, ——— 56
Bidwell, ——— 128
    Adonijah 46, 225, 232
Bilâtre, ——— 204
Biles (see Byles).
Bingham, Capt. 183

241

Blake, ——— 131
    Christopher 56, 59
Blanchard, ——— 157
Blaster, John 56, 57
Bliss, Ebenezer 130-134
    M. 34, 35
    Mary 9
Boin, Obadiah 165
Bollman (see Bulman).
Bosch (see Bush).
Bosworth, Nathaniel 137
Boulerdrie ⎱, (see de la Boular-
Boullarderie ⎰   derie).
Bourinot, J. G. 231
Bowman, Jonathan 168
Bradford, ——— 183
Bradish, ——— 128, 131
Bradstreet, Dudley 232, 237
    John, xvi, 45, 53, 92, 143, 160-162,
        170, 171, 176, 177, 202
Branham, Capt. 183
Brays, Nathaniel 160
Bret ⎱, Capt., 25, 123, 125, 150, 181
Britt ⎰
Broadstreet (see Bradstreet).
Brooks, Edward 58, 59, 91
Brower, Alexander 143
    I. 101
Brown, David 139
    Francis 152
    John 151, 165
    Peter 168
Browning, Robert 163
Bryant, Robert 154
Bull, Aaron 183
Bullman (see Bulman).
Bullock, Lieut. 142
Bulman, Alexander 42, 138-142
Burbank ⎱, ——— 40, 139
Burbanks ⎰
Burnhill, ——— 151
Burr, Andrew 9, 133, 134
Burrage, H. S. 231
Burry (see Burr).
Burt, M. 101

Busch ⎱, Capt. 45, 75, 182
Bush ⎰
Butler, Moses 53
Byles, Capt. 183
    Charles 124, 143

C., Col. 21
C., J. 41
Cahoone, Capt. 183
Calmady, J. 111, 181, 194
Call, Daniel 163
Campbell, ——— 141
Cannida, David 183
Card, John 54
Carey, Jonathan 138, 164
Carver, ——— 138
Cary (see Carey).
Casteen ⎱, ——— 63, 138, 162
Castine ⎰
Castle, ——— 101
Caule, ——— 162
Chamberlain, ——— 153
Chambon (see du Chambon).
Champion ⎱, Joshua, 145, 147, 149,
Champlin ⎰   156, 165
Chandler, Samuel 16, 32, 34
    Thomas 27, 54, 171
Chapin, ——— 2
    Howard M. 181, 231, 232
    Nathaniel 102, 106, 154
Chaplian, ——— 150
Chaplin (see Champlin).
Chapman, Capt. 183
    Daniel 132, 139, 165
Charly, ——— 153
Charties, ——— 161
Chattuck, Sergt. 154
Cheney ⎱, Lieut. 155
Cheny ⎰
    Thomas 160-165, 167
Chester, ——— 143
Choat ⎱, E. 139
Choate ⎰
    John, 31, 32, 46, 121, 122, 125,
      126, 128, 130, 132-134, 138,

INDEX 243

139, 144, 147, 153, 160, 169, 233
Church, Capt. 183
    James 40, 139, 148
Churchill, Sergt. 150
Clap, ——— 138
Clark, Capt. 62, 183
    John 159
    Josiah 149
Clary, Jonathan 20
Cleaves, Benjamin 233
Clinton, ——— 149, 216
Cobb, Sylvanus 73, 150, 167, 233
Coffin, Capt. 150
Cogsall, Joseph 152
Coit, Capt. 183
Colb (see Cobb).
Cole }
Coles } , Edward 151, 167
Coley (see Cooley).
Collins, Thomas 150
Colman, ——— 150
Colton, Charles 159, 161, 162
    Isaac, 32, 34, 40, 97, 99, 105, 122, 123, 126, 128-147, 149-151, 153-164
    Job 104, 136
Commins, ——— 167
Conant, William 161
Converse, ——— 129
Cook, Samuel 152
Cooley, Joseph 158-165
    Moses 101
    Roger 133-135, 137
    T. 101
Coolidge, Nehemiah 161
Cooly (see Cooley).
Coomes, William 56
Cooper, Capt. 183
Corbet }
Corbett } , Thomas 66
Coreah }
Coreh } , John 163, 164
Cornwall }
Cornwell } , Frederick, 25, 39, 118, 181, 210

Costeen (see Castine).
Cotton, Job 39
Cowell, Joseph 167
Craft }
Crafts } , Benjamin 233
    J. M. 233
    W. F. 233
Crossman, Ezekiel 152
Crow, William 159
Crowell, Joseph 136, 138
Crowfoot, ——— 140
Cumberland, Duke of 111
Cummins, Jacob 165
    Sergt. 144, 145
Currier, J. J. 235
Curwen }
Curwin } , Samuel 152-154, 233
Cutbridge, ——— 149
Cutler, Sergt. 157
Cuts }
Cutt } , Richard 53, 141
Cutter, Ammi Ruammah, 54, 158, 168
    Isaac 156
Cutting, ——— 148

D., ——— 87
Daggett, Capt. 183
Dakin }
Dakins } , ——— 38, 134
Davis, Capt. 149, 152, 183
    Gershom 152
Deal, Francis 163
Deering, Bray 53, 161
de Forest, Louis Effingham, 69, 229, 232, 236
de la Boularderie, ———, 68, 112, 217
de la Maisonfort, Capt., 20, 24, 90, 209
de la Perelle, ——— 26
Delboude, ——— 156
de Mézy, ——— 227
Deninson }
Denison } , Robert ... 127, 129, 160
Dennison }
De Salvert, ——— 122

De Thierry, Capt. 11, 113
Devotion, ——— 143
Dike, Nathaniel 40
Dinnison (see Denison).
Doan ⎱, Elisha 166
Doane ⎰
    Ephraim 42, 183
Dodd, Capt. 183
Dodge, ——— 141, 142
    Joseph 163
Dodgett, ——— 138
Dolittle (see Doolittle).
Donahew, David, 5, 7, 25, 33, 62, 73,
    74, 78, 82, 83, 89, 94, 105, 182
Done (see Doane).
Donil (see Donnell).
Donnahoo (see Donahew).
Donnel ⎱, Capt. 183
Donnell ⎰
    James 147, 148
    Nathaniel, 54, 147, 148, 151, 156,
        197
Donnohoo ⎫
Donoho   ⎬, (See Donahew).
Donowh   ⎪
Donowho ⎭
Doolittle, Charles, 133-135, 137, 143,
    147-154, 157, 159, 163-165, 167
Dotie, Thomas 164, 167
Douglas ⎱, James, 25, 111, 181, 182,
Douglass ⎰   194, 209, 219
    W. .... xvi, 231
Drake, Daniel 151, 233
    Samuel A. 231
    Samuel G. 231-233
Draper, J. 237
Drown, ——— 155
    Sergt. 154
du Bourzt, Marin Michel 78
du Chambon, Louis, 14, 26, 29, 115,
    234
    Mesillac 10
Dugless (see Douglas).
du Maisonfort (see de la Maisonfort).
Dumaresque ⎱, Philip 53, 146
Dumerisque ⎰

Duquesnel, ——— 220
Dural   ⎫
Durall ⎬, Philip, 24, 25, 74, 83, 111,
Durell ⎭   150, 181, 184, 194, 233,
        234
Durham, ——— 159
    John 164
Durton, Samuel 162
du Vivier, ———, 23, 170, 201, 204,
        205, 210
Dwight, ——— 47
    Joseph, 4, 53, 99, 107, 122, 123,
        138-140, 146, 150, 152, 159,
        161, 162, 164, 167, 168, 234
    Josiah 100
    Winslow 234
Dyke, ——— 138

E., ——— 40
Eastman, Ebenezer, 142, 145, 160, 161
Easty, ——— 151, 152
Eaton, ——— 48
Edmund ⎱, Ebenezer, 31, 125, 126,
Edmunds ⎰ 138, 140, 143-145, 149-
        151, 153, 154
Edward, ——— 145
Edwards, Abraham 161
    Richard ..25, 118, 150, 181, 210
Elis, Edward 54
Ellis, Corp. 142
    Eleazer 147, 148
Elwell, Zebulon 183
Ely, John 47
Emerson, Joseph 234
Enos, ——— 164

Faibanks, Joseph 167
Fairfield, John 53
Fairweather, ———, 34, 135, 136, 150-
    152, 154, 156, 157, 159, 161,
        162, 165
Fernald, John 74, 182
Fiske, John .... xvi, 231
Fitch, Adonijah 159, 163, 164

INDEX 245

Capt. 183
FitzGerald, Daniel 154
Flecher ⎱, William, 7, 8, 20, 25, 34,
Fletcher ⎰ 39, 61, 64, 66, 75, 77,
          82, 123, 138, 142, 148,
          149, 182, 187-190
Flood, Roland 159
Fogg, Daniel 53
Fones, Daniel, 40, 63, 74, 83, 139,
          143, 182
Foster, Jeremiah 124, 163, 235
Fox, —— 178
    Isaac 160
    Jonathan 40, 138
Freeman, William 223
Fry, James, 137, 143, 149, 159, 163,
          168
Fuller, Daniel 161, 167
    Joseph 139
Furnell (see Fernald).

Gale, Capt. 157
Gambell, —— 132
Gardner, Samuel 102
Garisun (see Garretson).
Garner, Maj. 102
Garretson, —— 38, 134
Gautier, —— 204
Gayton, Clark 182, 196
Gears, Capt. 183
Geary, Capt. 181
    Joseph 148
    Joshua 26, 36, 130, 132
George II 24
Gere ⎱, (see Geary).
Geree ⎰
Ghent, Gamaliel 149
Gibson, James 234, 235
Giddens ⎱, Capt. 183
Giddings ⎰
    Daniel 127-130, 235
Gillman ⎱
Gillmans ⎰, Ezekiel, 5, 129, 131, 136,
Gilman ⎰   138
Glover ⎱, Robert 42, 142, 163
Glovers ⎰

Gold, Capt. 168
Golden ⎱, (see Goulding).
Golding ⎰
Goldthawit ⎱
Goldthrait ⎰, Benjamin, 53, 145, 148,
Goldthwait ⎰   162
    Joseph ..145, 148, 162
Go—n, —— 144
Goodhue, —— 162
    Joseph 165
Goodsal, Amos 163
Goreham ⎱, Col. 64, 66
Gorham ⎰
    John 22, 64, 77, 87, 235
    John M. 235
    Shubael 64, 146, 147, 161
Gould, Zac. 40, 139
Goulden ⎱, Palmer ... 54, 141, 149
Goulding ⎰
Grainger, —— 154
Grant, Capt. 155
    James 54
Graves, —— 130
Green, —— 156, 165
    Benjamin 235
    Samuel A. 232
Gridley, Richard, xv, 109, 127, 152
          168, 236
Griffith, John 182
Grondy, —— 163
Gross, Lieut. 38, 134
Groton, Thomas 163
Gwinsey, Oliver 167

Haill ⎱, Daniel 18, 53, 86
Hale ⎰
    Robert 137, 166, 233, 235
Hall, —— 165
    Jeremiah 164
Hammond, Capt. 183
Hancock ⎱
Hancocke ⎰, Abner, 102, 106, 107,
Handcocks ⎰   162
Harmon, John 53, 124, 134
Harriman, Nathaniel 153

Harvey, —— 142
    Capt. 137
Hatch, Estes, 40, 54, 128, 131, 150,
    151, 153
Hathaway ⎫
Hatheway ⎬, Seth, 138, 139, 143, 144,
Hathoway ⎭   146, 152, 154, 165, 167

Hauley ⎫, Joseph, 4, 9, 13, 16, 32,
Hawley ⎭   125, 127, 129, 135, 141, 144

Hay ⎫, William 105, 145, 146
Hays ⎭
Haywood, —— 160, 161
Hedding, John 150
Herrick, Sergt. 156
Heuston (see Huston).
Hicks, Walter 167
Hildrick, James 152
Hill, Daniel 168
Hirstock, James 167
Hitchcock, Ebenezer 129
    Lieut. 105
    Reuben 106
Hoar (see Hore).
Hodge ⎫, —— 139, 143-146
Hodges ⎭
    Benjamin 161
    Ebenezer 161
    Maj. 150, 151, 155, 156
    Michael 183
Hoit, Sergt. 160
Holey ⎫, —— 146, 161
Holeys ⎭
Holms, John 155
Honiwell, Capt. 183
Hooker, John 20
Hoor ⎫, John 25, 123, 150, 181
Hore ⎭
    John Lar 101
    L. 100
Horan, George 165
Horton, Nathaniel 26
Hovey, —— 139, 141
    Amos 162

Howard, —— 148
    Oliver 163
    Sergt. 151
Howland, Joseph 107
Hoyt, A. H. 231
Hubbard, Jonathan 157, 162, 164
    Walter 130
Hungary, Queen of, ... 140
Hunt, —— 132
    Peter ... 141, 145, 149, 158, 166
    William 53
Huston, John, 40, 41, 54, 128, 138,
    139, 141, 142, 148, 151, 156, 157,
    161, 162, 164
Hutchinson, Thomas xvi

Indians,
    John Mommopuit 148
    John Sassiman 165
    Merrill 154
    Slate 162
Ingersol, Capt. 211
Inslie, Joshua 157
Iuial, Stephen 94
Ives, Benjamin 133, 139, 233

Jackson, —— 56
    William 183, 223
Jaques ⎫, Richard 53
Jaquesh ⎭
Jeffs, Thomas 161
Jillet, Isaac 106
Johnson, Capt. 142, 153, 155
    Caleb 99, 168
    Jonathan 29, 34
Jones, Capt. 183
    Lieut. 159
    Morrison 150
    Thomas 107, 150
Jonis, Joseph 160
Jonson (see Johnson).
Jordan, James 183
Judd, —— 131
    Philip 235
Jves (see Ives).

INDEX

Kalmady (see Calmady).
Karrer, ——— 24, 90
Keep, John 106
Keith, Robert 151
Kelly, ——— 163
Kemp, Capt. 25, 181
Kent, John 129
    Josiah 106
Kimberly, ——— 159
King, Capt. 155, 163, 166
    Charles 54, 167, 168
Kingberry, Capt. 145
Kinselagh ⎫
Kinslagh   ⎬, John 53, 155, 165
Kinslough ⎪
Kinslow   ⎪
Kirslough ⎭
Knowlton, Benjamin 106

Lakin, ——— 139
Lamb, Caleb ..97, 102, 105-108, 142
Lane, Capt. 42
Langdon, Samuel 6
Lanoo, ——— 204
Larkin, ——— 143
Lawrence, Capt. 158
    Ebenezer 56
    Jonathan 142, 154
L'Croix ⎫, John 2, 63, 138, 183
Le Croix ⎭
Lee, Capt. 183
    Stephen 150
Legraw, ——— 90
Light, John 136, 158, 159, 162
Lincoln, Charles H. 231, 235
Lite, John 159
Little, ——— 163
Littlejohn, Corp. 42, 142
Lommis, Mary 9
Long, Palatiah 152
Loring, ——— 134
    Joshua 183
Lothrop, Simon ..109, 155, 159, 236
Louis XV 228
Lovett, Capt. 183
Lowry, ——— 134

L'Roch, ——— 63
L'Vivier, ——— 62

M., ——— 163
M., H. 21
M., Lieut. 125
M., N. 101
Macgregory, Daniel 162, 163
Mackdonell, John 164
Mackdonald (see McDonald).
Mackfall, ——— 132
Macpherson, K. L. 231
Mac Sparran, ——— 155
Magiston, Nathaniel 163
Mahew (see Mayhew).
Maisonfort (see de la Maisonfort).
Mallett, ——— 124
Man, John, 2, 15, 32, 37, 43, 44, 53,
    132, 142-144, 156, 158, 160
Manning, John, 46, 93, 105, 145-147
    Samuel 153
March, ——— 135, 143, 160
Marin, Capt. 78
Marshall, ———, 150, 164, 166, 168
    Christopher 54, 153
Martin, William 164
Mascarene, Jean Paul 205
Mason, Joseph 164
Master, George 101
Mather, ——— 142, 157
    Roger 162
Maxey, ——— 157
Maxfield ⎫, Joshua 41, 139, 140
Maxwell ⎭
Mayhew, Elisha 183, 232
McDonald, James 24, 198
McLennan, J. S. 121, 231
Meechan, Isaac 106
Melvin, David 54, 144, 151, 156
Merell, Joseph 56
Merrick ⎫, Charles L. 97
Merrik ⎭
    David 101
    Jonathan 97, 107, 108
Metcalf, ——— 155, 159
M-fall (see Mackfall).

Miles, Capt. 142
    Samuel 183
Millar, Lieut. 156
Miller, ——— 122, 123
    Jeremiah 46
    Joseph 19-21, 24, 54
Millet, Sergt. 143
Mirick (see Merrick).
Molton (see Moulton).
Momford (see Mumford).
Monk, James 144
Montague, W. 181, 209, 215
Montique, ——— 25
Mood ⎫
Mooday ⎬ , Samuel, 6, 8, 30, 32, 53,
Moodey ⎭   84, 129
Moody
Moor ⎫
Moore ⎬ , Samuel, 55, 109, 126, 144,
             158, 163, 164, 197, 199,
                               236
Moors, Lieut. 131
Moran, Philip 145, 146
More (see Moore).
    Giffin 56
Morepang (see Morpain).
Morey, George ... 143, 145, 154, 165
Morgan, ——— 147, 148
    Samuel 159
Morpain, Capt., 10, 74, 112, 130, 217
Morris, Capt. 211
Morrison, ———, 20, 141, 151, 159,
                               163
Mose, Jothul 161
Moses 17, 24, 29, 30
Moses, Bildad 164
    John 159
Moulton, Jeremiah, 16, 54, 74, 75, 112,
          130, 160-162, 164, 166, 168
Mountford ⎫
Mountfort ⎬ , (see Mumford).
Mudget, ——— 162
Mumford, Capt. 183
    Richard, 141, 143, 149, 150, 152,
              155, 161, 163, 164
Mun (see Man).

Munson, ——— 128
Murphy, Morgan 161
Mygate, George 97, 106, 107

N., P. 105, 151, 154, 155
Nabby, ——— 169
Nash, Onisimus 40, 139
    Phineas 105, 137
Negroes,
    London 142
    Newport Cofew 163
    Peter 163
    Philip 143
Newcastle, Duke of ... 109, 176, 177
Newcome, Sergt. 136
Newman, John, 85, 88, 90, 165, 166
Newmarch ⎫
Newmarsh ⎬ , Capt. 94, 183
Newton, Maj. 21
Nible, Joseph 159
Nichols, John 168
Nicolls, ——— 142
    Ebenezer 154
Noble, Arthur 22, 53, 77, 87
    Capt. 158
    James 23, 53

Oliver, Samuel 223
Omstead, Jabez 20, 25, 54
Osborn, ——— 159
OSenr, ——— 162

P., Capt. 142, 169
Pa., ——— 21
Page, Phineas 160
Pain, Capt. 167
    Humphrey 167
Parkman, Francis, xv, xvi, 56, 122,
                         170, 231
Parry, Thomas 163
Parsons, U. 231
Partridge, Capt. 169
Pearce (see Pierce).
Pearson, Moses 53, 156
Peas ⎫
Peese ⎬ , James 107, 159

INDEX 249

Peirce (see Pierce).

Peperel ⎫
Peperell ⎪
Pepperel ⎪
Pepperrell ⎬, William, xv-xvii, 6, 9,
Pepprell ⎪ 13, 14, 23, 25, 29, 31,
Peppriell ⎪ 36, 45, 53, 55-57, 61,
Peppril ⎪ 84, 87, 89, 109, 110,
Pepprill ⎭ 122, 142, 170-172, 176-178, 184, 185, 187, 189-191, 194, 196, 198, 200, 202, 207, 210, 211, 216, 222-224, 228, 234-237

Perkins, Thomas 53, 141
Pernier, ——— 62
Peter 3
Peters, Math. 134, 135
Philipps ⎱, Richard ...170, 171, 177
Philips ⎰
Phips, William 173
Pierce, Joseph 159, 161
   Joshua, 12, 16, 18, 19, 54, 56, 86
Pierkins (see Perkins).
Pierpont, James 164
Pits ⎱, Samuel 136, 156
Pitts ⎰
Plats, Maj. 167
Pollard, Benjamin 2
   Col. 214
   John 129
Pomeroy ⎱, Seth, 1, 20, 54, 69, 229,
Pomroy ⎰ 236
Porter, ——— 131
Prat ⎱, Joshua 164
Pratt ⎰
   Philip 161
Prentice, John, 25, 47, 141, 143, 182
Prescoot ⎫
Prescot ⎪
Prescott ⎬, Jonathan, 124, 132, 163,
Prescut ⎪ 164
Prescutt ⎭
   Peter 16, 54, 87
Prince, ——— 48
Proctor, ——— 143

John 163
Prout, Ebenezer 148, 149
Prussia, King of 140
Puffer, ——— 159
Pyncheon ⎫
Pynchin ⎬, Charles, 4, 8, 16, 20, 23,
Pynchon ⎭ 36-40, 42, 46, 102, 104, 125, 127, 129-133, 135, 137, 138, 140, 142
   Joseph 38, 40, 134, 135

Quimbey, ——— 135

Rackwood, Capt. 147, 183
Ramsden, Joseph 223
Rand, William 165
Raynolds, Ebenezer, 141, 158-160, 163
Reddington ⎱, Nathaniel 21
Redington ⎰
   William 168
Reed, John 164
   Robert 165
Reynolds (see Raynolds).
Rhodes, Samuel, 54, 143, 144, 148, 151, 157, 159, 164
   Sergt. 160
Richard 83
Richards, Mathias 149
Richardson, ——— 148
   Jeremiah 54, 80
   Joseph, 54, 62, 63, 80, 84, 88, 89, 182, 183
Richelieu, Duke of 112
Richfor, ——— 97
Richman ⎱, ——— 134, 150
Richmond ⎰
   Nathaniel 163
   Sylvester, 58, 60, 124, 125, 127, 129, 134, 148, 150, 156, 160-163
Ring, Elkanah 223
Ripley, William 162
Robbins, Capt. 183
Robins, Thomas 162
Rogers, William 159, 162
Rogers & Fowle 237
Rolla, ——— 124

Rollins, ——............161
Roods (see Rhodes).
Root, Lieut. 136
    Richard 168
Roundbtt, —— 129, 131
Rous ⎱
Rouse ⎰ , John, 8, 22, 23, 45, 65, 66, 73, 74, 81, 83, 86, 93, 94, 110, 146, 182, 185, 187, 196, 202, 209
Rowsden, Joseph 151
Russell, —— 134

St. Croix, —— 14
    Samuel 34
Sanders, —— 158
    Gideon 164
    John 158
    Thomas, 4, 8, 74, 75, 93, 182, 199
Sanford, Capt. 183
Sanson, James 167
Saunders (see Sanders).
Savery, Robert 56
Sawyer, William 223
Sayward, Jonathan 183
Scammon, —— 136
Searl, —— 130
Sebury, David 46
Sergeant, —— 124, 126
Sewall, —— 150
    Thomas 159
    William 224
Sexton, Joseph 164
Shaw, —— 156, 162
    David 97
    John 63, 140
    Sergt. 157
Shearbarn (see Sherburne).
Shepardson ⎱
Sheparson ⎬, Daniel 223, 224
Shepherdson ⎰
Sherman, Abraham 151
Sherburn ⎱
Sherburne ⎰ , Capt. 130, 183
    Henry 55
    Joseph 55, 60

Shirley ⎱
Shirly ⎰ , Mrs. 61, 133
    William, xv, xvi, 23, 36, 45, 46, 57, 61, 103, 105, 109, 110, 133, 154, 170, 171, 177, 178, 197, 198, 215, 216, 231, 236, 237
Shore, —— 149, 158
Slarrow, Matthew 164
Sleeper, —— 129
Smead, Sergt. 137-139, 141
Smith, Capt., 46, 147, 149, 152, 155, 156, 207, 208, 210
    David 150
    Ebenezer 127
    George D. 1
    Joseph 183
    Preserved 158-160
    William, 141, 149, 155, 157, 161, 163, 164
Smithers ⎱
Smithurst ⎬, Joseph, 25, 182, 185, 196, 198
Smothers ⎬
Smythers ⎰
Snelling, Jonathan, 8, 25, 38, 82, 83, 94, 145, 151, 152, 182, 210
Sole, Cornelius 167
Spaulding, —— 154
Spear ⎱
Spears ⎰ , —— 166, 169
Spry, Capt. 62, 157, 183
Squire, Joseph 163
Stafford, Henry 236
Stanchfield ⎱
Standifield ⎰ , —— 129, 130
Stanford, Thomas 154, 155
Stanly, —— 102, 126, 130
Stanton, Benjamin 164
Staples, John 161
    Peter 53, 153, 154
Stark, Thomas 161
Stearns, Benjamin 237
Stebbins, Benjamin 5
    Thomas 157
Steel, —— 34
Stephens, —— 149
    Ebenezer 162

INDEX

James 41, 53, 54, 141
John 166
Stereter, Josiah 223
Stevens (see Stephens).
Stinson, John 183
Stoddard, Francis Russell 223
    John 169
    Mrs. Francis Russell 223
Stone, Capt. 183
Storer, John, 40, 53, 124, 139, 143,
    159, 223, 237
Stow, Edward 98, 183
Street, Nicholas 167
Stuart, James 132
Swan, Capt. 83, 133, 182
Swet, ——— 142, 146-148, 151
Symonds, ——— 167
Symons, Philip 105, 106

T., S. 105, 151, 154, 155
Talcott, Capt. 183
Tarbell, ——— 141
Tayler ⎫
Taylor ⎬, Gillam, 153, 154, 158, 159,
    161, 163
    John 1, 37, 130-133
    Sergt. 42
Teal, Asaph 105, 107
Temple, ——— 151
Terry, John 7, 54
    Samuel 101
Thatcher, Joseph 142
Thomas, ——— 142
    Nathaniel 128, 136, 146, 147
    Richard 164
Thompson, Thomas 182
Thornton, William 168
Throops, William 159
Thurrell, ——— 146
Tiddeman, Richard 181, 194
Tiffany & Co. 228
Tilton, ——— 156
    Jacob 146
Ting (see Tyng).
Titcomb, Moses, 57, 77, 78, 91, 118,
    143, 145, 150, 154, 156, 163

Tiyng (see Tyng).
Torey, Samuel 144
Totman, ——— 150
Toub ⎫
Toubbr ⎬, (see Zouberbhuler).
Town, ——— 143, 144
Tracy, Philip 167
Trow, Bartholomew, 54, 143, 152,
    158
Trays, Stephen 164
Trumbull, ——— 236
Tufts, ——— 140, 143
    William 12
Tuscany, Duke of 140
Twing, Nathaniel, 142, 143, 148, 155,
    157, 159, 160, 167
Twitchell, ——— 125, 126
Tyng, Edward, 5, 8, 25, 32, 34, 40
    47, 61, 81, 83, 104, 134, 138,
    149, 150, 152, 161, 165, 182,
    184, 186, 188, 194

Usells, George 223

Varnum, ——— 136, 137
Vaughan, William ... xvi, 11, 12, 57
Verrier, ——— 113

Wadham, John 56
Wadlin, Capt. 183
Wait, ——— 158
    Corp. 152
    Ebenezer 167
    Joseph 165, 167
    Sergt. 159
Wakes, Joshua 150
Waldo, ——— 150
    Samuel, 53, 80, 85, 109, 136, 149,
    150, 154, 155, 162, 164, 189, 236
Waldron, N. L. 184
Walker, Sergt. 41, 141
Walldrow (see Waldo).
Walley, A. 168
Walter, Nathaniel 14, 19, 26
Ward, Andrew 131, 135
    Capt. 183

Wardwel,
Wardwell, —— 42, 137
Warner, Capt. 142, 143, 145
  Israel 162, 164, 165, 167
  John, 40, 41, 54, 139-141, 163, 232, 237
  Jonathan 144
  William, 40, 53, 132, 139, 143, 145, 148, 158
Warran,
Warren, Mrs. 61, 133
Warrin
  Peter, xvii, 2, 6, 9, 13-15, 19, 24-26, 29, 40, 42, 43, 45, 46, 51, 57, 61, 65, 66, 72, 74, 76-79, 81, 83, 89, 101, 110, 111, 117, 121, 122, 170, 171, 174, 176, 178, 181, 184, 185, 187, 189, 190, 194, 196, 197, 199, 200, 202, 206, 207, 210, 211, 216, 222, 228, 233, 234
Warriner, J. 107
  Jonathan 43, 142, 143
  Joseph 106
Warringer, Gedion 106
Warrington, —— 126
Watkins, Andrew 144, 145, 164
Watts, —— 4
  John 53
Way, Matthew 167
Webb, —— 167
Webster, J. Clarence 226
Wendell, Col. 214
West, —— 137
  Capt. 183
  Judah 135
  Sergt. 143
Westen, John 53
Weston, —— 128
  Jeremiah 151, 160, 162
Wheatin, —— 147
Wheeler, E. P. 231
Wheelock, —— 143
Wheelright, —— 2
  Thomas 40, 139
White, Lieut. 151
  Robert 183

Whiteing, Charly 159
Whitelock,
Whitlock, John 56, 57
Whittemore, Joel 224
Whitworth, —— 161, 166
Willard, J. 177
  Samuel, 1, 8, 18, 40-42, 54, 83, 129, 131, 139, 142, 148, 149, 151, 163, 164, 232, 236, 237
William, S. 101
Williams, —— 141
  Benjamin 129
  David 143
  Edward 160
  Elijah 169
  Elisha, 19, 32-34, 36, 38, 39, 43, 44, 46, 122-124, 126, 127, 129, 130, 132, 133, 135-138, 140-142, 144, 146-148
  John 136
  Nathaniel 131, 135, 137
  Stephen, 32-37, 39-41, 43, 46, 102, 104, 121, 122
  Warham 39
  William, 127, 135, 137, 144, 149, 150, 152, 153, 158-163, 165, 166, 168, 169, 223
Williston, —— 152
Winchel,
Winchell, —— 141, 142
  J. 21
Winslow, Samuel 41, 140, 141
  William 140
Winsor, J. 231
Witherby,
Witherley, Capt. 150, 155, 156
Withevin, James 167
Wolcott, Roger 9, 238
  Samuel 238
Wolfe, —— 227
Wood, ——, 40-42, 157, 160, 163
  James 158
  Nathaniel 153
  W. 231
Woodberry, —— 134, 166
Woodcock, Jonathan 223

INDEX

Woodward, John 152
Wormwood, ——— 147
Worth, William 160
Wooster ⎱
Woster ⎰ , David 32

Wrong, George M. 231, 236
Youngman, ——— 139
Youngs, ——— 143
Zouberbhuler, Sebastian 107

www.ingramcontent.com/pod-product-compliance
Lightning Source LLC
Chambersburg PA
CBHW070724160426
43192CB00009B/1309